THROUGH YUP'IK EYES

through
Yup'ik
eyes

AN ADOPTED SON
EXPLORES
THE LANDSCAPE
OF FAMILY

Colin Chisholm

ALASKA NORTHWEST BOOKS ™

FOR MY FATHER, JOHN PETER

Text and photos © 2000 by Colin Chisholm

Published by Alaska Northwest Books™
An imprint of Graphic Arts Center Publishing Company
P.O. Box 10306, Portland, Oregon 97296-0306
800/452-3032
www.gacpc.com

Chapters 1 and 2 were published in different form in *Hope*
magazine (December 1996) and the *Utne Reader* (April 1997).
Chapter 14 was published by *Audubon* (August 1995).

Library of Congress Cataloging-in-Publication Data
Chisholm, Colin, 1967–
        Through Yup'ik eyes / text by Colin Chisholm.
           p. cm.
        ISBN 0-88240-533-0
           1. Chisholm, Colin, 1967–   2. Yupik Eskimos—Biography.
        3. Adoptees—United States—Biography.   4. Yupik Eskimos—
        Alaska—Kotlik—Social life and customs.   5. Kotlik (Alaska)—
        History. 6. Kotlik (Alaska)—Social life and customs. I. Title.

        E99.E7 C532   2000
        979.8'6—dc21
        [B]   00-038117

PRESIDENT/PUBLISHER: Charles M. Hopkins
EDITORIAL STAFF: Douglas A. Pfeiffer, Ellen Harkins Wheat,
                        Timothy W. Frew, Tricia Brown, Jean Andrews,
                        Alicia I. Paulson, Jean Bond-Slaughter
PRODUCTION STAFF: Richard L. Owsiany, Susan Dupere
DESIGN: Carol Haralson Design
MAP: Gray Mouse Graphics

Printed on acid- and chlorine-free paper in Canada

ACKNOWLEDGMENTS

I AM ESPECIALLY GRATEFUL to Nicky, for her many readings of this book, and for her never-ending patience.

Also, thanks to William Kittredge, Deirdre McNamer, and Glendon Brunk for their encouragement and advice.

Thanks to Denise Shannon, my agent, for believing in this story; to my editor, Ellen Wheat, for nurturing me along; to Jon Wilson, for publishing the essay that led to this book; and to Alicia Paulson, for her humor.

I am indebted to many Yup'ik relatives, especially my cousin Larry Mike, who provided me with crucial information about our family tree; and my cousin Fred Mike, who always writes back.

And to Joan Stone, who once believed in a poem of mine.

The following resources were indispensable during the writing of this book: The Alaska Native Language Center's *Yup'ik Eskimo Dictionary*, by Steven A. Jacobson, and their *One Must Arrive with a Story to Tell*, edited by Eliza Cingarkaq Orr and Ben Orr. Also *Yupik Lore: Oral Traditions of an Eskimo People*, published by the Lower Kuskokwim School District.

Well into the publishing of this book, it was brought to my attention that another book of the same title was published in 1974 by the Van Cleve Printing Company in Anchorage. A collection of St. Marys High School student poetry and photography, the book was coordinated by Richard Fagnant. I respectfully recognize this precedent.

Finally, a note of clarification: for simplicity I've used the village names of St. Marys and Mountain Village throughout the book, when in fact these names for those sites were not in use until after 1950.

CONTENTS

When I was eight years old I came, distraught, to my mother, weeping about magazine photographs I had seen of coyote pups burned to death by ranchers trying to extricate them from their dens. My mother took one look at the burned carcasses and pulled out a sheet of paper and a pencil.

"Here," she said. "Write about how this makes you feel."

I did, and when I was finished she helped me address an envelope to our senator, gave me a stamp, then walked with me to the post office where I slid the letter into the mail slot with a sense that I was sending a message to God.

What I gathered from her lesson was perhaps not what she intended: not that I could make political change through small acts, but that words had power. By writing that letter I believed, on some level, that I was resurrecting those pups. Through me, the dead could live again.

Nearly twenty years later I sat down to write my first reflections on my mother's life and death. I had just returned from her birthplace in Alaska, and I was reeling from what I had discovered there. As her story unraveled, I began to realize how little I had really known her. It is an old cliché, but for me perhaps true, that I came to know my mother better in her death than I had known her in life.

What began as a journal became an essay, then flickered into the beginnings of a book. All along, people have asked what the book is about, a question I began to dread because, like my mother's life, the answer is complicated. The book metamorphosed from a simple memoir into a biography, then a fictional history. In the end, *Through Yup'ik Eyes* is all of these at once.

Early in the process I realized that my mother's Alaskan history—as well as the history of her parents—was largely erased. Justina Mike, my mother's aunt and the only living person who had known my mother as a small child, graciously recalled for me many crucial details, including the mysterious death of my grandfather. However, I came to realize that between the need for translation, a reluctance to discuss the past, and simply not remembering, Justina could not tell the story for me.

Faced with the prospect of abandoning the project due to lack of documentation, I began experimenting with fiction as an avenue to exploring my mother's Yup'ik past. I did so naively, without a clue as to where it would lead, what problems might result. Immediately the characters took root, and before I knew it a book had emerged.

From the beginning it was a two-headed creature, one head nurturing me along while the other snapped at my heels. While fiction solved the problem of an unrecorded past, it inevitably risked accuracy. For undoubtedly the lives of the characters I have described in the fiction sections of this book were different than I portray them. In Yup'ik culture—inherently respectful to ancestry—I risk blasphemy.

Furthermore, I am writing about a culture that is not my own. Though I consider my mother's Yup'ik family my relatives, I am not Yup'ik. As my mother once asked me to do, I am trying to see the world through different eyes; in this case my mother's eyes, her Yup'ik eyes and her childhood eyes.

My truths may differ even from my immediate family's. To this day my father claims he never saw my mother drunk. He saw through different eyes than I did. We all—Yup'ik and non-Yup'ik—have different levels of need, different ways of placing ourselves in the world, and different paths to healing.

I live in a kind of borderland, between where I came from and what I've become.

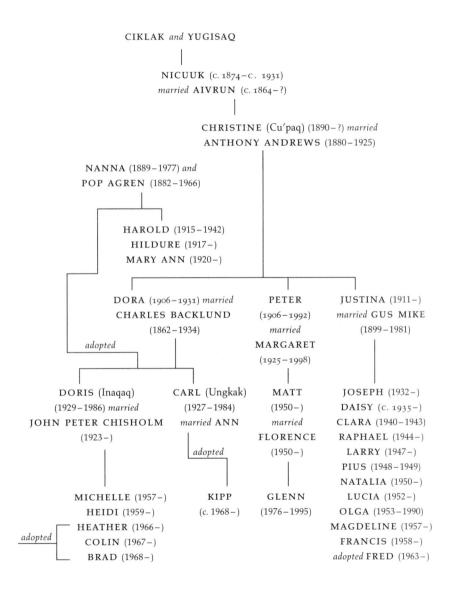

CIKLAK *and* YUGISAQ

NICUUK (C. 1874–C. 1931)
married AIVRUN (C. 1864–?)

CHRISTINE (Cu'paq) (1890–?) *married*
ANTHONY ANDREWS (1880–1925)

NANNA (1889–1977) *and*
POP AGREN (1882–1966)

HAROLD (1915–1942)
HILDURE (1917–)
MARY ANN (1920–)

DORA (1906–1931) *married*
CHARLES BACKLUND
(1862–1934)

PETER
(1906–1992)
married
MARGARET
(1925–1998)

JUSTINA (1911–)
married GUS MIKE
(1899–1981)

adopted

DORIS (Inaqaq)
(1929–1986) *married*
JOHN PETER CHISHOLM
(1923–)

CARL (Ungkak)
(1927–1984)
married ANN

MATT
(1950–)
married
FLORENCE
(1950–)

JOSEPH (1932–)
DAISY (C. 1935–)
CLARA (1940–1943)
RAPHAEL (1944–)
LARRY (1947–)
PIUS (1948–1949)
NATALIA (1950–)
LUCIA (1952–)
OLGA (1953–1990)
MAGDELINE (1957–)
FRANCIS (1958–)
adopted FRED (1963–)

adopted

MICHELLE (1957–)
HEIDI (1959–)
HEATHER (1966–)
adopted COLIN (1967–)
BRAD (1968–)

KIPP
(C. 1968–)

GLENN
(1976–1995)

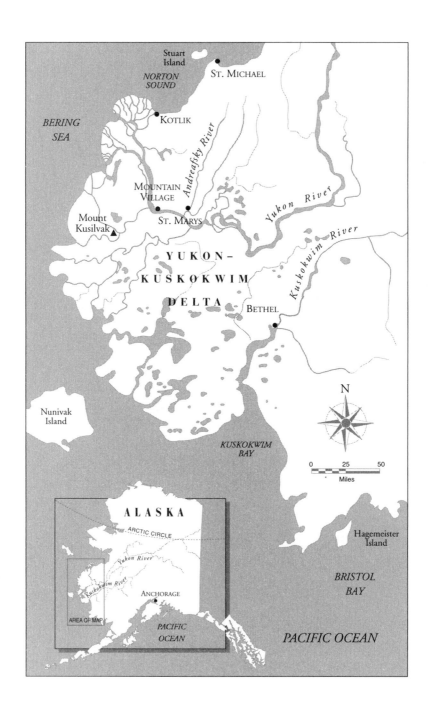

Stuart
Island

NORTON
SOUND

ST. MICHAEL

BERING
SEA

KOTLIK

Andreafsky River

MOUNTAIN
VILLAGE

Yukon River

Mount
Kusilvak ▲

ST. MARYS

Kuskokwim River

Y U K O N –

K U S K O K W I M

D E L T A

BETHEL

Kuskokwim River

N

Nunivak
Island

*KUSKOKWIM
BAY*

0   25   50
Miles

ALASKA

ARCTIC CIRCLE

Yukon River

Kuskokwim River

ANCHORAGE

AREA OF MAP

*PACIFIC
OCEAN*

Hagemeister
Island

*BRISTOL
BAY*

PACIFIC OCEAN

THE GREAT RIVER broke into little fingers as it neared the Bering Sea, one of these fingers jutting north where it spilled silently into Norton Sound. Salmon country, tomcod, burbot, whitefish and pike. All the fish in the world. The village of Kotlik lay along both sides of the river not too far from the sea. Cloven by the river, spliced by fishing boats in the summer and ice in the winter, the village lived and died by fish, their comings and goings, their ritualized migratory lives. In the summers the people lived along the river's banks, the men out on boats catching the fish they would bring to the women and children waiting and working at fish camp.

One of these children was Inaqaq. Too young to work, she wandered along the banks of the river with her brother, Ungkak, playing in the high grass, catching white butterflies and cupping them in her willowy hands. She peered between her fingers and watched the twitching of legs, the cleansing, the dark globes of eyes. Then she uncupped her hands and waited for the silky white wings to flutter into the sky.

She and Ungkak tossed sticks into the current and ran alongside them downriver, pretending they had missed the boat and were running to catch up. "Wait for us," they yelled. "Wait for us." But always the boats kept going, down one, two, three bends in the river, until Inaqaq and Ungkak collapsed in a laughing heap on its banks. The sticks floated on and on, past fish camps and boats, around widening bends and out into the open sea, where the salt smoothed them and the tide washed them to shore, to be collected as firewood in the coming fall.

Inaqaq had a doll named Nina, with brown bear hair and seashell eyes. She kept it with her always, careful to keep it clean because it was a present from her grandmother, Cu'paq, who had made it for her over the long winter. One day, running along the banks of the river just a step behind Ungkak, Inaqaq let Nina hang too low and dragged her through the muck. When Inaqaq saw Nina's face covered in mud and her dress torn, she looked at Ungkak and began to cry, quietly, her sobs no louder than small stones dropping into water. Ungkak smiled a small, shy smile, shook his head, took Inaqaq by the hand and walked her upriver where the reeds grew tall. There he took Nina and bathed her, pushing and pulling her through the rough water grass, until the doll came out clean and dripping, her eyes sparkling with the sea's glitter.

They walked back to fish camp, Inaqaq holding Nina above her head to dry in the sun and wind. Ungkak skipped stones across the river, counting under his breath, *one, two, three, four*. "Five!" he yelled, and Inaqaq screamed in delight. When they neared the stilted log structure that was fish camp, their mother's sister, Justina, hunched over a pile of fish, called out to them. Inaqaq ran ahead, Nina trailing like a sister behind her.

1

A D O P T I O N

You might look at me and think you know me. You see my white skin and my tall, thick frame, and you guess at who I am. You see this nose, long and hooked like a hawk's beak, and you imagine from where I come. I have light brown hair, blue eyes angled like a cat's, the pupils often dilated so that my eyes appear as black holes in my face. I slouch. My bones are big, my limbs heavy with muscle and protruding veins. In sixth-grade science class I learned that I was a mesomorph, which explained my ungainly hands and disproportionate feet. My father called me "Bigfoot." In fourth grade my forearms grew like zucchini and kids called me "Popeye," until I discovered that those same forearms could be used like jack-hammers and kids stopped calling me any names at all.

You might see me and guess that I am a Slavic Jew with some Neanderthal thrown in. When you met my family you'd really start to wonder. Five children and three of us adopted. My short, brown-skinned mother with her wide, angular face. My tall, wiry father, his red hair kept alive by Grecian Formula 44, his icy blue eyes, pale freckled skin. You would look at them, especially my mother, and back to me, and you might not say but you would think, "What happened?"

I would wonder too when I saw your parents. I would marvel at the mirrored face, the same crease running from the lip, the dimple, the same big fat toe. I would stare at your sister not just because she was beautiful but because I saw your face in hers and it was a wonder to behold.

To be adopted is not rare. Nor, for me, was it a hardship or disadvantage. On the contrary, ever since I was old enough to understand what it meant, I saw adoption as a wonderful mystery. I had some sense that who I was could not be determined without knowing where I came from. But I had no concept of how complex and expansive the word "family" would turn out to be.

BRITISH COLUMBIA, 1971. The tan Volkswagen Squareback sputters its way up and over the pass that will send the car and its occupants hurtling down the mountain to Lake Louise. The man at the wheel has red hair and he is driving too fast, not because he likes to drive fast but because he loses himself in ideas and forgets that he is the captain of a small German ship that wasn't made to exceed seventy miles per hour without disintegrating; in addition, he has forgotten that he is the father of five children who are packed into a car designed for four. The smallest of these children, a three-year-old with sandy hair and green eyes as wide as quarters, sits on his mother's lap in the front passenger seat and wails at the top of his lungs. His screaming joins the cacophony coming from the back, where his brawny four-year-old brother is pulling the hair of his pug-nosed five-year-old sister. Both of them have light hair, which contrasts sharply with the red and dark brown hair of their two older sisters, who are crammed in next to them. The red-haired sister is eleven. She has a mask of freckles, and fierce eyes when she yells at the boy and pulls him off his pug-nosed sister.

The mother screams at her husband, "For Christ's sake, slow down!"

At which point the father wakes from his reverie and frantically pumps the brakes that were never meant to stop this much weight on this tight a corner on this steep a grade. The tires screech, the rear end of the Squareback fishtails toward the abyss; silence reigns in the sardine-can car.

"Just a little gravel," mumbles the father as he guides the car around the next curve. "Nothing to worry about." But beads of sweat speckle his furrowed brow. He slows the car.

The mother, a dark-skinned woman who might be Native American or Filipino, glares at the man. The children stare at their mother, waiting. The father does not meet her stare, but he knows with certainty that it is there. The Squareback creeps down the highway, the smell of burning brakes in the air.

The mother turns from her husband to comfort the boy on her lap, then whirls around to warn her other son, whose fist is poised to drop again on pug-nose.

"You don't hit, do you hear me? The next time I catch you, this car is pulling over and you know what's next."

The oldest sister is pretty, skinny, and aloof. She looks like her mother, the same broad face and angled cheeks, but with her father's ivory skin. She stares out the window, trying to ignore the humiliation a thirteen-year-old feels when she is forced on vacation with snot-dripping siblings and arguing parents, when she'd rather be back in California listening to records or talking with her friends on the telephone.

At the campground the car erupts, the children scrambling to escape. An old man watching from his Winnebago shakes his head and wonders. The father unloads while the mother washes the boys in the rest room. In the car all day, they are smeared with peanut butter, dirt, and the hair of their dog, Flossy, who'd been left behind at the last minute because there wasn't room. While the mother cooks dinner and watches the kids, the father sits in the car writing on a yellow pad of paper. Past dusk he writes by flashlight, stopping only for dinner. He looks up from his work when he hears his older son attacking his red-haired sister. The mother pulls them apart and takes the boy aside to scold him, her voice low and patient. Later, around the fire, she tells stories.

Her three-year-old asks, "Mom, tell me about Boheema, where I come from."

"No," says the older boy. "Tell about me and the Bigfoots."

She tells both stories again, and they all laugh and let the tension of the day rise into the starry sky.

When the children are asleep she sits by the fire drinking red wine from a glass. The father leaves his work to join her at the fire. He places his hand on her shoulder.

"Beautiful, isn't it, the stars," he says. And he means it. He doesn't notice the tension in her shoulders.

"Sure," she says, her faraway voice barely a whisper. "It is." She sips her wine and stares into the fire.

My family comprised eight completely different ethnic backgrounds, four breeding pairs, and fifteen or twenty mixed ethnic origins. Because three of us were adopted and knew our ethnicities, our imaginations blossomed as we created stories about where we came from, our home nations, why we were the way we were. My mother, Doris, told and retold the stories of our adoptions in the same spirit that she recounted the coming of her biological children, with an eye for the inner beauty and uniqueness of each child. Her stories were meant, I think, to teach her children how wonderfully different we all were, and how we could laugh—and cry—at our origins. The intricacy of her children: this was everything to her.

The seven of us laughed at each other's stories as we sat around the large octagonal dining room table, specially built for a family of seven and one guest. I remember wondering if that extra place at the table was there in case my mother happened to find another child looking for a home. More often than not that chair was filled.

My mother's inclination toward adoption came naturally. Her upbringing prepared her, in no uncertain terms, for a life of bringing people in. She was half Yup'ik Eskimo, born in 1929 in a fishing village named Kotlik, which is split by a small slough arm of the Yukon River as it drains into Norton Sound on the Bering Sea. Her mother, Dora, was Yup'ik, and her father a Finnish trader named Charlie Backlund, who owned the village store. Forty years Dora's senior, Charlie had helped her family in hard times. Their relationship may have been based more on necessity than true love, but perhaps it was both.

In the harsh Alaskan bush where the Yup'ik lived, adoption — *yuksagute* — occurred naturally and necessarily. People often died young, leaving their children to be raised by family, friends, or, in some cases, strangers in distant villages. When my grandmother, Dora, died of tuberculosis at the age of twenty-five, my mother was two years old and her brother was four. Both were raised for the next two years by their maternal aunt, Justina. My mother's journal speaks of the entire village as family, a unit that took her in and made her a child of everyone. That custom continues to this day, and there are many examples of Yup'ik children being transferred from one home to another, for reasons as simple as the birth parents being unable to afford another child. A child might grow up in one family knowing his birth parents live two houses away. Inaqaq and Ungkak would have remained with Justina indefinitely, had Charlie Backlund not sent them away.

This he did two years after Dora's death. He was worried about tuberculosis, a common killer among Natives; in addition, he wanted his children to have a "proper" Western education. With the intention of joining them the following spring, Charlie hired a nurse to escort the children to the Lower 48, where a former business associate had found a home for them to stay. But with Charlie's mysterious death not long after, my mother was separated from Alaska and her Yup'ik family for the rest of her life.

She and Ungkak were taken in by a Swedish family that lived on Vashon Island, a short ferry trip from Seattle. Vashon was a mostly white farming community, where my mother's high, sharp cheekbones were noticed. She fit in better with her Japanese immigrant classmates than with her new family, the Agrens, but whether it was a sense of responsibility or simply an openness of heart and mind, the Agrens raised my mother to believe she was one of them.

In the short term this allowed my mother to find home and family in a foreign place; in the long term it cleaved her from her origins. She became intensely aware of her brown skin, and she tried to hide everything that was Eskimo about her. Her mother's picture vanished; her beaded sealskin slippers, chewed soft by her grandmother's worn yellow teeth, lay hidden in the back of a closet; her favorite doll, Nina, disappeared. She soon blended into the community, and the memory of her old life faded away. She did well in school, grew into a beautiful all-American girl, went to college, became a nurse, and married at twenty-seven. Her Yup'ik name and her brother's disappeared with the stories of their past. They became Doris and Carl.

I NEVER KNEW POP AGREN, my grandfather, a quiet old Swede with a love for sweets. I imagine his eyes sparkled when he looked at my mother, and I have no doubt that he loved her as one of his own. I remember Nanna Agren, my grandmother, always treating my mother so gently—as if she were still the shy, scared Yup'ik child just arriving on Vashon—softly telling her to sit as she pushed plates of homemade raspberry pie in front of her. Nanna died when I was ten, and I cried myself to sleep at her funeral. Genetic bond or no, I had lost my grandmother. Mourning knows nothing of DNA.

The Agrens were a big family—seven, including my mother. I believe that's why my mother wanted to have many children. After marrying my father she gave birth to my two oldest sisters, Michelle and Heidi, but soon after that she was diagnosed with a tumor and underwent a hysterectomy. Her hope for five children diminished until she came to a natural conclusion, given her upbringing: adoption.

Six years later, in 1966, she adopted my sister, Heather, light-skinned and blond. I wonder if my mother found it strange, at first, to view Heather as her own. Without morning sickness, swelling, or painful contractions, her family grew by one. My mother used to laugh when people asked if she had missed giving birth to us.

"You must be crazy," she'd joke. "It's the best way to go! You can wake up and say, 'I think I'll have a baby today!'"

And as my father tells it, that's pretty much how I came into the family. "I was in Washington, D.C., on business," he recalls, "and I call home to check in with your mother. She says to me, 'John, how would you like to have a baby boy?' I didn't quite know how to respond, but that's okay because she beat me to it with, 'You're now the father of a ten-pound baby boy!' All I could think to say was, 'I'll be home as soon as I can.' I wanted to get home before she rushed out and got another one."

Brad rounded out my mom's magic number, five, in 1968. I shudder to think what it must have been like for my parents to raise three babies, each arriving within a year of the next, plus two young girls (not to mention three cats, our dog, Flossy, and Heidi's pony, Princess, as well as the entourage of friends who wanted to ride her). I look at an old black-and-white photograph of the three adoptees with their parents: Heather is giving her camera smile that hasn't changed in thirty years; Brad's lips are puckered with concern and con-stipation; and I am gazing up at my dad, who is looking at my mom, whose smile threatens to swallow us all. This is how I want to remember her, glowing with children, her own, someone else's, any that would come.

THOUGH MY FATHER JOKED about his powerlessness in our adop-tions, he was my mother's compatriot in inviting strangers to our home. One rainy November night our family was driving home from Reno when a bearded man wearing an army coat appeared out of the drizzle as we sped by. Before we had time to protest my father swerved the VW van off the road and backed down the highway shoulder.

I piled into the rear seat with Heather and Brad, wide-eyed, leav-ing the seat behind my parents for the man. He slid open the van door, said, "Thanks much," and sloshed himself down on the seat. The smell of whiskey, cigarettes, and urine filled the van.

"Where you going?" my father asked as he pulled the van back onto the highway.

"Sacramento," the man answered, his voice scratchy and raw.

"We can take you as far as Truckee," my father offered. "That's where we turn off."

"Much appreciated," the man said.

He was soaking wet, his medium-length brown hair stringy on his neck, his shoulders slumped. He looked about forty, and the only thing he carried with him was a large plastic garbage bag. I flinched every time his hand moved near it. I pictured him pulling out a gun or a knife and forcing my father to drive off on some side road where he'd kill us all.

After a few long minutes of silence, my mother and father began asking the man questions, and as the rain turned to snow on the asphalt, we heard a small part of his story. It was the first time in my life that I glimpsed the world beyond the protective circle of my clan.

After serving in the army in Texas, the man had moved to Las Vegas. He was some kind of electrical technician, and for a while he worked fixing the casinos' neon signs that light up the desert sky. After he was fired for drinking he worked odd jobs until his money was about gone, then in one desperate effort risked his last two hundred dollars on a poker table in Reno. He lost, and for the last month he'd been living under the Virginia Street underpass, begging during the day so he'd have enough money to eat a ninety-nine-cent buffet breakfast at Harrah's.

But winter was here and he was cold. He had a sister in Sacramento, though he hadn't talked to her in years. He just wanted to get somewhere warm. I didn't know how to feel about this man. I felt sorry for him, but I was afraid that my father would ask him to come home with us. Which he did.

The man declined, thanking my father with a handshake when we pulled off at Truckee. Before the man stepped down my father said, "You know, it'll be snowing like hell over Donner Summit. We can drop you at the bus. Take this." He put a bill in the man's hand.

The man's eyes glazed over as he stared at the ground. He said thanks, sat back down, and ten minutes later was sitting on a bench outside the bus station, nodding good-bye to us. It was snowing hard by then.

All the way home none of us talked. I thought about what the man's sister was going to say when he knocked on her door. When we turned into Squaw Valley the sky filled with great sheets of snow covering everything.

WHEN MY FAMILY sat around our dinner table, the topic most often repeated was our genetic history. We took great pleasure in discussing the countries of our origins, and we learned at a very young age that being adopted was a privilege, not a stigma. I knew, for example, that I was half Yugoslavian, and the joke in my family was that everyone in

Yugoslavia had huge hands, noses, and feet. "Land of the Bigfoots," my dad liked to say. I was grateful to also have a quarter each of English and Irish, because I thought that it somehow connected me to my dad's Scottish blood. Brad was half Bohemian, a quarter English and Irish; Heather was French, English, Italian, Dutch, Apache Indian, and who-knows-what-else. We three would argue about which of our homelands was the best, and I dreamed of someday going back to the land of the Bigfoots.

Years later, when I was twenty, I studied in Yugoslavia. I thought that somehow I was returning to my homeland, that I would see people who resembled me. I couldn't have been farther from the truth—genetic makeup in Yugoslavia was almost as mixed as in America. Still, I wandered around the streets of Zagreb watching for my twin; I was sure he was out there somewhere.

FIVE YEARS AGO IN COLORADO a friend introduced me to a forty-six-year-old artist who lived in the mountains making stained-glass windows for a living. I spent a few days watching her at her craft, trying to learn a thing or two.

We instantly liked each other, and it wasn't long before our talk rambled beyond the intricacies of stained glass. On the second day I watched her creating a large glass montage, a jumble of colorful figures gathered by a stream. On one side of the glittering indigo creek a little boy flew a kite in the shape of a yellow hummingbird hovering over a blue green tree. Downstream a little girl in red knickers pulled in a violet fish, and behind her a shimmering black bear watched, salivating, from behind a marigold boulder. An ominous black sky contrasted sharply with the brightness of the scene.

Almost finished with the piece, she lifted it away from the table just as I mentioned, in the course of the conversation, that I'd been adopted; she flinched, let out a muffled cry, and dropped her work onto the cement floor, where it shattered at our feet. When I looked up, she was weeping.

Later, after we had both calmed, we sat on stools over shards and splinters of glass, like two ships marooned on a broken sea. "I'm sorry," she said. "It's not your fault. Let me explain.

"I was nineteen when I got pregnant. And I was in love. I wanted the baby but Tim would have nothing to do with it. When I said I was going to have it, he left. That was that. I don't know, I guess I was just too young . . . I was so scared.

"I had the baby, but I put him up for adoption. It was the hardest thing. I was in labor for twenty hours, and a mind gets to do a lot of thinking in that much time. I started doubting whether I really wanted to give my baby up. I was pushing and pushing, and finally he came out, and I was so filled with relief and joy. But I was bleeding badly. I passed out, and when I woke my baby was gone. I never even got to see him."

She began to weep again. I sat there, numbness coming on. I wanted to console her, but I didn't know how.

After a minute she continued. "All that work, a month's worth, gone. I'm not sure why I reacted like that; I mean, it's been a long time and it's not like you're the first adopted guy I've ever met. Maybe it's because he'd be your age now; I mean, he is your age.

"And I've never had another child. I registered with an adoption computer—you put in all your personal information, and if the other party registers then a match is made. I registered eleven years ago. Every day when I check the mail I'm looking for a letter from that damn computer. Every day."

I've never talked to her again, but I wonder often if her child thinks about her, if someday they'll meet again. And I wonder if somewhere out there a woman I met briefly in the early hours of dawn is checking her mailbox for me.

I have a family that seems infinite, a collage without borders, always growing to make room for more. Every time my mother or father brought someone home the walls stretched, and our universe expanded. So I register with the central adoption computer; I place my being in a microchip and wait for a match. Not so my life will somehow become magically complete, but simply to allow for the possibility of reconnection, of closing circles, of building a bridge between wandering broods.

My family was a living mosaic of DNA. Seen all at once we were identifiable as a clan because of the way we interacted. Seen individually, there was no physical resemblance between, for example, my mother and me. As a child it didn't bother me, but the older I got the more often people who didn't know I was adopted would say to me, "You know, you don't look anything like your brother." Or your mother. Or your father.

Because of this, over the years I've become fascinated with meeting relatives of people I know, just to pick out the similarities, both obvious and subtle. "You have your mother's nose, but your father's lips." "You're built like your dad, but your coloring is your mom's." "You and your sister have the exact same chin—it's so weird." Of course it's not weird. It's normal to resemble, at least vaguely, your biological family. This is something I've never experienced. To my knowledge I have never met another person who is packing around the same kit of DNA.

Years down the road I still wonder if my twin is out there, if he hurts or loves in the same way that I do, if he grows bunions on his heels, if his beard is patchy in places when he lets it grow out in the mountains. As I get older I have more and more questions, and far fewer answers. I love my adoptive family, but the apathy I felt about my birth parents as a youngster has vanished. The same thing happened to my mother a few years before she died: Yup'ik voices started calling to her in dreams, and she woke up listing and lonely.

BIRTHING,
1929

THAT NIGHT the dogs wouldn't calm. *Wolves or bear,* Charlie thought. *Or maybe just the cold biting at their eyes.* The wind blasted through Kotlik harder than Charlie had ever seen. When he locked up the store he had a hard time getting the door shut, pulling with all his weight to get the lock in place. The freezing metal burned his fingers as he pushed the rod into the hole and turned the key. He'd barely had a customer all day, and he'd been tempted to close the store at noon and go home to Dora.

Charlie pulled on his mittens, cinched the fur hood tightly around his face, and bent himself into the wind. All the dog teams were whining, some in half-hearted moans, others in full-force yaps and howls. Charlie saw the Andrews' team, restless and heaving against their ropes behind the store, and down the street he saw other dogs straining their pegs. Nobody else was outside, except old man Nikolai feeding his dogs two houses down. The dogs ignored Nikolai, as well as the buckets of fish he threw in front of them. Charlie waved as he passed, but Nikolai either didn't see him or didn't care to wave back. The old man was cursing to himself, at the dogs, the cold.

Charlie hurried down the wooden boardwalk, turned right, and came to the small log cabin that was his home. He heard muffled talk within, and as he opened the door a shriek tore through the air, blending with the cacophony of the dogs. He knew it was Dora, and his heart quickened. Justina, Dora's sister, came to him, holding two-year-old Ungkak in her arms.

"She's been in labor four hours now," she said. "We thought to come get you, but the storm is bad and we thought you would come sooner. She is fine, but her labor is hard. My mother and the nurse are with her." Charlie felt his tension ease. He had always felt comforted by Justina's presence. He nodded.

"Thanks," he said in his deep, lazy voice that was often mistaken for mumbling. He removed his coat and mittens, hung them by the stove, and fed wood into the fire. He heard Dora's heavy breathing coming from the other room.

After stoking the fire he asked Justina if he could go in, and she nodded. He turned, took a deep breath, and clumsily tiptoed to the doorway, where he peeked around the corner toward the bed. He saw Dora, breathing easier now but her eyes closed and her head back, her forehead glistening in the lamplight. Christine, or Cu'paq, his mother-in-law, turned and saw him, then motioned with her hand for him to enter. The nurse, a plump white woman, frowned and said that Dora was doing well, but that this baby wasn't making it easy.

"Powerful stubborn," she said. "Seems like it don't want to come out into this cold. Neither would I, I have to tell you."

Charlie nodded and replaced Cu'paq at the head of the bed, across from the nurse. He took a handkerchief from his breast pocket and wiped Dora's forehead. She opened her eyes and saw him, tried to smile through the next contraction but it was too much and she gritted her teeth and moaned. Charlie held her hand and Dora squeezed it until his fingers turned purple. His balding head gleamed with sweat, the remaining white hair hanging in damp strings. By village standards he was an old man, in his sixties, and at Dora's bedside he appeared more a father than a husband. But his soft caress on her forehead and the way he flinched at her pain belied the impressions of age. Charlie focused on Dora's contractions, held her hand, and whispered in her ear.

"Think of the sea, the tide and its easy ebbs and flows, the way water washes the world."

He stayed with her until near the birth, when Cu'paq replaced him at Dora's side and he went to sit with Justina and Ungkak in the other room. An hour later a shriek woke him from a sitting sleep. Justina bolted from her seat, handed Ungkak to Charlie, and rushed into the birthing room. Charlie held Ungkak against his chest and patted him on the back, trying to calm him back to sleep. His crying softened into broken speech and hiccups, and in a few minutes he was snoring and drooling onto Charlie's sweater. Minutes later the wind suddenly ceased its wailing and the dogs stopped their crying. Charlie heard whispering in the next room. Justina appeared in the doorway and motioned him in. He didn't notice if she was smiling or not as he passed by her, still holding Ungkak.

"You can tell Ungkak he has a baby sister," the nurse said, and Charlie looked at Dora, who watched him with a tired, relieved smile. In the crook of her right arm, bundled in fur wrappings, a wrinkled brown face showed through. Charlie took Ungkak, still sleeping, and placed him next to the baby. He leaned over and kissed the baby on the forehead.

"I'd tell you to protect her, Ungkak, but she seems pretty tough herself," he said as he pulled away. He turned to Dora, kissing her on the cheek. "She gave you a tough time, eh?"

She nodded, but her eyes were glad.

"Sleep," Charlie said. "The dogs will let you sleep now." Dora closed her eyes and slept while Charlie sat and watched over them for the rest of the night and into the darkness of the next day. It was the first morning in years that the store opened late.

2

GOING BACK

My mother died too young, of cancer, when she was fifty-seven. She was just beginning to know herself, at least that's what she said in her final days. She wanted to return to Kotlik and know her Yup'ik relatives, but it took her more than fifty years to understand this yearning. Just before she died, in 1986, she gave me a fetish: a small bear carved from stone, a blue arrow strapped to its back with sinew. The fetish is supposed to protect the traveler on his journey, and the arrow brings good hunting. I'm not sure where she got it, or why she gave it to me. Perhaps she thought that I, her most troublesome child, needed more protection in my travels. Or maybe it was simply intuition. Maybe she knew I'd go to Kotlik.

Three years after her death I clasped the bear in my sweaty hand as I boarded the small plane from Anchorage to Bethel, the city nearest Kotlik. Flying in Alaska was a humbling experience, the largest, emptiest expanse of snow I had seen in my life. I expected mountains; instead, I saw rolling hills and flatness, dissected by thousands of frozen rivers and streams, dotted by a million little lakes. Every so often we passed over what looked like a settlement, clusters of buildings tucked into bunches of trees. I thought I saw a person on a snowmobile, a speck of black moving fast down a river, then swallowed up by the curving whiteness.

As the plane began its descent, I saw the lights of Bethel flickering out of the limitless dark. I had never been to a place so far from anything. My doubts about coming resurfaced: What would my relatives think of me, a white man posing as family? Would they know that I was adopted? Would they care? I wondered if they expected an Eskimo formed in the image of my mother. All they knew for sure was that I was Inaqaq's son, home to meet the family.

The plane landed and I was shocked into the twenty-below reality of Bethel. My contact met me at the luggage claim and soon we were cruising down the main street in her pickup, past bars, video stores, a bowling alley, all of it temporary and tacked up, like army barracks. Few people wandered the streets, but the bars and bowling alley were lit. I fell asleep that night listening to dogs howling and sheet metal flapping in the arctic winds.

The next morning I flew due north, the only passenger in a small, single-engine Cessna. My pilot, Earl, had left his wife and kids in Texas and swore he'd never go back. He liked to hunt. I asked him if flying up there was dangerous, and he answered, "Shit, the flyin's safe. It's the not-flyin' that'll kill ya." He went on to tell me about a friend of his. Lost his engine north of Nome, landed smooth as silk in powder, got out of the plane, and sank up to his neck in snow. He ended up burning parts of his plane to stay alive before a search party found him four days later. And he was lucky. Earl told me there were more plane crashes per capita in Alaska than in any other state. I asked him why and he explained, "Look around ya. There's nothing to guide by out here. You can fly for a day without seeing a damn thing. Combine that with a white-out blizzard and you can't find your pecker to piss. You fly around in circles till your fuel runs out."

Looking around, I saw what he meant. Flying over Kotlik I sensed a seed of loneliness taking root in me, one that grew throughout my stay and may never fully leave me. I felt, for the first time in my life, my own smallness; I was a tiny shoot in the midst of immeasurable wilderness.

From the air Kotlik didn't look like much. It ran about a half mile down both sides of a slough arm of the Yukon River. The small airstrip sat on one side of the slough, the cemetery on the other. There were no cars or streets. A wooden-planked boardwalk connected house to school, school to store, store to house. People huddled at the end of the runway, waiting for the plane.

The plane taxied down the dirt airstrip, stopping just before the people, who shielded their faces from the blowing snow and ice. There were about fifteen of them, all wrapped in heavy coats with fur-lined hoods, faces barely visible. Some were hunched and old; a few were children, feet covered in miniature fur mukluks.

Before I was completely out the door they surrounded me. One man came forward and introduced himself as Matt Andrews, my second cousin. He shook my hand, then shyly embraced me. Through his fur hood I saw dark eyes behind thick glasses, fine black hair, a mustache. His skin was brown and wind-burned. He introduced me to the others, each of them embracing me in turn. Some said, "*Waqaa*," which means hello, some said, "Welcome," and one, my great-aunt Justina, said, "Welcome home." My pack and I were loaded on the back of a snowmobile and minutes later I sat in a warm house that smelled of smoked fish, eager faces all around.

The family is large and complex, and over the next month I would struggle to get all the names right, trying to understand the family tree. It seemed everyone in Kotlik was related, and therefore wanted to meet me: son of their long-lost relative, Inaqaq, who left as a child and never came back. They didn't seem to care that I was white—a *kass'aq*—though I suspect I was the tallest person Kotlik had seen since Charlie Backlund. I was a relative, and that was all that mattered. I could have been leprous, crippled, antennaed, and I don't think they would have flinched.

I was overwhelmed by how firmly my mother had remained in their memory. Justina—her serene face crevassed like summer glaciers and spotted from age, her hair as silver as salmon—spoke to me in Yup'ik, a clicking and clacking from deep in the throat. Her daughter, Olga, translated. "She says your mother looked like her mother, Dora. She says your mother was old for such a little girl. She is glad you have come. She says she has been waiting a long time." Olga finished just a moment after Justina. The room was quiet except for the fire popping behind us.

"She wanted to come back," I said. "But she got sick, and . . ." I didn't know what to tell her, but she nodded as if she understood and spoke again for a moment. Olga translated. "She says thank you for coming. You are part of our family. It is good that you are home. You must call me Grandmother."

I remembered the bear and retrieved it from my pocket. Over the last three years it had always been near me. I handed it to Justina. There was recognition in her face, her lips softened into a sad smile, and tears formed in the deep creases of her eyes. "*Paugnaq*," she whispered. *Bear.* She closed her hand around it, and shut her eyes.

I breathed in deeply, the fish smell new and soothing. In the silence that followed, I let go of my fears and watched my grandmother sleep.

IN NATIVE AMERICAN MYTHOLOGY there are stories of children lost in the wilds and saved by animals. In one of these stories, a young girl is lost while playing hide-and-seek with her brothers. She is near death when a great bear finds her and takes her home to raise as his own. One day he marries her, and they have children, half human, half bear. Years later the brothers kill the bear and take the sister and her cubs back to the village, where she is welcomed by all. But eventually she begins to transform into a bear and, fearing she will harm her family, she takes her children and returns to the wild. I like to think that this story implies a certain power of adoption, of nurture over nature, a belief that our stories define us even more than our genes do. Adopted by the bear, Bear Woman becomes a bear; there is no going back.

The night before I left Kotlik, Justina told me the story of Bear Woman. As she spoke, her old body became young again. Her hands and arms moved gracefully in circles, and her chair wobbled with the motions of her body. Her voice changed pitch dramatically, most tense when the bear was slaughtered by the brothers. The clicks and clacks of her voice receded to gentle murmurs as she described the fate of Bear Woman. The ending went something like this:

The early morning sky is dark about the sleeping village, though the northern horizon is alive with dancing light. A woman pokes her head out the hide door of her home, glances around, smells the air. She is afraid, this woman, but somehow strong and determined. Her eyes are sad but fierce. She moves out into the morning, followed by two children wrapped in furs. The three of them move toward the edge of the village, toward the trees and the hill where they picked berries all summer long. The dogs watch silently as they pass, but their teeth show behind curled lips and the fur is erect on the backs of their necks. The woman moves into the trees. Her children wade in her growing footprints as they climb the hill and drop into home on the other side.

The Trading Post, 1932

INAQAQ AND UNGKAK loved going to the trading post to see their father, his heavy Finnish frame seated behind the counter, his huge clunky hands punching the keys of the oversized bronze cash register he'd imported all the way from Seattle. The door's bells would jingle as Inaqaq and Ungkak scampered in, and Charlie would glance at them out of the corner of his eyes before going back to business.

They came for two reasons: one, to see their father; two, equally alluring, for candy. Inaqaq especially craved candy. She loved standing below the counter where all the colorful glass jars were stored. Charlie would lift her and set her down next to the long row of jars containing peppermint, jelly beans, licorice, toffee, chocolates, and lemon sours. She'd wait for Charlie to finish with his customers, then ask politely, as if he might even say no, "May I have a piece of candy?" And Charlie would laugh at the begging look on her face because he knew it was a game, and he knew she knew it was a game, one which never tired. Ungkak would grin knowingly as he watched.

Eventually, after a number of customers came and went, Charlie would capitulate, saying, "Oh, all right, just one piece. But you're gonna drive me outta business—you know that, don't you?" And Inaqaq would nod like she knew and then reach in to snatch her licorice or peppermint, while Charlie went back to his work. Sometimes Ungkak and Inaqaq sat for hours watching people come and go, buying everything from toilet paper to gum balls, shotgun shells to tins of beans. From Inaqaq's perspective the store sold everything imaginable, and in fact it did sell most everything the villagers needed, as well as much that they didn't need. Its stacked shelves exposed Inaqaq and Ungkak to the outside world in ways that many Yup'ik children would never experience. They were materially privileged because their father owned the store, and because he was white. Of course at the time they had only a vague notion of this; they just liked to eat candy and be near their father.

As the children sat there watching, people greeted them with smiles and teasing jokes. "Hey, Ungkak, those mukluks is about to explode, your feet is growing so big." Or "Inaqaq, you save some of that candy for the rest of us, okay?" And they'd tousle the children's hair, or touch them gently on the shoulders. Half of the customers were relatives, and if they weren't they might as well have been. Every Yup'ik child had a home in every house. Nearly everyone who walked into Charlie's store was like an uncle, a sister, a cousin once or twice removed. It was a warm place to sit and eat candy, and to watch the family come and go.

Charlie Backlund left Kotlik once or twice a year, traveling by boat up the slough to St. Michael, where he'd catch a steamer to Seattle to buy goods for the store. Inaqaq and Ungkak always begged to go along, but Charlie would say no, he had business to attend to, and off he'd go, bundled up for the long journey. He was gone five or six weeks at a time. He'd return with a fleet of fishing boats sunk low in the water with goods. Inaqaq and Ungkak waited patiently while Charlie and his men unloaded the boats, carried the goods to the storage shed, and restocked the store. Only when all of that was finished would Charlie take them both in his thick arms and growl like a bear. Then he'd pull some treat from his ear, a new kind of candy or a special marble. Once he pulled a shiny rainbow-colored yo-yo from Ungkak's ear and a giant blue jawbreaker from Inaqaq's. For the next week anyone who saw Inaqaq wondered why her jaw was swollen. Her tongue was blue for a month. Ungkak became the first Yup'ik child in the village to perform one hundred Around-the-Worlds with his yo-yo. People gathered outside the store to watch him, the bright colors orbiting his calm, large head. Charlie joked that buying Ungkak a yo-yo was the best thing he could have done to bring in business.

Inaqaq and Ungkak were lonely when Charlie was away. Their uncle Simeon tended the store. He was a short, stout man with thick fingers that reminded Inaqaq of the miniature sausages that Charlie brought back from Seattle. Simeon was a faithful employee who never succumbed to the begging of friends who wanted a deal while the boss was out of town. He took his responsibility seriously, and while in the store he rarely even talked. This made for a stoic atmosphere, and Inaqaq and Ungkak usually stayed away. Not to mention that Simeon would never even think of giving away candy. Thus there was cause for great celebration when old Charlie Backlund came home.

Everyone welcomed Charlie's return, but perhaps none as much as the people waiting for whiskey. He didn't sell it in the store, not only because of Prohibition but because it was considered inappropriate, if not unethical. And if anyone was asked on the street, "Where can I buy liquor?" no one would say that Charlie Backlund sold it. Charlie never talked much about his trips to Seattle, but he spent more time there than buying goods for the store required. He had "business partners" there, and he built up a small fortune in his dealings with them, possibly during Prohibition. Whatever the case, he didn't get rich selling candy and canned tomatoes, and soon after he sent Inaqaq and Ungkak away, his mysterious death would belie the clean, simple facade of his life in the bush.

3

October 1995. I stand with my father and Brad in the Kotlik cemetery. We hunch in a line, facing the grave. We are bundled in borrowed clothes: Brad in a heavy sealskin coat with a fur-lined hood and intricate embroidery running down both sides of the zipper, rubber boots three sizes too big; my father in an army-green snowmobile jacket, rubber boots, a hunter orange wool cap; I in a coat like my father's but two sizes too small.

Typical *kass'aq*, we came to Alaska underdressed, even though we've lived in the mountains most of our lives. Already winter is well on its way, though the river isn't yet frozen. Our cousin, Papa Joe, brought us across the slough in his fishing boat. He stands respectfully behind us with another cousin, Angela, who helped us find Dora's grave.

My grandmother, Dora, after all these years. Her bones lie beneath my feet, those same bones that became my mother's bones. Immersed in the tundra sea for sixty-five years.

The sky hangs heavy with clouds; a mist envelopes us and veils the river flowing by only feet from the graveyard. The river's banks erode yearly, and before long the villagers will be forced to abandon Kotlik. There are some who swear they would rather drown; they will never leave their ancestors.

We do not speak. A strong wind scours the tundra with the first dusting of snow. Boats motor upriver behind us. A tension fills the air. I am acutely aware of my mother's absence, and I know the same is true for Brad and especially for my father. I can see him out of the corner of my eye, the cigarette moving neurotically in and out of his mouth. While my mother was alive he was a closet smoker, partaking only when he was stressed and beyond the reach of her disapproving stare. Even after her death he tried to hide it from his children, but we all knew he was smoking many packs a week. This is the first time he's smoked in my presence. The smoke wafts toward me, and for once I like the smell.

Our visit wasn't planned. Brad and I spontaneously decided to come to Alaska, and we invited our father along, fully expecting him to decline. Since her death we have rarely spoken of my mother, though she has been gone nine years. If we do speak of her the conversation is brief and superficial. Nothing heavy, nothing hard: that is the rule. At least when my father is around.

But this trip is different because we cannot escape the presence of my mother anywhere we go. Relatives resemble her, people ask about her, and now we are standing at her mother's grave. If I could reach over and hold my father it would be easier, if we could all embrace and weep together. But that is not this family. Not now, not ever. I have rarely seen my father cry. On this trip I see him choking back tears every day. I see pain in his furrowed forehead, in the perpetual glassiness of his glacier blue eyes.

Again and again I read the words on the tombstone. I imagine my mother standing next to me. I see her as a little girl in the arms of Charlie Backlund as he stands over the freshly covered mound. She holds paper flowers because the real ones haven't bloomed yet. Maybe she cries and maybe she doesn't. But she knows that something is wrong. She can see it in her father's face, in his sagging skin and glassy eyes. She knows.

I wander away from Dora's grave. I need space. I stroll around the graveyard examining dates and names, mostly Yup'ik and Russian. I run my hands over the smooth, timeworn Russian Orthodox crosses, bulbous and painted. More recent graves are less ornate, some well tended, others merely driftwood held together by wire. A child's bicycle hangs from a cross. Plastic flowers litter the ground. I am bent over a grave, shivering, when Brad appears behind me.

"I think Dad is going to lose it," he says.

"I've never seen him smoke like this," I answer. "How are you?"

"All right. I just keep thinking that it's not fair, that I'm not the right person to be here, you know? All these years that grave just sitting out here. Mom never, she never . . ." He pauses, waiting for words.

"Yeah," I say. "I know what you mean."

We walk back to our father, who has pulled a ski mask over his face so that all we can see are his pursed lips sucking a cigarette and his eyes magnified by glasses; he reminds me of a cartoon character, eyes bulging and surreal. A single tear dangles from his eyelash, but I look away quickly so he won't see that I've noticed.

Papa Joe is telling us that many of our relatives are buried here. He points out some of the oldest graves, tells us how most of the family used to live in Kotlik but are now spread throughout many villages in the delta.

I ask him about Charlie Backlund's grave, and he tells us it is not here. He thinks it is far upriver, near Mountain Village.

"Why?" I ask. "What was he doing up there?"

Papa Joe shrugs. "Don't know," he answers. In Yup'ik he asks Angela, who is much older, if she knows. She shakes her head, but something in the way she averts her eyes makes me feel as if she is holding something back.

As we putter back downriver, snow begins to fall. My father sits in the bow, hunched, taking long draws on his cigarette and staring north to the sea.

THREE MAJOR WAVES OF NEWCOMERS came to the Yukon–Kuskokwim Delta, where Kotlik is located on its northern shores. First came the Russian fur trappers and missionaries, who immigrated in large numbers and soon integrated with the Native populations. Russian Orthodox missions were established, and as Natives converted, intermarriage became common. Many Yup'ik families today are of partly Russian blood, and the names of many of my cousins confirm this blending: Natalia, Olga, Ivanoff, and Yuri. My Yup'ik name, given to me by Justina, is Aivrun, after my great-great-grandfather. Even the village dress bears traces of Russian influence, the old women's colorful babushkas covering their heads. My cousin Angela has yellow eyes, and her hair hangs golden beneath her scarf.

My great-great-grandfather Aivrun—or Ivan as he would have been called in Russia—was probably full-blooded Russian, as far as anybody knows, for there is no record of his ancestry on the family tree, which was researched and drawn by my Yup'ik cousin, Larry Mike. Aivrun married Nicuuk, my great-great-grandmother, a Yup'ik woman who spawned this family tree that sprawls twenty feet across my study floor, well over five hundred names long. My name lies about halfway down the list, beneath my mother, Inaqaq, and her parents, Charlie and Dora. The Yup'ik world is somehow integral to my own, yet so foreign that I wonder how I can even begin to understand.

Most of the names on the family tree have lines drawn to them connecting ancestors to descendants, but like Aivrun, Charlie Backlund's name has no predecessor. Such ancestorless names are usually those of newcomers, men of different ethnic origins. My father, John, belongs on the family tree only because he married my mother. Regardless, all of these names are family, genetics notwithstanding.

The second wave of newcomers to the delta were Americans, mostly scientists and explorers seeking a route for the North America–to–Europe telegraph line in the 1860s, when much of the bush was mapped and explored. Diseases from the outside world began infiltrating the villages; tuberculosis, which killed my grandmother, was pandemic. But unlike in the Lower 48, interaction between the Natives and the whites was generally peaceful, leading the whites to invent the stereotype of the passive, jovial, rosy-cheeked Eskimo living in an igloo made of giant ice cubes.

My grandfather came with the third wave of newcomers, the gold seekers who viewed the Yukon River as a route to the gold fields in the Yukon Territory and Alaska's interior. I don't know if Charlie came for gold, and if so whether he found any or not. Regardless, sometime between 1900 and 1910, Charlie first appeared and opened his store in the village of Chaneliak, which was later flooded and moved to where Kotlik lies today. He may have come from the gold fields, because when he came to Chaneliak he had money in his pockets, enough to build and stock a one-room log store. He was a tall, bulky Finn in his forties, with large hands and a long, thin nose. Nobody with whom I spoke, even the elders, had any notion of Charlie's past, except that as a young man he had come to Alaska from Finland. One day they woke and he was there, his entrance as baffling as his departure would be twenty-five years later.

Charlie became known throughout the Yup'ik villages as a generous man, readily giving to those in need. That is why he met and married my grandmother, Dora, the story goes. When Dora's father, Anthony Andrews—the half-Russian son of Aivrun—died, her mother,

Christine, was left with six children to care for. Charlie took her family in, and when he moved his store from Chaneliak to Pastolik, they went with him. When Pastolik flooded they moved to Kotlik, where Charlie and Dora married and a year later gave birth to my uncle Carl, or Ungkak. Two years later my mother was born, named after her great-uncle, Inaqaq, brother of Nicuuk.

My mother barely remembered her father. She remembered the store, the candy, the size of his arms and chest when he picked her up to hold her. She remembered his resonant, baritone voice, like her brother Carl's. But Charlie was gone to her by her sixth birthday; therefore, the memories she passed on to her children were little more than the dead roots of a plant that has dried and crumbled into dust. This was true for all of the family tree that is spread over the floor of this room; she had so slight a memory of her childhood, and what she did remember was difficult for her to discuss because it belonged to a life that was no longer hers. She knew she had been an Eskimo, but only in the abstract, a long-ago dream. She knew her name had been Inaqaq, but it was a name from another life. So she lived her life half aware of herself, struggling, I think, to understand the empty place inside her. She had only Carl to remind her of that other life, and maybe that is why they lived three thousand miles apart and rarely talked. She remembered eating fish eyeballs, the slippery jewels her father brought home after a good day's fishing. She remembered his herd of reindeer, and the fish wheel that plucked salmon from the river. She remembered fish camp in summers, playing in the dense willows that lined the shore of the Yukon for a thousand miles.

Meanwhile the family tree kept growing, with or without my mother in it. Justina married Gus Mike in the Catholic church and raised twelve children, two of whom resemble Doris, one who could be Carl's twin. Meanwhile her great-aunts and -uncles—Cus'aaraq,

Yugisaq, Cu'paq, Kumagaq, Qumigan, Aparsuk, Yuqutaq, Taqitaq, and Ciklak—had all died and left behind children and grandchildren who were fishing and hunting and dancing to the beat of the drum. Meanwhile her aunts, Justina and Cecilia, struggled to raise their children in a traditional way while Michael Jordan and Skidoo and Budweiser became the new cultural icons, and the young children ceased learning Yup'ik. During my mother's lifetime the Yup'ik culture was being squeezed tight in the fist of the American dream, the same dream that my mother was living.

THE OLD WORLD, 1930

THE OLD WOMAN'S NAME WAS NICUUK, and she was as old as the great white bear—*nanuaq*—who stole children as they fished carelessly too far out on the ice. This is what the children whispered to each other when they saw the old woman shuffling out of her mud house built from the tundra. She emerged only in summers now, when the days were long and she could warm her brittle bones down by the river, watching her daughter and granddaughters and great-granddaughters clean and hang the fish that the men brought in their wooden boats. *This day*, she thought, *I will go to the river and cover my tired feet in mud. It will do me good.*

The winters were hard for her, each new one longer than the last, and she wondered how it was that she had made it through so many frozen days, months, and years. She remembered when she was young, how she used to go ice fishing with her husband, Aivrun, the tall yellow-eyed hunter whom she had married so many years ago that it seemed another lifetime. He was not the first white man she had seen, but she hadn't seen enough of them for his coming to be ignored. She was afraid of the white men, not from personal experience but from the stories she had heard about what they had done to the Inuit farther inland and to the north. Entire villages had been destroyed.

But she knew the Inuit way, the fighting and fierce rivalries between tribes, and she was not surprised that they had chosen to fight back. She was glad that the Yup'ik were friendly with the white men. When they came they brought things she liked: shiny metals, colorful cloth, and sugar. Whiskey, too, she believed, was not so bad, although she'd never tried it. There was reason to celebrate when the Russians came, for the men would drink and laugh and many new goods would come to the village by way of trade.

Aivrun, Nicuuk thought, as she carefully lowered herself onto the grassy riverbank, *today would be your birthday and you would be even older than I am, which is to say, too old.*

She removed her leather slippers and cradled her feet in her hands. *My feet look younger than I,* she thought. *I wonder how that is.* And she was right: her feet appeared youthful hanging there above the green-brown water of the Yukon. She had calluses like thick leather on her soles from walking barefoot over the tundra and along the riverbanks every summer of her life. But her toenails were cut neatly and her skin was tight where she thought it should be wrinkled. She massaged these feet with her wrinkled hands, her fingers like spiders crawling as they worked themselves into the flesh.

She submerged her feet in the river and felt the cool water between her toes. She pulled them out, dug a small hole in a shelf of the river's bank into which she splashed water, and she stirred until a thick mud was formed. Finally she sank her feet into the dark pool and leaned back onto the grass, staring up at the sky and the high satin clouds speeding across the blue. She heard laughter from her daughter's fish camp a short walk downriver, and she thought it was her grandson, Ungkak, playing with his little sister, Inaqaq. Nicuuk felt good knowing they were so close by, and she let her mind wander farther into the past, as it did more and more often on these never-ending summer days. She hardly slept anymore, and it was good to recall her life. *That is why my feet are young,* she thought, *because I tell them stories of my youth.* She chuckled at this thought, and anyone wandering by would have seen a fat and very wrinkled old Yup'ik woman jiggling as she laughed at the cerulean sky.

She remembered meeting Aivrun, his yellow eyes staring out at her from the cave of his hood, a freshly killed fox dangling from his shoulder. He'd been out hunting, and she'd bumped into him while carrying a load of driftwood from the shed. She was frightened by his eyes, but she saw the white glint of his teeth as he smiled. *"Waqaa,"* he said. She wasn't known to be shy. She stared him straight in the face and returned his greeting before quickly moving around him and up the hill toward home. He watched her go.

Many days later he came to her house to speak with her father, Yugisaq, who had heard of Aivrun's prowess as a hunter. Yugisaq and the Russian sat facing each other across the fire. Nicuuk and her mother, Ciklak, sat behind, sewing a coat from the caribou leather Yugisaq had brought home the week before. Moose sizzled over the flames, and the men ate dried salmon and drank tea from leaves gathered over the summer. The warm, single-room dwelling smelled deeply of fish. Circular in shape, the clay walls were hung with various provisions: animal skins, dried salmon, baskets filled with spices, tea, and sugar brought to them by the Russians. The fire pit burned in the center of the room, dug low into the earth and covered with a thick plaster of mud. A low bench surrounded the pit, and it was here that people gathered to tell their stories late into the night.

Nicuuk remembered for the rest of her life that single moment when Aivrun parted the skins covering the door and descended the ladder to the grass-covered floor. He was welcomed by her father, and Nicuuk noticed that the white man spoke Yup'ik well, though with a sharp accent that reminded her of northern people. He spoke his name, Aivrun. His huge sealskin coat was lined with wolf fur and sewn with colorful threaded designs that Nicuuk envied. She was taken aback by his face, by how handsome he was for a white man. *For one thing,* she thought to herself, *his skin is not white. It is colored like clay from the riverbank.* Aivrun's skin was the color of light mud, a deep walnut tone made by years of sun and wind. Though he was young, maybe ten years older than Nicuuk's sixteen, his face was not youthful. But it was a good face, full of strength and emotion. His skin was grainy and pitted, as if by windstorm, and a long pale scar ran from the edge of his lip to the corner of his left jawbone.

But his eyes! Nicuuk thought. Like none she'd seen before. They reminded her of a lynx, bright yellow teardrops angling sharply back to his ears. She watched them as she sewed, and she liked the way they squinted when he laughed, the wrinkles spreading from his eyes like the tangled roots of a tree. He laughed easily and often, which was good in the presence of Yugisaq, who in Nicuuk's estimation took everything too seriously. Before long the two of them were like old friends, exchanging hunting stories and laughing and shoving meat into their mouths as if they hadn't eaten for days.

Yugisaq told the story of a hunt last winter. He was up north searching for moose when his dog team fell through the ice. He jumped from the sled just in time, but not before getting soaked from the waist down. He stood on the bank shivering as his dogs struggled to get out of the water, their front paws up on the ice, clawing desperately but every time slipping back into the water. Six dogs, all fighting to escape, but in less than a minute they were tangled in their harnesses like flies in a web, dragging each other down. Their mad howling raised the hair on Yugisaq's neck, until suddenly they stilled and their crying stopped. All six dogs regarded one another with frightened eyes before slipping soundlessly beneath the surface.

All of this Yugisaq was helpless to prevent. Blocked on both sides by gaping holes in the ice, his only avenue of retreat was back the way he had come. It wasn't until his dogs were gone that he realized he couldn't feel his legs. He had managed to grab one small pack as he jumped from the sled, and as he walked to a nearby clump of trees, he began fumbling around in it for something with which to start a fire. He found his flint and stone, and before long he was sitting under the trees, warming his toes over the flames and thinking about how he was going to survive the journey home. A full day's sled ride from home, he figured he could walk it in three days if he didn't run into trouble. His provisions had gone down with the sled, as had his rifle. He had his hunting knife on his belt, and in his pack he found tea, sugar, a roll of rawhide string, and a bag of beads that he had planned on trading when he passed through neighboring villages.

"A lot of good these are going to do me," he said out loud to himself. But he kept them because he had, at that point, nothing to lose. He figured if he was going to die, he'd pour the beads over his body like water, and when they found him come spring they'd know that he had died in beauty. This thought soothed him.

His clothes dried by the fire overnight, and the next morning he began walking at first light. He'd spent the majority of the night constructing snowshoes, cutting branches from the few nearby trees, shaping and notching them with his knife. He had tied them with rawhide and made crude bindings which he'd laced over his mukluks. *They aren't pretty,* he thought, *not nearly as nice as the ones Ciklak makes. But they'll work.* For good luck he'd threaded beads onto the rawhide on the tip of each snowshoe, four tiny slivered moons on each side, red, green, blue, and yellow. He wasn't sure why he'd done so, but two days into his journey, trudging through a blinding snowstorm, he was thankful for the bright shapes. The colors gave him hope.

On the second day he found no shelter, so he walked through the night, a splinter of moon lighting the lonesome winter shapes. Near dawn a figure appeared out of the darkness. At first he thought it was a wolf, but as he came nearer he saw a wounded moose calf standing alone, its rear leg broken and dangling. Dizzy from hunger and lack of sleep, Yugisaq wondered if he was dreaming. The calf stared at him with fear and knowing. Yugisaq drew his knife and cut its throat. He slit open its belly and placed his hands inside the warm bowels. He ate the liver first, giving thanks. He packed as much meat as he could carry. Under each eyelid of the slain calf he placed a bright purple bead, and a blue one in its belly. He trudged on, knowing he would survive.

It took Yugisaq five days to slog home. When he arrived, his family was in mourning. Some people claimed he'd returned from the spirit world. He gave the rest of his beads to Nicuuk and told her to use them wisely. He never hunted again without a few of them tucked into a pocket of his coat. The snowshoes remained his favorite pair; he expected he'd have them on his feet when he walked into the next world. He had much to be thankful for.

When Yugisaq finished telling his story, silence filled the room. Aivrun had listened intently, nodding gravely from time to time, and now he stared ahead at Yugisaq as if expecting him to continue. His eyes flashed bright in the firelight, and for a moment Nicuuk found herself in his gaze. Aivrun looked at her and smiled, close-mouthed; Nicuuk looked away. The magic of the story hung in the air between them. The fire crackled, and Yugisaq faded off to sleep. Aivrun whispered good-bye and thanks to the older man, then rose to put on his coat. Before he climbed the ladder he turned and nodded thanks to

Nicuuk and Ciklak. Nicuuk watched him ascend into the night. She listened to his feet crunching through the snow. She heard his last footstep, and faded off to sleep.

THE OLD WOMAN NICUUK woke with a start from a dream. She felt her feet in the cool mud, and she noted the sun dropping low and the air chilling. *I must have some tea,* she thought. She dried her feet on her skirt, feeling the stiffness of her legs and a vague, sad feeling in her belly. *I wonder what I was dreaming,* she thought, and she tried to remember. Only when she pulled on her leather slippers did it come back to her: sewn onto each toe was a lazy red moon, surrounded by brightly colored beads like rings around a planet. *How could I forget?* she thought, as she rose creakily from the riverbank. All the way home she thought of beads.

4

C hristmas Eve, 1985. My first visit home from college. The seven of us stand in front of our Christmas tree. I can't say exactly what has changed, but I feel older and get along with my family as if we are old chums. It's after dinner and we're stuffed from the feast my mother had prepared, the entrees spread across the counter of her kitchen like a new constellation. I don't remember who's taking the photo, one of the many guests: Heidi's boyfriend, Richard; the Turkish engineer, Fatih; the speed skater, Ed; the skinny runner, Kim, from up the hill—the list goes on. One of them looks through the lens and sees us: my mother front and center, the rest of us crowding around her like we are cold and she is the fire. She wears a blue silk blouse and a black vest. Her hair is graying, her sea green eyes shine in the light. We lean and stretch to be near her, but she stands straight, poised, alone. She is independent, supremely confident in our dependence on her, in her own magnetism. All of our lives people have gathered around her table to listen to her words, listed inward to be caught in the glow of her smile. She gives selflessly, pulls the stragglers and wounded souls into her home, asks little in return.

Her only rule, unspoken but written in the lines of her face, is a certain distance; she will receive your problems, but do not try to be the receptacle of hers.

We stand many inches above my mother. Heather, nineteen, is to her right, wearing a green silk dress and lime green eye shadow. Her thick, wavy nest of hair is tamed by a curling iron. All evening I've been teasing her about the gobs of makeup, but she just cocks her head and says smugly, "To each his own," the same response she used to give me in high school when I hassled her about her Christian youth group. Heather's confidence is as steady and smooth as a river.

To my mother's left Brad gazes suavely away, as if he is looking into an African sunset. It's the model's pose that everybody tries at his age, seventeen. He's got freckled skin, thick hair just beginning to turn the reddish brown it will be in later years. Draped over his left shoulder is Michelle's arm; she hugs him from behind, her head extending from his right shoulder like a Siamese twin. But Michelle's face is different from Brad's, shaped from another cutter. She has my mother's wide smile and shelved cheeks. Her long brown hair contrasts sharply with my father's skin.

Behind, my father and Heidi appear as severed heads. My father is silver-haired, ruddy and smiling. Heidi's hair matches almost flawlessly the redwood walls of our house, her face freckled and her skin my mother's almond brown. Despite her brilliant hair, Heidi is an Eskimo; a blend of my parents' genes, I have always thought her unusually beautiful.

In back, I tower over them all, my hair cut short, a thick-lipped fraternity-brother grin on my face and my hockey player's neck wider than my head. I look a little drunk, stupid, something. In this melting pot of a family, I resemble your standard, empty-headed jock.

The photograph is the last of our family all together. The following Christmas my mother would be gone. We would gather anyway, trying to maintain a semblance of family. Heidi would prepare my mother's toffee; Michelle would cook the stuffing according to my mother's recipe. On Christmas morning we'd open gifts in the same order—oldest to youngest—as we always had. But our family was in real life just as it is in the photograph: drawn together and centered around my mother, like rings around a planet. Without her, we were only going through the motions, and we all knew it. The following Christmas I wouldn't come home.

ON MY FIRST TRIP TO KOTLIK in 1989, Justina pulled a torn, black-and-white photograph off her living room wall and handed it to me. I was speechless; I had known that photograph since childhood, when another copy had tickled my curiosity about my mother's ancestry. But until I learned that Justina had kept that very same photo for all of those years, my mother's Yup'ik past had seemed mythological.

"Inaqaq," she said. "Doris," and then a few more words in Yup'ik. Natalia, my second cousin, translated. "She says this is a picture of your mother with your great-grandmother Cu'paq, Ungkak, and herself. Your mother, she was just a little girl, but she was full of fire. Not like Ungkak; he was so shy."

In her eighties, Justina's wrinkled face beamed when she smiled. Her eyes grinned, as if she saw joy in everything. However, when she showed me the photograph her eyes glistened with tears.

"Why didn't she try to find us again?" Natalia translated. "Why didn't she come home?"

I shook my head. It was a question I could not answer. I stared at the photograph, into the eyes of the girl who was my mother, searching for an answer. How was it she never returned? Inside the tattered borders the subjects are smiling, all except the young girl sitting on Justina's lap: my mother, Doris. Inaqaq. She is three or four years old, dressed in a skirt with long johns underneath. Her dark hair is cut short; her lips curl downward in a pout. I recognize my mother in this girl, in the deep-set, evocative eyes. I cannot help but wonder why she looks so grim in this group of happy people. Her mother was recently dead, and perhaps she sensed the journey before her.

It occurs to me that my mother was always the free spirit I knew her as; even as a child she would have stood out in a room, if not for her beauty, then for her intensity. No matter what her mood or emotion she was rarely nondescript, and she wasn't afraid to stand against the opinion of a group. When she was angry her eyes flashed like lightning over a dark sea; in her joy those same eyes sparkled and suffused a room with light. I can see her at our table entertaining guests, all eyes focused on her as she weaves a story with her lithe, expressive hands and acrobatic words.

What I knew of my mother's Yup'ik childhood was limited before going to Kotlik. What I have gathered since then is piecemeal, small shards of knowledge that flicker and take shape as they begin to form a whole: her stories and journals, Justina's memory, a few photographs and the life I try to breathe into them with my own imagination.

In that first photograph, my mother sits on the lap of a young Justina, who wears a plaid skirt, leggings, and a wool cardigan. She has shiny black hair and a finely angled, gentle face. Her nose is long and well shaped, a fine ridge that runs from her brow to her smiling upper lip. She has thin eyebrows, large white teeth. Her arms enfold my mother, her hands covering my mother's hands in her lap. They could be mother and daughter.

To Justina's right is her mother, Christine, a middle-aged woman dressed in a fur coat, long skirt, and mukluks. She holds mittens in her lap. Judging by her clothing the photo must have been snapped in late spring or fall; they are sitting on long grass, not snow. Christine has the same long, narrow nose as Justina, the same thin lips. But her cheekbones are higher, more defined, and her eyes are more angled. Her hands are like my mother's: slight, bony, delicate.

They could be my mother's hands.

I stare at them for a long time and remember the grace with which my mother moved them through the air as she talked, her hands saying more than her words. I also remember those fingers running through my hair, pulling firmly on my scalp as she read to me late at night.

Next to Christine sits my Uncle Carl, Ungkak, dressed in a sealskin coat, knickers, and knee-length socks. To his left another young girl smiles coyly and leans into Carl, but he doesn't seem to notice. He stares steadily ahead at the camera, a bemused smile on his lips, thin and straight like Christine's. His cavernous eyes are gentler than my mother's, too knowing for his age. I always thought of Uncle Carl as wise, maybe because of his quiet demeanor. His expression rests somewhere between calm and concerned, as if he has guessed what his future holds and knows it won't be easy. Like my mother, he knew death. He must have aged well beyond his years in the time between Dora's death and when he and my mother were sent away from Kotlik.

When I handed the photograph back to Justina she held it against her chest. Again Natalia translated.

"I always thought that she would come back. She was like one of my own children." Justina smiled, turned and hung the photograph back on the wall.

We sat for a long time—Justina, Natalia, and I—not saying anything at all, just staring into the woodstove and listening absent-mindedly to the television blaring from the next room, where kids were playing Nintendo. Later we ate Jell-O pudding for dessert, and then Justina said she needed to sleep. I left her, the door banging behind me as I faced the stinging wind and walked into the luminous Alaskan night.

Leaving Kotlik,
1933

WHEN CHARLIE sent Inaqaq and Carl away from Kotlik, he believed he was doing what was best for them. He planned to have Miss Petril, a nurse, accompany them to the Agrens' on Vashon Island, while he stayed in Alaska long enough to settle his business affairs. He'd then retire to Vashon with his children.

Charlie had never met the Agrens, and in fact had only a vague notion of who they were: that they boarded children who were waiting to be placed in permanent foster homes. He knew of them through a Seattle banker, who had handled the trust Charlie was establishing for the children.

Initially Charlie had asked Justina to go with the children to Vashon. For the rest of her life she would remember Charlie's request as one of the hardest anyone had ever made of her. She loved Inaqaq and Ungkak as if they were her own, but she had never been farther from Kotlik than twenty miles downriver to the mission. To her people the delta was the center of the universe, where creation began with Raven carving out the Yukon, where their ancestors' bones danced again in the flickering winter lights. For Justina, leaving Kotlik was like mourning, all at once, the death of everyone she'd ever known.

Perhaps Charlie never understood the Yup'ik way, what leaving Kotlik might do to her, and to his children. Perhaps back then nobody had any idea how an Eskimo would fare downstates, how they would adapt to urban life and white cultural values. Charlie had no reference point from which to make that decision.

The day Inaqaq and Ungkak sailed away on the steamer out of St. Michael, Justina pulled her mukluks over her feet, wrapped a yellow babushka around her head, donned her light parka, and began walking upriver. It was early May, and patches of snow still lay melting over the low humps of soggy ground that sucked at her feet as she walked. She hummed to herself, a song she knew from childhood. She remembered her grandmother, Nicuuk, only a few years dead, singing the song to her as she cleaned salmon at fish camp. Justina didn't remember the words anymore, but she imagined Nicuuk singing, her voice soft and high. It soothed Justina to hum along with her grandmother, but Nicuuk's death still weighed heavily on her, and now the loss of Inaqaq and Ungkak only sharpened the pain.

She walked due east, toward the scattered lakes and streams that were constantly being reformed and rerouted by the flows of the Yukon. When she passed a small hummock where she had picked blueberries with Inaqaq the summer before, she sank to her knees in the marshy grass. She had told herself she would not cry. *I must be strong,* she said to herself. But the ground pulling her in felt soft and warm, and Justina thought how good it would be to be the tundra, how good it would feel to let it pull her until she swam in the mud and roots, her ancestors' blood and bones.

She thought of Charlie, all he had done for her family, and she wanted to forgive him. She wondered if she should have gone with the children to Washington, and she was filled with guilt. She pictured Inaqaq's scared, tear-streaked face as she boarded the steamship for Seattle. *Little Inaqaq,* she thought. *How I will miss you. Who will make me laugh anymore?* And then the tears came, at first restrained, then covering her cheeks with a shine that rippled like windblown water.

That morning she and her mother, Christine, had accompanied the children from Kotlik to St. Michael, where they met Miss Petril at the steamship dock. Charlie had stayed behind, busy with the sale of his store and his upcoming move to Liberty Landing, although Justina suspected that he hadn't wanted to witness his children's sorrow. Miss Petril boarded first and stood atop the gangplank, gesturing to the children to come aboard. The nurse's robust frame seemed withered so high above them. She frowned slightly, contradicting the cheeriness with which she had greeted Inaqaq that morning; she was angered by Charlie's absence.

Ungkak stared up at Miss Petril, then back to Inaqaq. He held Inaqaq's hand, which she kept trying to yank away in order to free herself and retreat to Justina and Christine, who stood stoically behind the fence that separated passengers from well-wishers. They stared unflinchingly at the children, sending silent prayers to protect them on their journey. Justina's lips trembled.

Inaqaq clutched her doll, Nina, clothed in a blue dress and tiny fur mukluks that Christine had sewn, as Ungkak held her arm and towed her up the gangplank. When she broke into a high wail that silenced the hustle and bustle of the dock, Ungkak gently but firmly lifted her and held her to him. At the top of the gangplank he handed her to Miss Petril, who whispered in her ear, kissed her cheek, then turned her toward Justina and Christine, standing in the shadows. It began to rain, at first lightly and then suddenly in arcing swaths that sent people scrambling for shelter. Justina's last vision of Inaqaq was one of grief, her tiny hand waving, her face pinched in tears as Miss Petril turned and carried her into the ship's cabin. Ungkak waved one last time before slipping behind Miss Petril.

Christine went for shelter, hiding under the wide awning of the shipping depot. Justina stayed alone in the rain, soaking wet, as she watched the *Anna Marie* slip out of the harbor, make a sharp turn east before heading out to sea. Though it was spring, the air was still winter-chilled and damp, and she began to shiver without realizing it. Christine pulled her under the awning and held her.

Later, out on the tundra, Justina remembered these things and mourned the loss of her dead sister's children. She sank into the brown grass and cried until no tears came. She lay back on the soft earth and watched the clouds form animals in the sky. She had done this with Inaqaq, taught her how to see animals in the clouds, bears and frogs and whales that the wind blew in. They had lain side by side on the tundra, pointing into the sky. Once Inaqaq had said, "I have a new animal, a fox with wings." She had shown it to Justina and they had given it a secret name and promised to tell no one.

As Justina lay there alone she looked for the flying fox, and she thought to herself, *If I see this flying fox again, then surely they will return to us.* She searched for hours, finding eagles, seals, beavers, caribou, bears, wolves, spiders. But there were no flying foxes. Finally she rose and squished through the tundra back to the village, feeling old though she was barely more than a child herself.

WHEN DORIS AND CARL first sighted the towering buildings of Seattle, their jaws fell open. Beside them, one hand on the railing and the other shadowing her eyes so that she could see, Miss Petril looked worriedly at the children. Carl held the railing and tried to force his head between the bars to get a better view. His eyes bulged, and Miss Petril warned him to stop before he crushed his head. Doris stood farther back, holding Nina above the railing to give her a better view of the fast-approaching city.

"Nina," she said excitedly in Yup'ik, "look at how the houses sparkle, how they rise into the sky like trees. This is where you're going to live! This is your new home!"

Miss Petril lifted Doris, holding her firmly against her round body and looking her in the eyes. But Doris was agitated and nervous, too busy staring at Seattle to pay attention.

"Doris," Miss Petril said, her voice urgent. "You must listen to me." She paused and waited for Doris to focus her impenetrable eyes.

"You must listen to me. It is important now for you to speak English. You must try very hard to speak all the time in English. And you must help Carl, because his English is not as good as yours, and it will be hard for him. You're lucky that you have learned, and now you must practice speaking it all the time. If you can't remember a word, or you don't know what to say, then you may ask me. Otherwise it is best for you to be silent. Do you understand me?"

Doris nodded and looked down at Carl, who watched them with curiosity, but who, in fact, understood almost nothing of what Miss Petril had said. Doris was afraid to say anything to him because she would have to speak in Yup'ik. She didn't want to upset Miss Petril, but she promised herself that once she was alone with Carl she would tell him everything.

A moment later Miss Petril surprised her by speaking to Carl in Yup'ik, repeating what she had told Doris, except that she told him he must work very hard to learn English, or things would be difficult for him here. She told him he must be quiet in public, and that Doris would help him if he couldn't understand. Carl nodded at everything Miss Petril said, but the inquisitive expression on his face hardened into fear. Before, he had watched Seattle grow larger while imagining all the pretty cars that he had seen only in magazines. Now he felt alone. Now Seattle loomed dark and ominous, and he wondered why Miss Petril had spoken so threateningly.

The steamship's foghorn blew, and Carl and Doris flinched in fright, though they had been hearing it for the entire two-week journey. A flock of seagulls perched along the railing rose at once into the sky. Doris and Carl watched, momentarily distracted. Doris raised Nina into the sky and whispered in English, "Look, Nina, look, a whole cloud of birds, shaped like a flying fox!"

Miss Petril smiled, remembering Justina playing with Carl and Doris out on the tundra. She had not stopped thinking about Justina's mournful face as the steamship pulled away from St. Michael. It was a face she would never forget, even years later when she wondered whether she had done the right thing, taking the children away from Kotlik.

WHEN THE STEAMER DOCKED in Seattle, Carl and Doris were nearly paralyzed by the din and rush of the wharf. They clung to Miss Petril as she plowed through the throng of people. Voices blasted from loudspeakers, men and women clung to each other and kissed, a red-nosed man tried to sell them steaming apples, a policeman barked orders from high on a horse. Everybody seemed to yell. Most startling, however, were all the white people. For the first time in the children's lives they were surrounded by people who resembled their father—white skin, light eyes, yellow hair—rather than the darkness of their mother. White men of all shapes and sizes rushed around with crates and baskets and bunches of fruit on their backs and heads. One carried a cage with a rainbow-colored bird, which Doris could have sworn was speaking English. She looked at Carl, but he hadn't noticed. He was too busy staring at a crate of bananas, which neither of them had ever seen. Miss Petril noticed Carl's fascination and scuttled over to the man standing beside the bananas. She bought one and brought it back to Carl, who was wide-eyed.

"It's called a banana," Miss Petril said, speaking very slowly in English. She pointed at the banana as she said its name. "It's a kind of fruit, from a very warm place far away, across the ocean. It's good to eat."

With a few quick motions she peeled it. Doris thought of the walnuts Charlie sometimes brought back with him, which she decided were similar. Miss Petril took a bite of the banana and handed it to Carl, who nibbled a bite. His face grew a small, tentative smile; for the first time since leaving the ship he relaxed a bit. Miss Petril asked them to wait while she located the bus, then she was gone into the crowd.

Carl took another bite of the banana, then passed it to Doris who, to Carl's disgust, licked it. She smiled. She liked the color, the way it glowed out of the fog and slow drizzle of the dock. It made her feel warm, if only for a moment. They finished it and huddled together in the thickening rain. The yellow peel hung from Carl's hand, cold and limp, as they stood dumbfounded by the crowd.

Carl pointed at a woman strolling by with her nose in the air. She wore funny shoes, tall and skinny in the heels, like walking with small sticks underfoot. Carl thought it must be difficult to walk with shoes like that, and he wondered why the woman wore them. Doris giggled with him as the woman passed, but she was more entertained by the woman's dog, trailing on a leash. Or at least she thought it was a dog. *Not like the dogs in Kotlik,* she thought. It was as small as a muskrat, with curly ivory hair shaped in strange little balls on its head and tail. Its back was shaved bare, and Doris thought that it must get cold. Carl chuckled at the red ribbons tied neatly on the dog's ears, its red nail-polished claws. It pranced along, its head high in the air, aloof. Carl and Doris restrained themselves until the woman was out of sight, then burst out laughing. Doris imagined the dog in Kotlik and laughed until her belly hurt. Then she thought of the sled dogs, and her laughter subsided as she imagined what those dogs would do to the muskrat dog, tearing it apart like a piece of fish. But the laughter had felt good, the tension of the journey finally released. Doris slumped against Miss Petril's duffel bag, exhausted.

Carl kept watching while Doris nodded off to sleep. The rain stopped and long slivers of sun pierced the low clouds. Huge crates of sweet-smelling, bright orange and yellow orbs were lowered from a ship. A juggler threw bananas in the air; people dropped money into a black hat in front of him. The familiar smell of fish wafted from the boats. Carl thought of fish camp and Justina cutting and hanging salmon in long, pink strips. He felt like crying, but he knew he shouldn't. He was hungry by the time Miss Petril returned ten minutes later, her brow glistening with sweat.

"I'm sorry," she said, as she approached them. "It's very crowded. But I found the bus. Everything's okay. Follow me."

Miss Petril carried Doris, still sleeping, while Carl struggled behind with a duffel. He was exhausted by the time they reached the bus, the first one he'd ever seen. The driver looked friendly enough—with a thick mustache twisted and curled at each end—and he helped them load their luggage. But as Miss Petril moved to board the bus, he stopped her and nodded sternly at the children.

"You'll have to ride in back, you know, if you're their keeper," he said.

Miss Petril's face blushed, her lips twitched. She squeezed her purse and her thick arm shook. Carl thought she would hit the man, but he didn't understand why.

"How dare you!" she said, then snatched Carl's hand and pulled him past the driver to the rear of the bus, where two Indians stared indifferently out the windows. The bus jerked away from the dock, and instantly Doris awakened and broke into a scream so shrill that everybody covered their ears. Miss Petril held her and spoke gently into her ear.

"Inaqaq, it's okay, you're okay now. Hush, my little bear. Nina is here with you." She pressed the doll between them. Carl clung to Miss Petril's leg. Doris screamed and screamed.

5

ESKIMO DANCING

T ired from all the visiting, our father goes to bed while Brad and I join our cousin Natalia in the upper row of the community center bleachers in St. Marys, a village about a hundred miles upriver from Kotlik. Many of our relatives moved here from Kotlik when the Catholic mission school was established. Children of all ages scamper around the open floor of the community center, dressed in clothes of popular culture: Raiders' jerseys, Nike Air Jordans, backward baseball caps, sweatshirts hanging to their knees. In contrast the old women wear babushkas over their heads and colorful, shin-length Yup'ik dresses, or *qaspeq*. The older men wear blue jeans, wool shirts, and baseball caps declaring CAT: DIESEL POWER, or SKOAL, or ANDREAFSKY EAGLES, the name of the local high school's athletic teams. Despite the chaotic wrestling of children everywhere, a sense of calm prevails. The dancing is about to begin.

The children scatter as our cousin Fred Mike begins the first dance. Short and thickly muscled, broad in the shoulders, he kneels in the center of the room. He has short black hair, deep eyes, and a wide, sharp jaw. The young women watch him, one giggling as she whispers into another's ear. In each hand Fred holds dancing fans, circles of wood from which six long eagle feathers protrude. He breathes deeply, stares at the floor in concentration; he is "Waiting for the Drums." He waits for the story to begin.

A younger man, maybe sixteen years old, kneels to Fred's right and follows Fred's motions. Pimpled, he wears a White Sox T-shirt and 501 Levis. He stares, like Fred, at the floor.

With the first beat my ears tense, then settle into the rhythm of five drummers beating their walrus-stomach drums. They hold the drums away from their bodies, above their heads, and beat them with long, thin wooden drumsticks. On the third beat Fred begins his dance, his hands flowing with the beat of the drums and the singing drummers. He sways from the waist, but the dance emanates primarily from his arms and hands as he moves the dancing fans with and against the motions of his body. As the rhythm increases, the feathers seem rooted in his hands, and his arms slice the air like wings.

The beat quickens, the drums boom louder, and, one by one, women join Fred on the floor, each with her own reed dancing fan, woven by grandmothers and passed from one generation to the next. Facing the bleachers, they stand in a semicircle behind Fred, their eyes either downcast or focused on him as he leads. Natalia joins them, then Justina, who knows the dances by heart. Her arms swing gracefully from side to side, synchronized with the others, four generations dancing the same dance. Ages merge. In Justina I see a young girl learning from her elders; in a little girl I see an old woman dancing with her eyes closed.

Every few minutes the drummers reach a deafening crescendo, then abruptly they stop. If they like the dancers, they wait only a moment before drumming again. The length of the song reflects the drummers' pleasure in the dancers. Sometimes the drummers make the young dance for a long time, teaching discipline and endurance.

In this dance, the drummers go easy on the dancers because many are as old as Justina. After two sets the dance ends. Fred steps back to sing with the drummers and the women leave the floor, many of them passing their dancing fans to the girls walking on, high-school students practicing to dance for the governor in Mountain Village next week. Two brothers kneel in the lead positions, the girls standing behind, all of them waiting for the drums. The younger brother watches for a cue. Both wear red shirts, the older boy a Chicago Bulls tank top with the number twenty-three on his chest. Basketball rules in the villages because it can be played indoors all winter.

The drums thunder; the kids flicker to the beat. The girls' feet are stationary, but their knees bend like reeds swaying in the wind. They glance at one another, nervous and giddy. The rhythm grows fast and intense, the singing a high, wailing keen, as if the drummers are trying to pass on a sense of urgency and need. The boys momentarily falter, but recover after a few beats, their confidence unshaken.

This dance continues for a long time. At the end of each set the dancers move immediately toward the bleachers, but before they get away the drums begin again, calling them back. They must dance until the drums stop. Seven times they're called back. The drummers look on, amused. By the last set the kids are slick with sweat, but glowing with pride. To dance is one thing; to be called back is an honor. A crucial part of village life, the dancing defines them just as they define the dance.

I try to imagine students from my high school performing in such a setting, four generations intermingling, kids of all ages playing together without obvious hierarchy. The dancers don't appear self-conscious. I can't imagine myself up there dancing, not because I would be laughed at, but because I am afraid I would be. I sense that for my relatives and other Yup'ik, dancing is selfless, an expression of the whole. When the child in tiny mukluks dances by her mother, she begins to learn her story, where she came from, where she will go. I see this in the smallest children watching, some imitating the dancers' movements. During one dance, Fred holds his two-year-old daughter, Josephine, on his lap while he sings, his hands guiding her hands through the mirrored motions of the old women.

After the high schoolers' dance, all the dances begin to blend together for me, until I feel I'm on a river of sound, gently drifting to the sea. Hypnotized by the rhythm, I sit watching while dancers come and go, the keening voices settling over me like an elixir. I imagine my mother among the dancers, and for a moment I believe that she is there. In the girl, in the old woman, in all of them.

I turn to Brad, next to me on the bleachers. His fingers are stuffed into his ears. He yells that he needs to leave, his ears are hurting. I realize that I can't last much longer, either. We are just getting up to leave when another cousin joins us. He recognizes me from my first visit six years earlier and welcomes us warmly. As he bends too close I smell whiskey, strong on his breath. St. Marys, like many of the villages, is "dry," but as Natalia told us earlier, it is more damp than dry. Again my mother is near; I grow hot with a confusing blend of pity and shame.

I ask this cousin if he is going to dance. He laughs loudly and mutters incoherently. I look at Fred singing to the drums. These two are similar in age and circumstance, both facing the same issues inherent in straddling two incongruous cultures. Yet one responds by learning the old ways, while the other takes to drink. I look around the room at the children playing or dancing or staring or sleeping. Some will not learn this dance. Or they will learn it and soon forget. Or they will remember but not believe. They will hear the drums, but they won't be called by them. When the drumming becomes just noise, the dancing ends.

LATER THAT NIGHT I walk home with Fred. We are about the same age, and since my last visit I have come to feel close to him, despite the distance that separates us and the very different lives we lead. The October night is cold. I see Fred's breath rising, sweat still glistening on his brow from four hours of dancing. I never saw him leave the floor. Below us the Andreafsky River shimmers in the moonlight. Fred asks me how I liked the dancing, and I tell him I am learning to like it, that it is very different for me. I joke that the drumming makes my ears ring. He laughs, says that most Eskimos must be half deaf. I compliment him on his dancing, his smoothness and endurance. I tell him I wish I understood the singing so that I would know the stories.

"The stories, you know," Fred answers, "they are important, but maybe not the most important. I don't even understand all of it— some of them are very old. Maybe nobody could tell you the story no more. But the dance it still goes on; I listen to the drum and that's enough. The dance tells a story even if the words are lost."

I listen to Fred's voice, passionate about dancing. I ask him why some people don't dance, such as our other cousin.

"I didn't used to dance either," he says. "For a long time I thought I was too cool, that my friends would laugh at me. But then bad things happened. It was . . . "

He pauses, searching for words. He looks at me, then down to the river.

"Lots of people die here, you know, when they're young. Something is hard, I don't know what, but many of my friends, people I know, they end up killing themselves. Too much drinking, no luck. Things go bad."

We are nearing the fork in the road, where he will go up to his house on the hill, and I will go down to the old Catholic mission, where Brad, my father, and I are staying. We walk in a comfortable silence for a minute, until he continues.

"Dancing saved me, I think. I went one night, came out feeling a little better, a little stronger. I kept going back. The elders, they teach me, help me to see how good it is, how it shows respect to our ancestors, how it gives me pride. Now I know I have to follow more the old way, try to live how we used to, gain strength from my ancestors. Your ancestors. One of these times I will get you to dance. Okay?"

"I will try," I say, not believing it. I have never been able to dance. We laugh comfortably together, shake hands under the moonlight. His hand is thick and warm. We say good night, make a plan to go jogging the next afternoon when he gets off work at the St. Marys airport, where he unloads cargo planes. He turns and heads up the hill to his house.

I go down, past rows of dilapidated houses, the post office and docks, then up another small rise to the sheet-metal mission, which looks more like an airplane hangar than a Catholic church. Back in the fifties they opened the mission as a boarding school for the Native population, removing children from their families in order to immerse them in a Western education. It didn't work for long; the Yup'ik families simply packed up and moved to St. Marys. That's how St. Marys stumbled its way onto the map: people coming to keep their families intact. The school closed more than a decade ago, replaced by a modern public school. Now they rent dormitory rooms to visitors. The place feels eerie, haunted.

After three days of drizzle, the dirt road leading to the dormitory is thick with mud. I slosh through it, avoiding the deepest bogs. As I near the building I hear rustling in the bushes to my left. I freeze, startled. Staring me straight in the face, less then ten yards away, is a red fox. I'm afraid I'll scare it off, but after a few minutes I realize this fox may not be afraid of me. It regards me with what I take to be curiosity, even longing. Perhaps it has been fed by village children and is only begging for food, but I want to believe it is something more than that. I begin to see, in the fox's eyes, that it somehow knows me, and wants me to know that it knows me. I think of Dora and Charlie Backlund, who died just downriver from here. I feel foolish, but I can't let go of the thought: *This fox knows me.* I shiver.

Writing this, years later, I doubt what I felt then. But I know, in those moments, on that muddy moonlit night, the sound of drums resounding in my ears, I believed that fox was my grandmother. Dora.

A door slams, distracting me. I look around and see the old priest waddling down the dormitory stairs. I turn back to the fox, but it has vanished. "Good evening," says the priest as he walks by me.

"Yes, good evening," I stammer, relieved that it's too late for conversation. I stand a while longer in the deepening silence. I hear the endless movement of river water, and somewhere deep in my ears the echo of drums. I will search for fox tracks in the morning.

Winter Potlatch, 1879

NICUUK WAS KNOWN, AT A VERY YOUNG AGE, for her dancing. When she was two years old she stumbled out onto the dance floor at a winter potlatch and began imitating the movements of her grandmother. Nicuuk loved watching her grandmother dance, loved the way the caribou hair flowed through the air like clouds around her grandmother's calm, focused face. At two Nicuuk was already dreaming of the fans she would someday hold in her hands when she danced. She imagined them with colorful beads sewn into the shape of her doll, Itsaq, whom she held as she bounced up and down, bending at the knees to the steady beat of the drum. Woven from grass, Itsaq was given to Nicuuk on her second birthday. She had black, waist-length hair and a red-and-blue dress painted with berry and charcoal dyes. Nicuuk took Itsaq everywhere. When they were alone she made Itsaq dance as she tapped lightly on her father's drum and swished the fans she had fashioned for Itsaq out of leftover caribou hair. By moving Itsaq through the movements, Nicuuk learned the village's dances and created dances of her own that would one day be absorbed into the village tradition.

During Nicuuk's tenth year a spring potlatch was held twenty miles upriver, to celebrate the end of a long, unusually brutal winter. Many people had died of starvation and the white man's disease, which had caught them by surprise. Confined for months on end, Nicuuk had practiced dancing all winter. When she was called to the floor she felt nervous, but easily settled into the rhythm of the drums. She danced so beautifully that the drummers wouldn't stop. Again and again, with the throb of their drums, they called the dancers back to the center of the qasgiq, the communal house. Nicuuk thought she might faint, but she kept dancing as if the din of the drum were the pulsing of her own heart. The people sat mesmerized around the dancers. Even the children watched in dreamy-eyed silence. When Nicuuk waved her fans gracefully through the air, the people saw caribou running across the soft tundra. When she swayed her body from side to side, her feet rooted in the earth, the people saw trees bending in the wind, or grass quivering in waves of summer heat.

The dance was old, so old that nobody knew when it had begun. It told the story of a family that lived alone up in the North Country, where caribou roamed thick as mosquitos beneath mountains by the sea. They were caribou people, and their lives revolved around caribou. They moved long distances to follow the herd, and sometimes they went hungry when the caribou were scarce or hunting was bad. One winter long ago, no caribou came to the family's home, so they lived on fish until the sea froze and winter closed them in. The children were dying when the father heard a strange scraping outside. He went to see what it was, and rubbing up against the driftwood of their home was a huge caribou with antlers as tall as small trees.

"I am here to bring you life," the caribou said. "We are brothers. You know what you must do." The man gave thanks and cried as he pierced the caribou's heart. He fed his children its meat, and with its bones he fashioned tools for the hunt. With the great antlers he carved a herd of tiny caribou. When his children and grandchildren were grown, he gave each of them one of these caribou, and he told them they were sacred and would bring them good hunting for the rest of their lives. And the people lived and died by caribou.

When Nicuuk waved her fans above her, touching the sky, the drummers' voices rose to meet her. The people thought of sunshine, the months to come, fish in their nets and caribou sweeping across the land. When they saw Nicuuk dance they forgot, if only for a moment, the loss of winter. They let the dead slide into the next world like salmon slipping back into the sea.

When the dance was finished, people brought Nicuuk gifts. Some wept as they reached out to her. She felt shy, unused to such praise. She wasn't yet old enough to see that the tears she had made were tears of joy, even those shed in farewell to the dead. Potlatches, she knew, were about *catngu*, which meant to be helpful, essential. And she knew that dancing was *catngu*, like blood flowing to the heart. Later in the potlatch, a powerful shaman came to release the spirits of the dead through the hole in the *qasgiq*'s roof. But for years afterward people would say that Nicuuk's dancing had let the spirits go. People said she had strong medicine, though she was never asked to use it in the way the shamans were. Mostly her dancing blunted the vicious teeth of delta winters, brought light where there was none before.

Just after Nicuuk's seventeenth birthday she danced at the spring potlatch in Chaneliak, where she saw Aivrun again for the first time since he had come to visit with her father more than a year before. She had thought about him many times, remembered his yellow eyes and the scar across his face. That winter her father had trapped a lynx and brought it home for her to skin. The lynx reminded her of Aivrun, and it made her sad to see the fire in its eyes faded to smoke, lusterless and gray.

She was dancing when he entered, the only *kass'aq* in the *qasgiq*. Seeing him broke her rhythm, imperceptibly to most people in the room, but she knew that he had noticed. A faint smile crossed his face. She looked at the floor and continued dancing, mesmerizing the audience. Aivrun, too, was caught like a fish in the ebb and flow of her gestures, her tidelike bending of knees. He had heard about her dancing, and he remembered her unflinching stare the first time he met her in the village. He had thought her intriguing, but he was busy with hunting and trapping, and he'd spent the last six months prospecting for gold upriver. He had tried, all of his life, to avoid women because he didn't believe he could settle down long enough to be a decent husband or father.

Nevertheless, he watched Nicuuk, spellbound, until nearly an hour later when the dance ended. Gifts of seal oil, caribou hair, and wolf pelts were laid across the floor. A family from Alakanuk gave a kayak with a whale bone protruding like a spear from its bow. Dancers from other villages took the floor, the drums drummed on. All night into the early morning they boomed through the walls of the *qasgiq*. Dancers came and went, children slept on the floor or in the laps of their mothers, food appeared and disappeared again and again from the long bench, men retired to the nearby bathhouse, a mud and grass hut with a deep fire pit in the middle around which the men sat and sweated, pouring water over red-hot rocks and exchanging endless stories. Everything that happened in the village during the potlatch seemed framed by the sound of the drums, a deep throbbing that shook the ground and echoed off the riverbanks and hills for miles around. The animals knew when it was potlatch, and sometimes they wandered in to the edge of the village and watched from a distance. Ravens perched on the highest homes, or soared above the *qasgiq*. A new energy was born, year after year, no matter how hard the winter. The river was breaking up; life was beginning anew.

Nicuuk danced many dances that night, well into the morning. Aivrun would one day joke that the dancing became a test of wills: who would give up first, the dancer or the dance. Aivrun watched every dance, every move Nicuuk made. She knew he was there, felt his eyes, but never once, since that first fleeting glance, met his gaze. Nicuuk's father, Yugisaq, was aware of the game, and he approved despite the fact that Aivrun was a *kass'aq*. They sat together, watching the dances and talking about Aivrun's journeys upriver. Nicuuk's mother also saw, and she worried. She was distrustful of the Russians, especially when it came to Nicuuk, who was well into a marrying age. Nevertheless she brought Aivrun food. He thanked her, but only nibbled at the dried salmon and whale blubber. He had no appetite.

Soon after midnight a dance began that was like no other dance the people had ever seen. Nicuuk was among the eight female dancers behind Kitluk, the old master known far and wide for his drama and skill. The drums began telling the story of how the world began, how the great Raven, using his talons, carved out the Yukon and Kuskokwim Rivers, the mountains and streams of the delta. The story was familiar, one heard every year again and again with the changing of the seasons. But this time it was different; this time Raven flew endlessly, until it seemed that creation was eternal.

The air was charged. Kitluk arched his back more than anyone had ever seen. His ribs pressed tightly against the skin of his chest, his spine bowed backward, his body convulsed to the drums. His knees sank into the floor, his old but well-muscled arms fanned out like wings, and his face twisted in agony. Ever after people would swear that Kitluk nearly took flight that night, that Raven had tried to break free.

The second time around the drums grew louder, the pace quickened, the room heated until people dripped with sweat. Following Kitluk, Nicuuk closed her eyes and swooped into Raven's world. Her fans sliced at the floor, like giant talons bringing forth the river. As the singing shrilled, her jaws clenched, her lips parted, and her bare feet clawed the dirt floor. Watching, people worried. Aivrun stared, knowing only that he was changed, that he would never leave this place again. He was afraid, watching her, yet more afraid not to.

There was never a longer dance. The drummers endlessly called the dancers, until all but two had fainted to the floor. Many people had gone home to sleep, others dozed around the room, the drums steady but distant in their ears. Nicuuk and Kitluk danced until the sun's first light fell on the raven perched atop the *qasgiq*. When it lifted into the silver dawn the drummers knew the dance was over. Kitluk slumped forward onto the ground, Nicuuk buckled at the knees. The last thing she saw were Aivrun's eyes, staring at her from the shadows of the room.

6

Charlie Backlund was a mystery to me. In Kotlik he was remembered as a kind man, but little else was said of him. My mother said his voice was deep and slow, like Uncle Carl's. I remember being lulled to sleep by the sound of Uncle Carl's voice as he spoke to my mother late into the night during his brief visits with us. It was a low voice, soothing, with the rasp of a smoker's throat.

I imagine Charlie Backlund with that same voice. Like Carl, he was a big man. By the time my mother was born he was old, overweight and balding, but with clear, thoughtful eyes. I know from photographs that he smiled with a frown.

My mother rarely spoke of him. As a child when I asked her about my grandfather, she said he had died of cancer or tuberculosis, she couldn't remember which. And no wonder. I suspect that his death finally cut the gossamer strings that connected her to Alaska. Her past may have faded into dreams, Kotlik receding into the shadows of her imagination, Justina a whisper in the night.

Until I journeyed to Alaska, Kotlik was a fairy tale and my grandfather a ghost. Over the course of my time there, on two month-long visits, I heard many stories about my mother and Carl, but few about Charlie Backlund. Everything said about him was respectful but superficial, the kindling of a stick figure. Justina seemed to tense when I asked about Charlie, especially when I focused on his death. She would change the subject or pretend that she didn't understand.

"Your grandfather was a good man," she would say repeatedly. "He would never turn anybody down who needed help. Everybody liked him."

But Justina understood better than she let on, and I was convinced after each visit that having a translator was more habit than necessity. Justina could read me like a book. She understood what I wanted to know, but she wouldn't tell me.

Finally, only a few days before Brad and I were leaving, she summoned us to her house. Natalia was there to translate. I had given up asking about Charlie, so her admission seemed to come out of nowhere.

"I don't know this for sure," she said, "but it was spoken like this for many years after your grandfather died." She paused for what seemed like minutes. I heard the wind pounding against the plywood house, dogs howling, the strained breathing of time.

"When Charlie died," she said, "his legs was all swelled up, that's what the people said. He died in pain, bleeding inside. It took many days, and nobody could help him."

Justina paused again and looked at me with pity. Her eyes filled with tears, her lower lip trembled. I looked back, blankly. I didn't know how to respond.

She began speaking again, but Natalia, instead of translating the words, looked at her mother in surprise and asked another question in Yup'ik, as if to clarify what Justina had said. Justina nodded. Natalia turned to me, her face pinched.

"Charlie, my mom says, was poisoned. He opened a store upriver from Mountain Village, and someone put broken glass in his drink. He bled to death inside. That's why, the people used to say, his legs swelled up. My mother says nobody knew this for sure, but she believes it is true. The elders said this was so."

Justina stared at me, her half-moon eyes glistening with tears. I knew she was worried about how I might react. She had hoped for a happy reunion, one without unhealed wounds. Also, I discovered later, she had learned in her long life to accept the injuries of time. She resisted passing on painful memories.

Charlie Backlund had been murdered. I sat there with Justina and Natalia, and I didn't say a word. Of all the things she might have said to me, this was the farthest from my imagination. Justina rose to make tea. Natalia and I remained in silence, both of us, I think, wandering the past. Somewhere out on the tundra not too far from where we sat, someone had buried my grandfather, her uncle, the large white man with the soft face and radio voice.

TWO DAYS LATER Brad and I travel downriver to Mountain Village to see our cousin Matt. In his mid-forties, he has neatly cut hair, a trimmed mustache, and is well dressed in clean blue jeans and a button-down shirt. He has a keen sense of humor that shines through when he plays with one of his three grandchildren or five children, who all live with him and his wife, Florence, in a three-room apartment above the town store, which he manages.

As a boy he'd heard the story of Charlie Backlund's death, but more as myth than truth. When we tell him about Justina's story, his interest is sparked.

"There's a place upriver from here, called Liberty Landing, where your grandfather is said to have moved his store from Kotlik. It's not there anymore, just a bunch of broken-down old buildings, but high up on the hill just downriver from there is a cross—I have seen it from the river—and people used to say that Charlie Backlund was buried up there."

Matt has never been there, nor does he know anyone who has. But he offers to help us find the place, and the next day we pile into his SUV and drive out of town on the only road that goes anywhere, two lanes of dirt that connect Mountain Village to the airport ten miles away, and to St. Marys another eight miles. Matt thinks it easier to approach the supposed burial site from inland rather than hiking uphill from the river. Five miles from town he turns off onto an obscure jeep trail that I wouldn't have noticed. We bump and grind another few miles over tundra, Matt chain-smoking and recalling his high-school days.

"We used to come out here to get away from town, a whole group of us, and drink and sing and . . . you know, all that kind of thing. It was easy to get away. When I was a little kid my dad, your Uncle Pete, he used to take me hunting out here. He knew this land like the back of his hand, could walk blindfolded from here to St. Marys. One time we did, too. We were hunting, didn't find any game, just kept on walking. We walked all the way to St. Marys without seeing so much as a ptarmigan. Spent the night up there, walked back the next day. I was little, just six or seven years old. My dad carried me most of the way home. I remember looking over his shoulder as he walked, and it seemed like we were walking to the edge of the earth. My dad, he could walk a long ways—they were a lot different back then, you know?"

I think of Pete Andrews hiking over the tundra with Matt on his back, his feet squishing and sinking, every step like five on solid ground. And here we are bumping along in a Ford Explorer, Matt's cigarette smoke curling out the window to the twang of some radio cowboy. The autumn colors are sprinkled across the land, as if the earth is burning. As far as I can see, the tundra glistens with swirling shades of flame, a soft breeze bending the yellowed blades of grass and crimson tips of barren, low-slung bushes. Here and there, Honda four-wheeler tracks crisscross the tundra, deeply grooved and slicked with patches of oil. Every bit of it, on this day, looks right to me, organic.

A few miles down this so-called road, we stop. Thick willows block our way, and just beyond, the land drops steeply to the Yukon River. We step from the car onto the soft soil, where Matt flicks his half-smoked Marlboro.

"This is it," he says. "We walk from here."

We duck through the willows on a barely discernible trail. We walk uphill, Brad leading the way, until we break through the brush and top out on the highest hill around, a bald spot on the back of the earth's head.

Brad's mouth drops open. "Colin, you won't believe . . . "

And I don't. Before us, the tundra turns from red and yellow to undulating orange, the sun just dropping below distant, snowcapped hills. We had grown up in mountains, where winter alpenglow had tinted our skin shades of indigo and pink, and we had stood on high Sierra peaks and gazed into the gray-green deserts of Nevada. But we have never seen so far. From this lowly hill, a few hundred feet above the sea, we see the curves of the earth. We stand as if sea-bound, the tundra transformed into waves of orange that drain off the horizon like water cascading into a bottomless sky. I feel upside down; I balance on the blue earth and touch the burning sky with my toes.

Matt, lagging behind, emerges from the willows, his skin shimmering with sweat. We stand, the three of us, side by side in silence. Matt stares south toward the Kusilvak Mountains, and I wonder if he is thinking about his teenage son, Glenn, who is dying of intestinal cancer. Matt hasn't spoken of it much, but I have seen him and Florence as they watch Glenn, dying quietly at home, watching television late into the night.

Cancer is no stranger to the three of us standing on the hill above Liberty Landing. It runs through my mother's Yup'ik family like a plague, often the same cancer of the liver and small intestines, irrespective of age and gender. My Uncle Carl died of this cancer when he was fifty-seven, my mother two years later. My cousin Olga, Natalia's older sister, two years after my first visit. My Uncle Pete, Matt's father, two years after that. And the list goes on. With every one I feel it again, the loss of her; it burrows into me and stays through the winter. I can feel it there, another smaller heart of mine.

"I used to come here a lot, a long time ago," Matt says, breaking the silence. "My dad took me here the first time, to look for game. You see how far you can see. And after that I'd come here by myself, or with a friend. Later with my sons, with Glenn. He loved . . . he loves to hunt. I should tell you both, Glenn is going to die. You probably could tell. But it's bad. We took him to Anchorage a couple months ago, doctor said there's nothing we can do. Glenn wanted to come home, die here with his family."

Brad and I nod and look at the ground. A boat horn honks somewhere down the river. Matt tosses his cigarette butt on the grass and smashes it with his shoe, takes another from his breast pocket and lights it. A breeze blows upriver, whipping smoke into my face. I breathe in his used, tired breath, knowing it came from him and that somehow this means something.

Brad breaks the spell with a cough. Matt feels the change, says "I think the cross is down that way," and he points. We split the circle of willows, Brad first and Matt behind, our hands protecting our eyes from slapping branches. We weave in and out of willows, up and down the slope, finally spreading out to cover more ground. We've been searching for an hour when I hear Brad's voice below.

"Colin, Matt, down here."

I'm surprised. I hadn't been expecting to find anything, not a cross, not a grave, definitely not Charlie Backlund. I hurry down the slope, the willows scratching my arms. The bushes thin as I move downhill, and in a few minutes I break into a clearing, a small plateau perched above the river. Brad and Matt are standing by a long, fenced grave, both of them looking at a weathered wooden marker, six feet tall, a small cross delicately carved on its crown. Green lichen glows in the twilight.

"There's no name," Matt says. "It's been weathered off the marker. But I'll tell you one thing, Charlie Backlund was a big man, and this sure isn't a Native grave. At least no Native I ever knew. Too big, too rich. This person had some money."

Each fence picket is weathered gray and spotted with light green lichen. The wood appears hand-carved, the fence held together by tiny nails. It's the softest wood I have ever touched, like the skin of a woman's forearm. Inside the fence a long rectangular box shelters the grave. A layer of canvas dangles in strips, revealing wood. Matt is right; it looks like an affluent grave.

The three of us amble around it a few times, taking photographs and noting details. I try to imagine the funeral, who had come here to mourn for him, what words had been spoken. I wonder why he was buried on this hill. I wish that my mother were here to mourn for him, that she could touch the green-gray cross and see the twilight dancing like fireflies on the river below.

Just downhill Brad finds another seven graves, all with Russian Orthodox crosses, the points ornately bubbled, stained and streaked in different shades of brown and gray. They're covered in thick tundra grass and overgrown with bushes. A thick willow juts through the middle of one, and I wonder if the willow grew up through the corpse, if its roots are entangled with ribs and bones. Better than lying alone, I think, embraced always by the moist tethers of sky-seeking buds, an umbilical cord to the sun.

We explore the graves for a while, Matt speculating that this site was used for the small settlement of Liberty Landing, which didn't last long and therefore didn't have much of a cemetery. We hike back to Charlie Backlund's grave. It's nearly dark, and the wind carries a chill. I know we need to go, but I want a moment longer with my grandfather. I may never come again.

Matt lights another cigarette and walks to the edge of the clearing while I kneel by the grave. Brad stands beside me, and though we don't speak I know we are thinking the same thought: *Here is the man who was our mother's father. This long-dead man. What do we do with all of this?* Just as I did at Dora's grave in Kotlik, I feel close to my mother. I imagine her fingers caressing Charlie's cross as if it were his skin. The wind swishes in waves through the willows and tall grass, and I know, if only for a moment, the wind my grandfather felt on his face as he walked to the place where his bones would someday lie.

When I rise from my knees a few minutes later, Brad is halfway up the hill. Matt stands nearby, watching the river. A barge moves slowly upstream, its wake wide and frothy.

We thrash up the hill, the day's light gone. I am tired of thinking about the dead, ready to drink a beer or drop into the brain-dead haze of television. Matt smokes as he hikes behind me, gasping at intervals for air. I feel closer to him, as if visiting Charlie's grave is proof of our relatedness. Brad and I are foreigners, whites, and just because our mother was born in this country doesn't make us Yup'ik. We're a couple of *kass'aq*, related to Matt only through the shared memories of a displaced child. Nevertheless, we are here, and he makes us feel at home.

Staggering up the hill, our silence is easy. In darkness we reach the car, and I sag into the seat. We bounce back through the tunnel of the headlights.

Moving Upriver,
1933

The children had left three weeks before. Charlie Backlund stood on the bow of the old barge as it carried his house up the Yukon River. Not long after breakup, chunks of ice still bobbed in the current, sporadically smashing against the barge's hull. His broad shoulders hunched, Charlie leaned on a wooden crate marked with bright red letters, FRAGILE. It was a sleepy, gray afternoon, and he passed the time by watching small icebergs far upriver and guessing whether they would hit the barge.

He thought about how fast everything had happened: the children leaving, selling the store, moving upriver. How arduous it had been to lift the house from its foundation and roll it on logs to the barge. Folks thought he was crazy, selling out to the Bering Commercial Company and going where nobody lived. After twenty years in or around Kotlik, people were used to him. "He has family even," they would say. "Why would he leave for no good reason?" They had stood watching as the log house was hauled away. It was a big event. Charlie Backlund was leaving town.

He had his reasons, some clear, some foggy in his head. For one, the magic had gone from Kotlik now that Carl and Doris were gone. He missed them hanging around, asking for candy. Even after Dora had died he'd felt like his family was whole, Justina filling some of the space where Dora had been. But after he sent the children away, things weren't the same with Justina. She kept her distance, wouldn't look him in the eyes. He understood; he harbored no illusions about his relation to her. She needed to raise a family of her own. He remembered when she was a girl, when the floods came through Pastolik and left her family homeless. He'd been glad to take them in. He enjoyed their company, and he'd fallen for Dora right away. But all of that was over now. He was moving on.

He often questioned whether sending the children away had been right. He wasn't sure, and he sensed that he never would be. He'd wanted them to have a good education, a civilized education. And though he loved Kotlik and many of the people there, he'd never gotten over feeling that Kotlik could never give his children what he felt they needed. He didn't want them to grow up believing that the delta was the center of the world. He disliked this part of himself, the civilized, Western person he'd been raised as in Finland, his father an aristocrat and his mother a patron of the arts. As much as he'd resisted them his entire life, they seemed to resurface as inevitably as the river reemerged from the ice. Charlie justified sending his children away by convincing himself that their lives would be greatly enriched. He foresaw them spending the school year down there, and summers in Kotlik. He hoped to join them downstates just as soon as his affairs were settled up north.

This settling of affairs was the second reason Charlie was moving to Liberty Landing. He'd sold the Kotlik store at a good profit to Bering, knowing they would have come anyway and built a store of their own. He figured it was a good time to cash in, use a chunk of the money to open another store at Liberty Landing, a prime location just upriver from Mountain Village, good fishing and an excellent landing site. He reasoned he'd draw a lot of summer business from folks at fish camp, who normally had to go all the way down to Mountain Village for supplies. Timber was hard to come by and expensive, so he was bringing his house with him to convert to a store. He'd run the store out of the front room and live in the back. A few folks had already settled at Liberty Landing, and the way it was going he figured he could run the store for one summer season, maybe two, then sell it for a huge profit before joining the children on Vashon. All of it, he thought, was good business. He'd leave Alaska a wealthy man. The plan was almost too simple, he thought, and in the back of his mind small doubts flickered like beacons out of the fog. He pushed it from his mind because if he dwelled on it too long he doubted whether any of it made sense. The only thing that surprised him anymore was losing the conviction of youth.

The barge had one stopover at Mountain Village before it continued on to Liberty Landing and its final destination, St. Marys on the Andreafsky River. As it rounded a long bend in the Yukon, Charlie could make out the skyline of Mountain Village, the bowl-shaped ridge that sheltered the village from high winds. Having seen the mountains of the Interior, Charlie chuckled at the naming. It was called Mountain Village because by delta standards it was, in fact, surrounded by mountains, but to foreigners these mountains were merely hills.

As the barge drew closer Charlie could make out the sod houses clustered at the base of the hills. He smelled wood smoke coming from chimneys. Far above the houses on the southwest side of town, the cemetery's crosses speckled the hillsides like winter flowers. On coming to Mountain Village one couldn't help but notice the cemetery and the winding path that curved its way through the willows. As the barge moved toward the dock Charlie sighted a group of people walking down this path. *Someone has died,* he thought, and he wondered who it was. He knew everybody in town.

A few villagers had gathered at the dock to see the log cabin being floated upriver. They waved when they recognized Charlie, and he waved back. He had seen all of them not too long ago, at the February potlatch in Kotlik, when all the villages within a hundred miles had gathered to celebrate the end of winter by dancing and gift giving. Charlie always donated a prize to the potlatch, once a sack of sugar, once a gallon of kerosene, and this year a new fishing net imported from Seattle. Through his marriage to Dora he was related to many of the villagers. That's the way it was in the delta, most everyone connected by blood or marriage. Charlie felt welcomed wherever he went, and it was a good feeling pulling into Mountain Village and knowing he'd have a place to sleep. The barge would dock overnight before continuing on to St. Marys the next morning.

As soon as the barge was secured, Charlie stepped off and was met by Igvaq, one of Dora's uncles or cousins or some such thing. Charlie couldn't figure out exactly how he was related to anyone, so he called them all his cousins and that seemed fine by them. Igvaq was a short, fat man with a thick head of curly gray hair. He was jovial and often smelled of whiskey.

"Hey, Charlie," he said with a toothless grin. "We been hearin' about you goin' to haul your house up this way. Wasn't sure if I should believe it. Word is ol' Lemon Head is all fired up 'bout it. Ain't real keen on you puttin' a store in so close to here. But we can talk on that later. You stay at my place, eh? Got a bed for ya."

"Ol' Lemon Head" was Vincent O'Leary, the manager of the Bering store in Mountain Village. The company had come to the delta years ago and gained a monopoly on trade and goods. A small, wiry, sour man, Vince had come from the mining town of Butte, Montana, where he'd run the mining company's store for fifteen years. He was used to doing things the hard way, dealing with Irish immigrants angry at their indebtedness to the company. His toughness was contradicted by his nervous, tenor voice. He was disliked by the villagers because of his fast-paced, unfriendly manner. He rarely stopped to talk, never looked anyone in the eye, and he smelled strongly of antiseptic, as if he bathed in Lysol. Vincent never once took part in village activities, and the villagers, in turn, avoided him.

Charlie grabbed his duffel and walked with Igvaq away from the dock. He thought of Vincent and the last time he'd seen him. Vincent was what Charlie considered a "hired gun," a sort of low-grade thug who took advantage of the villagers. Bering Commercial Company had sent him to Kotlik to convince Charlie to sell his store. He'd arrived unannounced, stomped into Charlie's store and declared that the B.C.C. was coming whether Charlie liked it or not. He'd presented an offer, said, "Let me know by Friday," then walked out the door without a good-bye, never once looking Charlie in the eye. Charlie accepted the deal, not merely because of the money, but because something in him told him it was time.

"Who died?" Charlie asked Igvaq, pushing Vincent to the back of his mind.

"That'd be Sam Hunt, no relative but close ties anyhow. You know him, young guy, seventeen year old, son of Al and Kristina. Real good hunter."

"Yes, I remember him," Charlie said. "Youngest drummer at the Kotlik potlatch. What happened?"

"They say he was drinkin'. Went out on his boat with a friend for some early season fishin', got clobbered by a chunk of ice. Both kids went over, boat all smashed up. His friend made it to shore, near froze to death by time he gets back. Sam's body they find a day later, down by Pilot Station. Real shame, you know, kid like that drinkin', dyin' that way. I'm not one to talk, half used up as I am."

Charlie didn't respond. He let the silence swallow Igvaq's words, like water swirling a leaf in an eddy.

"Speakin' of whiskey," Igvaq continued, "you wouldn't know how a guy could get ahold of some, would ya? It's been a pretty dry winter up here."

Charlie thought for a moment. He sold whiskey, but he didn't like to admit it. He especially didn't like others acknowledging his trade aloud. But Igvaq was an old friend, a relative, and the kind of person who didn't think before he spoke. Something flew into his head, and a split second later it was sliding down his tongue. He'd never asked Charlie for liquor before.

"I've got a bit," said Charlie. "On the barge. We can go back later, after dark. But don't be spreading that around. I'm saving my supply for Liberty."

"Okay, no problem. Dark's just around the corner. Meantime Ma is cooking up some salmon soup. We heard you was coming. 'Mazin' how things get around up here, like the river's got ears, ya know?"

"Yeah, I know," replied Charlie. "It's enough to drive a man crazy. But it'll be good to eat your mom's cooking, that's for sure."

LATER IN THE EVENING, after filling themselves with the old woman's salmon soup, Charlie and Igvaq headed back to the barge. They walked slowly, Charlie smoking his pipe and staring at the dark night sky. He didn't like this situation, supplying liquor in a clandestine fashion, but he felt obliged to Igvaq and he knew the risk was fairly low so far upriver. He wished Igvaq didn't drink, had seen him crazy drunk. Once, when they were younger, he'd met Igvaq by accident in Emmonuk on a fishing trip, and Igvaq had ended up breaking the nose of a Russian sailor in a bar fight. Charlie had rescued Igvaq from the sailor's mates, and had dunked him in the frigid Yukon to sober him. Twenty years later Igvaq was still drinking. Charlie figured it wasn't his job to tell Igvaq, or any other man, how to live his life.

When they reached the barge Charlie told Igvaq to wait while he went on board. He exchanged a few friendly words with the night watchman before continuing to the bow, where he found the crate marked FRAGILE. He opened it with a crowbar, the boards creaking into the night. A wolf howled from the hills. Charlie reached in, grabbed two bottles that glinted golden as he raised them to the light flickering from shore. He slid them into his coat pockets and secured the box lid with a hammer. The noise reverberated across the canyon, ricocheting from ridge to ridge. Charlie's pipe hung nonchalantly from his lips, its sweet smoke drifting back to Igvaq waiting eagerly.

When Charlie stepped onto the dock, Igvaq chuckled and patted Charlie on the back.

"Thanks," he said, his cheery voice misplaced among the night sounds: the howling dogs, the lapping water, the clinking of the barge's moorings against the dock. "Hope it ain't too much trouble. Been real dry around here."

"It's nothing, Igvaq. Here you go," Charlie said, handing him a bottle. "Just don't be getting yourself in trouble."

"You know I'm too old for that. Just helps me stay warm is all," Igvaq joked. He unscrewed the lid and took a deep chug of the whiskey, his pulsing Adam's apple shining in the glow of his cigarette.

"I have to be heading back," Charlie said, as Igvaq wiped his mouth. "I have an early morning. You coming up?"

Before Igvaq could respond someone stepped onto the loose wooden planks behind them. Igvaq and Charlie flinched and turned.

Stepping toward them in the low light of a kerosene lantern was Vincent O'Leary.

"Charlie," said Vincent in his nasal Irish voice, "Heard you was headed up this way. Figured I might find you down at the docks doin' some business. Mine's been a bit slow lately." He shot a glance at Igvaq.

"Evening, Igvaq. I got whiskey down at the store, you know. No need to wait for Charlie. Specially since your tab is runnin' high. Mind if I talk to Charlie . . . alone?"

Charlie turned to Igvaq. "Feel free to mosey on home," he said. "As far as I'm concerned you can stay or go as you please. I'll be up shortly."

Igvaq smiled embarrassedly, excused himself and shuffled into the dark, clutching his bottle like it would warm the chill of meeting

Vincent on the dock. Every time Igvaq went to the store Vincent hassled him about his tab. Igvaq wasn't alone in feeling that Vincent looked down on Eskimos.

"Is it true you're openin' a store in Liberty Landing?" Vincent asked bluntly.

"Well Vincent, I may be, or I may not be. Either way I figure there's no reason I need to be telling you, nor is there any reason for you to be asking, especially in such a rude manner." Usually low and calm, Charlie's voice growled, so charged and thick that Vincent was thrown off-balance.

"No offense," Vincent whined, "but Bering bought you out down in Kotlik for a reason. They won't be happy to hear about you comin' in up here, takin' away their business. Seems to me you're gettin' a pretty good jump on it tonight, sellin' whiskey off the dock."

Already a large man, Charlie seemed to grow as Vincent spoke, as if the words were fueling him.

"You know as well as I do, Vincent, that Igvaq's my cousin, and I wasn't selling him my liquor, I was giving it to him. As for Bering, we cut a fair deal with no strings attached, except that I stay away from Kotlik. There's no law that says I can't open a store right next door to yours if I choose to. What you're saying sounds a bit too much like a threat, and I'm warning you, Vince, I don't like threats. What I do is my business, what you do is yours."

Vincent's eyes darted like minnows. The lantern jittered in his left hand.

"I'm not speakin' for myself, but for the company," Vincent stammered. "I just know they won't like it, and . . . "

"I don't give a damn," Charlie broke in. "Hear me, Vince, don't say another word." He turned abruptly and walked into the blackness. He stopped halfway up the hill to light his pipe, breathing deeply as he inhaled, calming himself.

Vincent stood for a moment on the dock, his eyes finally focusing as he stared at the seal from Igvaq's bottle of whiskey, red and smashed into the dirt. His eyes were angry, his lips pressed tight. He extinguished his lamp and slunk back to the store by the moon's dim light.

THE BARGE PULLED OUT early the next morning, Charlie again standing like the ship's mascot at the bow. He smoked his pipe with one hand and held up the other, palm out, in a single gesture of good-bye to Igvaq, who waved from the dock.

Charlie took one last look at the sod houses of Mountain Village, the boats and fishing nets and various tools of the trade strewn about the borderless front yards. Many of the homes were in disrepair, and Charlie wondered how their inhabitants had survived the past winter, one of the harshest in years. He saw the graveyard on the hill, and the Russian Orthodox church just up from the docks. He saw the old clay school, constructed by missionaries in the early days. He looked once more to the ridge surrounding the village, noticed the dark, gathering clouds, and turned his attention upstream, to the next long bend in the river.

A few hours later they pulled into Liberty Landing, which amounted to little more than a few docking posts driven into the grassy bank. A few small sod houses sat farther back in the protective crook of the river's elbow, and above them the banks of the Yukon rose hundreds of feet into rounded hills. Perfectly protected from winds, the river flowed serenely by. It was only lack of flat ground that had kept Liberty Landing from becoming a real village; unless one wanted to build on steep hillsides, there were few home-sites. *Still,* Charlie reasoned, *plenty of room for a small store, and a store is why people will stop here.*

He took it as a good sign that as the barge landed he saw a red fox watching from the hillside. It seemed to be staring right at him. He even thought he could see it grinning, and it made him feel welcome and that he had done the right thing by coming here. But it also made him momentarily sad, because he remembered Doris and how she loved animals, often coming home with wounded creatures. Once she had brought a frog—a *bluq-bluq* she called it, because of its sound— pulled it gently from her coat pocket and asked Justina to heal it. The frog's rear leg was nearly torn away, dangling by a few fleshy threads. Justina explained that the frog's leg was dead, and that without it the frog couldn't survive. It would be a sad life for that frog, she had said, and without another word she cut off its head with an *ulu*. She had cooked the legs and told Doris that by eating them she would become part frog, just as she would always be part fish because of all the fish she had eaten. Charlie laughed to himself thinking about it, how after that day he had often seen Doris hopping around the tundra with her friends, each trying to better the last one's jump.

It took most of the day for Charlie and the crew to unload the barge. They rolled the house on logs across the tundra, leaving deep tracks in the grass, as if some prehistoric snake had slithered through the settlement. More than once the logs sank too far into the soft ground and the men had to lever the house back out again using steel poles from the barge. Charlie was pleased with the location, the back of the house nestled against the hillside, its front windows facing east to a low spot on the horizon that allowed the sun's first light. He liked the place all the more because he had spotted the fox on the hill just above the house. Charlie was a man who believed in omens, though he would never have admitted it.

Charlie's goods and personal belongings were carried to the house, and soon after the barge pulled away from Liberty Landing. Charlie had invited the captain and his men to stay the night, but they had declined. The days were already long, they had said, and there was plenty of light. A tiny crack of moon rose over the hill just as the barge pulled around the bend.

For the rest of the evening Charlie unpacked. He set up a cot in the back room, organized a makeshift kitchen in which he made his first meal: canned kidney beans on crackers. He hung two photographs, one of Carl and Doris, and one of Dora. Finally, almost too tired to stand, he rummaged through his boxes until he found his old store sign, which he hung over the front door of the house. CB MERCANTILE it read in big red letters, and in smaller letters below, KOTLIK, ALASKA. He was pounding a nail when out of the corner of his eye he glimpsed a fox scurrying beneath his doorstep. His last thought before falling asleep was that he needed to change his sign to read LIBERTY LANDING.

THE MEANING OF WINE

7

There it is, the sound of her VW Rabbit in the driveway, gravel under tires. I hear our dog, Inaq, running down the stairs— *clickety clickety click*—to greet my mother, as she does every day when my mother returns from work. I'm excited, too, because I'm hungry even though Brad and I have eaten a box of Raisin Bran and a whole loaf of wheat bread with mayonnaise. We call them mayonnaise sandwiches, and I like them even though my friends make ugly faces when I ask if they want one. There's no food left in the house, and Heather is mad at Brad and me for eating all the cereal plus a jar of sweet pickles and a can of olives. The only thing left is a bag of carrots, but we don't like carrots.

I want to run down to greet my mother, but some other things have happened today that hold me back. First I got in a fight with Heather on account of the Raisin Bran. She poured water on my head when I wasn't looking and I got so mad that I picked up the phone and threw it at her and it hit her on the cheek and cut her. Plus the phone cord ripped out of the wall and I stuffed it back in but it still doesn't work. Heather locked herself in her room and screamed that she is going to tell on me. Which she will.

So Brad and I decided to play a game of floor hockey which we aren't supposed to play in the house on account of breaking things. But Mom was at work and Dad's on a trip so we figured why not. I was the goalie and it wasn't my fault that Brad shot high—our rule was no shots above the knees because we weren't wearing cups—but anyway he took a high shot and I went to stop it with one of those stretch saves like the pros where my legs split and my glove goes up and my goalie stick flies to my right. And crash. My stick goes through the living room window, one of those big ones that you don't want to break.

So that was it. Heather's face was my fault and the window was my fault and no matter what I'm in trouble. Sometimes I can lie and Mom can't prove anything but this time the evidence is there in glass and blood. The truth is that Heather poured the water and Brad took the shot, but it isn't going to matter. Not unless my mom's in a very good mood.

I run down to help her with the groceries to get me on her good side before she climbs the stairs and sees the glass and hears Heather crying like she is bleeding to death. Mom is out of the car and petting the dog hello. She's wearing her gray business suit, the one with a jacket like a man's, but a long skirt instead of pants. She wears high-heeled shoes which means she had an important meeting today and I don't know if that's good or bad because it depends on how the meeting went. Sometimes she comes home saying we're going to be millionaires and giving us hugs. Usually the meetings are about money, which sometimes we have enough of and sometimes we don't. Last year she brought home a barrel of beans that we ate for three months, and at Christmas we couldn't buy presents but had to make them or give something of our own. Usually I can tell by looking at her how the meeting went.

But today I can't. Today she looks tired but not angry. I say hi and smile and even that feels like a lie. She smiles, kisses me on the forehead, says, "How was your day?"

"Fine Mom," I say, "okay. Do you want some help?" She nods. I pick up a bag with hot dogs in it which I like to eat raw. Brad comes down also and picks up his own bag, and he gives me a look that says the window isn't his fault. I can blame it on him but he never gets in trouble on account of he's twice as small as me even though he's eight and I'm only nine.

I run up the stairs with my bag and am back down for another before my mother is halfway to the house. For a second I think about running, just heading off down the street to Peter's house—he's my best friend—but sooner or later she'd come get me and it would be worse. Plus I spat on Peter's windows and his mom is mad (that wasn't my fault either because Peter locked me out and my trumpet was inside). I pick up another bag and inside is some fruit and two bottles of wine. That worries me a little because usually she only gets one and when my father is gone sometimes she drinks the whole bottle and cries and says things she wouldn't normally say. If she drinks just a little it's okay because then she likes me better and lets me sit on her bed and give her foot rubs while she reads or tells stories.

But two bottles worry me. Things aren't good when I look up at the house. My mother now looks like the meeting wasn't so good. She looks like maybe we have no money left at all. Her hands are on her hips and her eyes are dark. She looks pretty scary when she's like that, even Peter says so. He's seen her chase me around the house when I say something she doesn't like. Once she hit me on the head with a wooden block. Now she's looking that way and she yells, "Colin Donald Chisholm, get up here this instant!" Which isn't good because when she says my whole name like that only bad can follow. I hear Heather whimpering like a dog in the background and my mom storms back inside.

I plod slowly up the stairs, but no matter how slow I walk the top is coming fast. I go in and put the groceries down. I take out a bottle of wine and place it on the counter where she will see it.

"Colin!" my mother snaps as she comes into the kitchen. "What in the world happened here today?"

"I . . ."

"Don't lie to me! How many times have I warned you about hitting your sister?"

"But I didn't hit her, it was the phone, I mean she poured water on me and I threw it but she started it and Brad's the one who took the shot."

She looks confused. "What shot?" she asks.

I've blown it. She hasn't seen the window and if I'd just waited until the wine maybe she never would have.

"Well, uh," I say, "a window got broken. Brad shot a ball through the window."

Brad comes screaming. He's been listening just in case, and he comes in yelling. "I did not," he screams, "he put his stick through the window, Colin broke the window!"

I'm sunk and know it. But I'm mad as a cat at Brad and I raise my fist to scare him and before I know it my mom has me by the shoulders and is shaking me like she wants to knock out my teeth. Spit flies in my face as she yells, "How many times do I have to tell you not to bully your brother? What is wrong with you? I come home after a hard day and find Heather in tears with blood on her face and a window broken and how dare you lie to me! You're worse than Heidi!"

I see red. She's said this before and I hate it. Heidi rides horses and used to tickle me until I cried, but then she got in trouble so they sent her away to boarding school. When I was little I didn't get in trouble because Mom was always mad at Heidi and Michelle on account of boys and smoking and that kind of thing. They'd all yell and scream at each other for hours, just sitting there in the living room and I had to be there too because it was a Family Talk. Then Michelle, who's the oldest, ran away to live with a family up the street, and she was there for a long time until one night their house burned down and a baby died and I remember my mom holding Michelle in her arms out in the street and Michelle breathing so fast and screaming and the firemen holding back the baby's mom because she wanted to run into the fire. Mom said Michelle was in shock. It was a big fire and the next day Brad and Peter and I looked through the smoking remains of the house, searching for that poor baby's bones. We all agreed that freezing was better than burning if you were going to die. Michelle came home for a while but dropped out of high school and I don't know where she is now. Heidi has red hair which is why she has her temper and the temper is why Mom thinks Heidi and I are the same but I don't have red hair. So why do I have a temper?

"I hate you," I yell at my mom. I thrash free and run to my room where I slam the door so hard the windows shake. I jump into my bed and bury my face in the pillow and cry and scream and kick and punch and tear at the sheets until I can hardly breathe and just lie there crying. I wish my dad was here. When this happens sometimes he'll come in and sit on the bed with me. He'll rub my back and tell me everything's okay and ask why I make my mother so angry.

After a while I hear the TV downstairs. It's the theme song from *M.A.S.H.*, my mother's favorite show. I know she's down there watching it and drinking a glass of wine while dinner cooks. I smell food cooking—chicken pot pies?—and it makes me hungry and I wonder if I'll get any. I still think it wasn't my fault, the blood and the glass, so I decide to hunger strike. Even if she gives me dinner I won't eat it. Maybe I'll throw the plate at her. But it smells pretty good.

My mom puts the chicken pot pie outside my door. "You can eat in your room," she says. I peek out and see the pie sitting there, steaming.

I love chicken pot pies, even though it's frozen food and Peter's mom says frozen food is for old men, not children. But ever since my mom went to work at the company she doesn't cook as much anymore. Sometimes we go out to eat at the Water Wheel, which is Chinese food and her favorite restaurant, but it gives my dad an ulcer. I like it okay, but I could eat chicken pot pies every night and never get sick of them. I smell it outside my door and my stomach is growling like crazy but I'm not going to eat it. No way.

"Can I have your chicken pot pie?" Brad asks through the door. He's so much smaller than I am but eats just as much, which doesn't seem right.

"No," I yell and fling open the door to save my dinner. I eat the pie but still I'm hungry. I sneak downstairs to the kitchen, hoping for a hot dog. Brad and Heather are watching *Little House on the Prairie* and my mom is talking on the phone in the living room. She can't see me as I duck behind the kitchen counter. I hear my name and figure that she's talking to my dad. Her voice sounds like maybe she drank the whole bottle and then I see it empty on the counter and the second bottle open also. I can't hear her words but I can tell that she is going to cry. Her voice gets higher and higher. I open the fridge, spot the hot dogs and Heather's leftover chicken pot pie. I eat the pie first, quickly, then take three hot dogs and a jar of mayonnaise and hide in the pantry. My mom is crying now. I hear her say "goddamnit" and "your children" and "what do you expect me to do?" I dip a hot dog in mayonnaise and think it's pretty good, I've never tried this before. I eat all three hot dogs and am still hungry but I can't leave the pantry now because my mom slams the phone down and comes into the kitchen where I hear her wineglass chime against the bottle. She tells Heather and Brad to go to bed and sits in front of the TV by herself. I'm in the pantry for a long time and eat a little bit of cat food which isn't as bad as I thought, and the crying has stopped but I peek out and the second bottle is half empty. I'm sleepy and wish she'd leave so I can go to bed.

Finally my mom turns off the TV and walks upstairs. I hear her go into the bathroom. This is my chance so I slip from the pantry, sneak by the bathroom and into my room. Brad is asleep on the top bunk. I crawl into bed and listen. Horrible sounds come from the bathroom, my mother's voice gagged and moaning. It's a cry and a growl at once and then the sound of splashing water. I'm terrified and want to help her but I can't because I'm in trouble and she might smell the hot dogs. The sound goes on for minutes, her breathing loud and strained through the wall. Near the end she shrieks, like Mrs. Ingalls when she had a baby on *Little House*. I hear her brushing her teeth, then the bathroom door opens. I pretend I'm asleep when she comes in. My heart is pounding so loud I think she must hear it, but she just stands in the doorway, breathing. The light falls across my face. The door shuts and I hear her climb the stairs to her room. I listen. Brad is awake, I can tell because the little whistle is gone from his breathing. We say nothing. My heart stops racing and pieces of hot dog and kitty food come up my throat. It's hard to fall asleep.

OUR FAMILY, I suppose, was fairly normal in the larger scheme of things. Normal enough, at least, to maintain appearances. Compared to some families in Squaw Valley, we were traditional. Our parents were still married, still "together." They worked hard, made a decent living. We lived in a large, nice home, and we had luxuries. As far as I knew we had no major scandals, no infidelities, no glaring abnormalities. I knew the valley gossip, whispered it to my friends with the silken tongue of disillusion: one friend's mother having an affair with another's father; marijuana in so-and-so's sock drawer; a neighbor suspected of arson. Things happened in the valley that everybody knew about but that were rarely spoken aloud. I tried to put myself and my family above such depravity. Though we weren't the richest or the most esteemed, we were normal.

But we lived beneath surfaces. Like the frozen lakes I skated over as a child, our sheen eclipsed our murky depths, cracked dangerously in the morning light.

My mother had been dead for more than a year when the ice broke. I was having dinner with a new friend, who began talking about her father, a heart surgeon, who for years performed operations while intoxicated. He wasn't an obvious drunk; nobody except the family was aware of it. He would have a gin and tonic every morning before leaving for the hospital. He wasn't abusive, never made a fool of himself in public; but he drank, every day that his daughter could remember. It took the edge off of him, she said, calmed him down. One day on his way to an open heart surgery, he slammed his car into a telephone pole. His blood alcohol level was above the legal limit, probably had been every day for the last ten years. He died in the ambulance.

I thought of my mother. She was no reckless drunk, but for as long as I could remember she came home from work, poured herself a glass of red wine, and sat down to relax. She was a small woman, with fragile, birdlike bones and wrists like blown glass. Wine warmed her back to her nurturing self, and mellowed her after a long day of work at the engineering company she had pioneered with my father. We children vied for her attention, all yearning to be caught in her glow. When I was younger I was glad for the wine, because I knew it would soften the hard shell that sometimes covered her, revealing the mother I liked her to be.

But more than a glass was too much. After two glasses she would begin to slur her words. She would praise us excessively, embarrassing us because we knew it was the wine talking. During periods when she was drinking more heavily, I avoided bringing my friends home because I was ashamed. Once she grew furious when I asked her not to drink at my birthday party; she didn't see her drinking as a problem.

I never talked about it with anyone. I remember watching those commercials on television that showed humiliating scenes of alcoholics throwing things or yelling at their children, the narrator's voice asking, "Does this look familiar? If so, someone you love may need help—call 1–800–ALC–OHOL." I wondered if I should call, but the alcoholics they portrayed were so much worse than my mother.

My father's absence seemed to intensify her drinking. Sometimes when he called from cities like New York or Washington, they would fight over the telephone. If she'd been drinking, she might scream at him or cry into the phone. I don't remember why they fought; perhaps she resented being left to care for us alone, living a life she may not have dreamed of, in a place she struggled to love. Perhaps it was money, or love, or infidelity. I'd listen to my mother's sobs, wanting to help but not knowing how.

One night, after one of those phone calls, she finished a whole bottle of wine, then grabbed her car keys and started for the door. It was the middle of a Sierra blizzard. I was twelve years old, already bigger than her and old enough to realize she shouldn't go driving in a snowstorm. Brad and I stood in her way and pleaded with her to not go, but she pushed us aside, stumbled out the door and down the stairs. Barefoot, we chased her, and at the bottom of the stairs I tried to take her keys. She erupted in fury, and in seconds we were in the snow, Brad and I wrestling her, attempting to pry the keys from her fingers while she swung her fists wildly and kicked.

I remember the noise of that winter night, my mother's unnatural screams, Brad's sobs as he tried to hold her legs down. Thick snowflakes fell on us, melting as they blended with her tears. Her fingernails dug into my forearms, speckling the snow with my blood.

And then, suddenly, she stopped. The fight left her and the keys dropped from her hand, tinkling briefly before disappearing into the snow. We sat, stunned, listening to the soft hum of snow, millions of stellar flakes falling effortlessly through the night.

I don't even remember if she left or not. Confused and cold, Brad and I sat shivering by the fire. Whether we stayed up that night, as we did so many others, waiting for the sound of her car in the driveway, is insignificant. She went, or she did not.

More important than whether she went is why. What drove her into the night? What compelled her to drink? There are no easy answers. All these years since her death I have searched for reasons, stacking them like kindling for the fire of resentment that has flamed in me, abated, then flamed again. It wasn't until Kotlik that I began to learn forgiveness.

In Kotlik the answers were sometimes obvious, sometimes as hidden as her childhood doll. Two things seem clear: first, my mother had a loving family there, from whom she was taken too young. I know now, deep down, that she suffered from this separation. Justina's love was like a full moon hidden behind clouds, and my mother must have felt the pull of it in her dreams. Second, like many Natives, my mother had little tolerance for drink; it worked like poison in her blood. In the villages, I learned to look away. When my cousin, red-eyed and puffy-cheeked, approached me at the Eskimo dance and breathed whiskey in my face, I acted as if I didn't notice. Maybe he had no work, had lost his traditional values. Maybe he spent the long winter taking steam baths with friends more stoned than he. My age, he looked twice that. This cannot go on for long.

Alakanuk, a village of 550 people, upriver from Kotlik, once had twenty suicide attempts (eight successful), two murders, and four drownings in sixteen months, most of them alcohol-related. Nobody really knows how bad the drinking problem is, but the rate is generally acknowledged to be, per capita, twice that of the Lower 48. To combat the problem many villages are officially dry, which means that alcohol is banned. But behind closed doors nobody keeps track, and a few people make a lot of money smuggling. My cousin

Matt admitted feeling that Eskimos are more susceptible to alcohol.

"Alcohol and tuberculosis were the two worst things the *kass'aq* brought in. Tuberculosis, which your grandma died of, we've gotten over; alcohol will plague us forever. There's just no getting rid of it." Matt didn't drink, at least that I knew of. But he once had, and like most people in any Yup'ik village, he saw the effects all around him.

"It's hard not to be drawn to it," he said. "Times can get hard here, not much to do in the winter. I worry about my kids, what will happen to them. Soon as the Russians started bringing the stuff 150 years ago it began eating away at us. Now it's part of our history, our story."

And part of mine. I wonder whether my mother's alcoholism was predetermined. I see her face in so many Yup'ik faces: the wide smiles of women at potlatch, the bloated cheeks of a Native wino asking me for change in Anchorage. I remember how my mother used to look, sometimes, when she drank, her eyes watery and her face vacant as she stared out to the mountains or into a crackling fire. Perhaps drinking was the only way she knew how to get back to Kotlik, the only way she could conjure up those distant shadows, whose blood and bones were her own. I think, in the end, she was ready to go back to Kotlik. I want to believe that, if she had gone, she would have been healed.

Surfaces. I see her blue-green, hazel eyes, gentle and stubborn at once, and I wonder: Did I know her? She was kind, but hardened in ways that people outside of our immediate family would never have noticed. The more I search for the meaning, the more appearances I find. Is it unfair to judge the dead? I was a child then; now I see that the woman who raised me was not wholly the woman I understood her to be. This isn't to say she had no substance; on the contrary, she had too much, like a sunrise that cannot last the day. She couldn't share with me who she was because she wasn't sure herself.

As much as she denied her past, it was always right there with her. While many of her Yup'ik relatives were drinking themselves to death, my mother drank to ease a pain whose origin she didn't understand. Somehow, no matter how far she ran from Kotlik, she lived struggles similar to her cousins', although her symptoms were less clearly defined.

My first time in Kotlik, I heard the story of a young man who had died the previous winter. He was a promising young student from a village far up the Yukon. He'd received a scholarship to a university in the Lower 48 and, thinking he'd finally made it, he packed his bags and hightailed it out of there. But things weren't how he thought they'd be in the outside world. He was back six months later, wouldn't talk to anyone. He got a job at the post office sorting mail, took long drunken sweats with his high-school chums. He could smell the whiskey as it worked its way out the pores of his skin, which he licked to be frugal. He was fired in the fall and by winter was drinking all the time. By himself. One night he got on his snow machine and headed downriver with his rifle.

What are the final thoughts of a man who blows his brains out on the ice?

My mother's drinking wasn't nearly so dramatic, but it sprouted from a similar seed. To this day I can't hear the theme song of *M.A.S.H.* without remembering, the trumpets blaring out the tired story of my mother's small-time alcoholism. Our family ignored it because we hadn't learned a better way. I wish I had known then what I know now: that her struggle was not unlike that of the young man who died drunk on the ice, except that she had the luxury of a surrogate past. In the end I see them both caught between an old world that they cannot understand and a new one that will not let them in.

I'm not even sure where or when my mother learned to drink, or if it really matters. It's tempting to believe she had no choice in the matter, given how her life had been drawn. Every time she saw her reflection in the sparkle of a wineglass, she was looking back to Kotlik.

For my own part, Kotlik taught forgiveness. I realized, the moment I stepped off the plane in the middle of winter a decade ago, that my mother wasn't who I thought she was. I see her now, up there, in passing faces on the river or at an Eskimo dance. Sometimes I smile, or wave, or whisper small words that I hope may catch the wind and fly to her at fish camp. *Home*, I say. Or *Water*. Or simply, *Go*.

Making Fans, 1915

THE OLD WOMAN, Nicuuk, sat cross-legged on the ground outside the door of her home, long strands of grass in piles around her. Her grandchildren had picked the grass from the tundra so that she could weave them dancing fans. It was summer, and Nicuuk warmed her tired muscles in the sun. She was dressed in a blue *qaspeq*, with a yellow scarf covering her head. Her bare feet rested on a pile of grass. She hummed to herself as she weaved, singing songs from long ago: childhood lullabies and songs of creation. Sometimes she hummed church songs, though she had never been to a service. She had learned the words from listening on Sunday mornings when the songs came wafting out of the cracks in the church's old walls. She didn't even know what the words meant, but she liked the way they sounded. The Russian missionaries had come when she was a girl, but her family had never been converted. Her father didn't trust the missionaries, and had passed this distrust on to her. Still, she and Aivrun were married in the church because that was what he wanted. He wasn't a religious man, but he thought it was the right thing to do.

Nicuuk missed Aivrun. She often thought back with nostalgia to their early days together, the long creation dance, how he had come to her after and helped her walk home; she had been so tired she could barely stand. He'd supported her weight with one of his arms wrapped around her waist, and she had smelled him up close, a leathery, sweet tobacco smell that made her drowsy and strangely comfortable. He left her with her parents, who thanked him. Later, Aivrun had asked her father, Yugisaq, if he could marry her. Yugisaq had consulted with his wife, Ciklak, and they had given their consent. In those days it was unusual for a white man to marry a Native. Yugisaq knew it might be hard for them, knew his own friends might not approve. But in the end he said yes because he respected Aivrun, and because he believed Aivrun was a good man, Russian or not. Ciklak approved because she saw the way Nicuuk and Aivrun looked at each other; she knew they were in love. Though she distrusted Russians, she wanted her daughter to be happy.

Nicuuk breathed deeply as she remembered these things. Her thick brown fingers moved quickly, like little dancers, in and out, in and out, looping the grass through the other rows of grass. She slowed, focused as she came to a design, the outline of the sun. Here she stopped, tied off one piece of grass with a knot, then began again with another, dyed red, weaving the sun. *This will be for my favorite grandchild*, she thought, *Yuculquq*. Justina was the Christian name given to the child, but Nicuuk still called her Yuculquq. Nicuuk wondered which of her grandchildren would dance as she had so many years ago. She hoped that Yuculquq would be the one.

Across the path, two houses down from Nicuuk's, a door opened. She saw old Joe Tunakuk stumble outside of his house, where he pulled down his pants to urinate. He held himself with his left hand, and with his right raised a bottle to his lips, drinking deeply. The sun shone through the bottle, lighting Joe's face with sparkles and dirty yellow rays. Nicuuk pretended not to notice him as he turned to walk back inside, belching loudly. She saw it often, but never got used to it. Joe had been a childhood playmate of hers, and many years later one of Aivrun's hunting partners. She didn't like to think about Aivrun and Joe drinking; it hurt her to remember Aivrun in his later years.

At first life had been good with Aivrun. Nicuuk was happy when her parents told her of their approval. The wedding was joyful, and the whole village celebrated. She wore a long white dress like one she had seen in a magazine that Aivrun had shown her. He had ordered the dress from Seattle, had it sent up by steamer. It must have cost him a lot of hard-earned money. She didn't like the dress, but she wore it to please him. She felt uncomfortable in it, as if it made her someone she wasn't, someone she didn't want to be. The ceremony in the church was also strange for her; in the old days her people didn't marry in a ceremony. A marriage was arranged by a woman's parents, who taught her its meaning. There was unspoken ritual, but not the wild, public celebration of a white man's wedding. Nevertheless, most of the village came to the wedding, and to the party after. Yugisaq and Ciklak looked uncomfortable sitting in a corner most of the afternoon. There was plenty of liquor, and many of the men got drunk. A few Russians came and danced a strange dance that Nicuuk hadn't seen before. Aivrun was happy and laughed loudly. He drank a great deal. Nicuuk was worried when he took her home later that night; she realized she didn't know him. But in the end she learned to love him.

Aivrun became a famous hunter. On a whale hunt, when the hunters gathered on the shore with their kayaks and called out the name of their chosen leader, it was often Aivrun, even when he was young, and even though he was a *kass'aq*. Tales of his hunting became legend. He was said to be so accurate and strong with his harpoon that a second throw was rarely needed for the kill. He was humble about his prowess, and he was quickly accepted into the life of the village, welcomed in any home. Gradually even Ciklak became used to him, to his fearsome yellow eyes. It helped when Nicuuk's first child was born with the same eyes, and Ciklak was immediately drawn in by them.

It was a few years into their marriage before Aivrun revealed his weakness for whiskey. Liquor changed him, and the older he grew, the more he drank. One night, soon after their fourth child, Kumagaq, was born, Aivrun came home early in the morning yelling for Nicuuk to get out of bed and make him some food. Nicuuk, still the only one bold enough to stare Aivrun in the eyes, was furious. She'd been up much of the night with a sick child, and she scolded Aivrun to be quiet. Aivrun exploded, screaming insults in her face, waking the children. He yanked her outside into the snow and beat her, while the children listened, horrified, from the shadows of the room.

The next day, bruised but not broken, Nicuuk pulled Aivrun aside, looked him fiercely in the eyes, and warned him that if he ever hurt her again, she would leave him. Even in his hungover stupor, he knew that she meant it. For a year they didn't share a bed, and for just as long Nicuuk refused to dance. She hid her fans and her dancing dress away, she tied her hair up in a bun. At each potlatch people would look around and ask for her. And the people who knew would bow their heads.

Haunted by guilt, Aivrun never lost control again, though he could be violent with his words. His children feared and loved him at once. He was usually a warm-hearted father who spent more time with his children than most. He took his boys hunting and showed them how to make harpoons and kayaks, for which, in his old age, he was renowned. He told his children stories about his birthplace, the northern land across the ocean, and he wrestled and tickled them until they screamed. When their sixth child died soon after birth, he mourned with Nicuuk. He was tender, taking care as she healed from her wounds. When she rested, asleep in the afternoons, he allowed himself to cry.

One afternoon when Nicuuk woke, she saw Aivrun hunched in a chair, weeping into his hands.

"Aivrun," she asked, shocked, "what is the matter?"

Aivrun stiffened, embarrassed. But he was caught, and in some way relieved.

"Our little one," he answered. "He is gone and will never be back. I keep seeing the man he might have been."

He went to Nicuuk and sat with her, and they wept together as they never had before. Aivrun held her, and she slept. Later he went outside, wiped his tears and smoked his pipe. For the rest of their lives together, Nicuuk would never see him cry again. When times were hard between them, she remembered those moments, the man he had been; she held them inside her like tiny embers of warmth.

Nicuuk learned to hate liquor. She wouldn't allow it in her home, and Aivrun learned not to test her. More and more, as they aged, Aivrun wouldn't come home at night. His face grew red and puffy, his eyes bulged like a lynx caught by the neck in a steel-jawed trap. When he came home smelling of whiskey or vodka mixed with cigarettes, she made him drink tea to sober him. Twice he nearly killed himself, the first time when he wandered too far out on the spring ice and fell in up to his shoulders. Joe had been sober enough, for once, to pull him out. Still, Aivrun caught pneumonia and spent a month in bed.

The second time was more intentional. Too drunk to speak Nicuuk's name, he pointed a gun at his head and threatened to pull the trigger, "I'm gon' do ith, Nichoo, not worth a damn. I'm sor' fer doin' this. . . ." before he passed out, flat on his face, in front of the fire.

From then on Nicuuk hid the guns when Aivrun was drinking. Usually he just came home and carved in front of the fire, mumbling to himself. He carved little imaginary animals out of wood, animals "from another world" he called them, which he gave to his children if they were around. Otherwise he threw them into the fire as soon as they were finished.

The old woman Nicuuk still had one of those animals, which she had rescued from the fire. It was burned on one side, but was still easily recognizable—a fox with wings. Its mouth was open, showing tiny teeth that Aivrun had somehow carved despite his drunkenness. Its wings were spread as if in flight. On its back he'd carved a cross. When Aivrun had carved that, Nicuuk remembered, he'd been singing a song in Russian that she didn't understand. It was a sad melody, and when he'd finished with the fox he'd tossed it in the fire, taken a deep breath, and fallen asleep, the knife still dangling from his hand.

Nicuuk finished her fan, gathered her things together, and rose stiffly. She padded inside, her toes curled upward. She tried to remember her thoughts from the afternoon, but she could not, despite the fact that they were the same, day after day. It wasn't until late in the evening, as she sipped salmon soup, that she saw the flying fox perched on a shelf above her bed. She smiled when she saw it, a slight curve of recognition that lingered on her face until the darkness stole it away.

8

As a child I loved visiting my grandmother's Vashon Island farm, just a short ferry ride from Seattle. My mother grew up on Vashon, in the same house that my grandmother, Nanna Agren, bought after World War I, thinking that no matter how bad things got, she would always be able to feed her children. My mother loved going back to Vashon, the same way I now love going back to Squaw Valley. These places, our childhood places, became ripe with the magic of our child minds, our games and dreams etched into every piece of wood or rock, dripping like dew from the trees and bushes we scampered around like squirrels. On Vashon my mother grew younger, she laughed more often, and she took pleasure in simple things: picking raspberries for my grandmother's pies, climbing the ancient apple tree to pluck apples, washing laundry in the old ceramic basin, the same one in which she bathed us when we were babies. She helped my grandmother clean and cook, and when Nanna was too old to do either, she helped Mary Ann and Hildure do these for her. The three of them were very close, and I loved listening to them talk and laugh like they were schoolgirls again, sharing coffee and pie as they sat next to the woodstove in the kitchen.

Hildure was the oldest, still golden blonde into middle age with pale blue Swedish eyes. She reminded me of Princess Grace, tall and beautiful with an air of distinction. She was gentle, soft-spoken, and she loved to feed us sweets that our mother rarely allowed. She won my young heart by sneaking us off to Baskin Robbins for ice cream every time we came to Seattle. Her house was filled with *Mad* magazines and *Archie* comic books left over from her grown boys, and down in the basement were magnificent electric trains, her husband's hobby until he died. Brad and I spent hours in Hildure's musty basement creating scenarios for those trains. Built atop a wooden platform, a whole world waited for us: beautiful houses with glass windows out of which light flickered at night, cars driving the roads, miniature people going about their lives, trees and bushes, dogs and cats. And all around it went the trains, steam surging from their smokestacks and whistles blowing as they approached the crossroads. Sometimes we contrived crashes, sending the trains too fast around corners, where they would launch off the tracks and scatter the countryside with debris. We were secretive about it, for though Hildure rarely scolded us, she was very protective of her husband's trains.

My aunt Mary Ann was, like Hildure, beautiful, but in a more earthy, country way. She had brown, curly hair, and a warm, energetic smile. She reminded me of the Mary Ann on the television show *Gilligan's Island*—sweet, and pretty in a plainer way than the movie star, Ginger. Mary Ann and her husband, George, lived with Nanna Agren in the old house for many years before Nanna passed away. George was a short, stocky man who looked like Eisenhower, balding and stern. But he was funny, telling Brad and me jokes as he picked apples with us or drove us around in his old Ford pickup, which he swore he would keep forever. He loved automobiles of all sorts, and kept portraits of Indy 500 race-car drivers on his workshop wall. Brad liked helping George out in the garage. They'd return to the house greasy and satisfied, and I knew that Brad was George's favorite nephew.

My time on Vashon was spent less productively. The moment our car drove onto the ferry I felt as if we were in another world. Tires squeaked on the steel deck, horns honked, voices echoed off the high, cavernous walls. As soon as we were parked, Brad and I would bolt for the stairs, ahead of our sisters and parents, racing to the ferry's bow, our footsteps resounding off the metal stairs—*tonk, tonk, tonk tonk, tonk*—as we elbowed ferociously for position. I remember the smells of the upper deck: coffee and pretzels from the cafeteria, cigarettes, plastic seats, chewing gum. People sat reading newspapers or books in long rows of seats by the windows, and I wondered how anyone could read through all the excitement: crashing waves, gulls surfing the wind, the low blare of foghorns, the distant mountains of the Olympic Peninsula rising like Hydra from the sea.

My mother was quiet on those ferry rides. She might stand outside with my father, leaning on the railing, their arms around each other, gazing out over the ocean like young lovers. Or she might walk the deck, faintly smiling, taking deep, deep breaths and closing her eyes for seconds at a time. My mother wasn't overly attentive to her children, though neither was she neglectful. So long as we behaved, she granted us our freedom, allowing us to explore unmuzzled the ferry's nooks and crannies. Brad and I, and sometimes Heather, would play tag or hide-and-seek, while Heidi and Michelle read books or flirted with the island boys.

On one trip Brad and I stuffed notes into bottles and tossed them into the sea, watching until they bobbed out of sight. A few months later I received a letter from a man named Bob Little, who had found my bottle while walking on a beach in Puget Sound. We wrote back and forth for years, until I reached an age when I thought pen pals were for kids. Brad never got a letter, but I like to imagine his bottle still out there somewhere, floating across a distant sea.

When Vashon came into sight my mother would point things out to us: a cove where she used to swim, a beach where she collected shells, a distant hill where she picked strawberries. We loved that first view of the island, sometimes appearing ghostlike out of the fog. We stayed on deck until the very last moment, until finally our mother would herd us down the steel stairs to the car. Soon we'd be climbing the steep hill that rose abruptly just beyond the docks. The narrow road twisted and curved through forests thick with green under-growth, so unlike the dry Sierra forests from where we'd come. The road calmed to rolling hills, passing from time to time open fields with cows or hay or acres of berries. I remember driving with win-dows down, sticking my head out like a dog, the smells washing over me like rain. It was so different from Squaw Valley, wet and lush, spiderwebs hanging over the road in long gossamers of light. "How did that spider get across the road?" I once asked, in amazement. "Carried by the wind, like a kite," my mother answered. But I could hardly believe it.

I tried to imagine my mother as a girl playing in those fields or woods, or walking along the road to her school. Sometimes she would point out her childhood haunts, painting herself in the landscape for us, but I had a difficult time seeing her as a child. I imagined her with a child's body, but her eyes were deep and old, and somehow elsewhere. Years later I would begin to understand those eyes, but as a child they seemed impossible.

After five miles the road dropped down a long hill, at the bottom of which was the farm. We turned right off the road, past the tall hedge and over the gravel driveway to the white two-story Victorian house, a long, covered porch curving around the front. Often Mary Ann and George would be waiting for us on that porch. Brad, Heather, and I would bolt from the car, give them quick hugs, then scurry down to the raspberry patch. My mother would wander around outside for a while, smelling flowers, touching, breathing deeply. My father would drink a beer with George while Heidi and Michelle helped Mary Ann and Nanna in the kitchen. It was total chaos for the first few hours, all of us so excited to finally be there.

Nanna Agren would hold my mother for a long time when we arrived, her eyes moist and blue. She was an old woman already when I was born, so that is how I remember her: gray hair, yellow teeth, wrinkles. I remember thinking that in her youth she must have been beautiful because Hildure and Mary Ann were so pretty. In reality, Nanna had been a plain young woman, with gaps between her too-large teeth. She had a long, straight nose and an oval face that sagged at her chin, and she wore glasses. It was a kind, pleasant face, but not an especially pretty one. Perhaps it was a face better suited for old age, for in my mind's eye I see a beautiful old woman, holding her Eskimo daughter as tightly as she can.

Nanna was an industrious and tenacious woman. While Pop Agren was away working construction jobs wherever he could find them, Nanna turned the new place into a self-sustaining farm. They raised chickens, turkeys, and cows, as well as berries and fruit. She was successful enough at farming that friends and relatives were often sent away with baskets for their own tables. She kept her children busy helping, and my mother spent many summers picking strawberries at home, as well as at neighboring farms to make extra money. Times were hard, but Nanna made the best of them, and her children were never without food and clothing.

She was an outstanding cook, and we feasted whenever we were on Vashon. She cooked wonderful pies — apple, cherry, raspberry, blueberry, and my favorite, banana — which she fed to us at the kitchen table. She shuffled around as best she could, making sure we had enough, fawning over us, talking to my mother about our lives. I remember these things vaguely, as if from a dream, because I was so young when she was healthy. After her stroke, which confined her to a chair or bed for nearly nine years, she told us stories as she knitted socks and blankets that she gave to us for Christmas. But her condition worsened over the years until she was unable, near the end, even to speak. We would greet her, look into her eyes, but it seemed as if she was gone to us already.

Despite Nanna's demise in the old white house, our time there was happy. Many of my days were spent exploring the fields, woods, and bushes that made up the property. Down the hill behind the house were sheds and, at the end of the driveway, a big barn filled with treasures: an old wagon, rusty tools, car parts, locked trunks that churned my imagination. An owl lived high up in the rafters and scared me with its strange, ghostly sounds.

Just beyond the barn was the field, which yielded hay when Papa Agren was alive and healthy, long before I was born. It was a small field, five acres of infant rolling hills, which Brad and I rolled down again and again. Summer gold when we were there, the grass was long and soft, filled with mice and birds and spiderwebs. My favorite activity was sleeping out there with my family. We'd go to the top of the hill—sometimes all of us, sometimes just my dad and I—roll out our bags in a row, and watch the night come. I remember stars, comets, full moons, wind rustling the grass, the chirping of the crickets, the whole field erupting in melodious, high-pitched sound. Once I asked my mother why the crickets only sang at night. "They sing to the stars," she had said. "And sometimes the stars sing back, too quiet for us to hear." For many years after I continued listening for the stars, lying so, so still in the dark, irritated by my heartbeat disturbing the silence.

In the morning we'd wake, laugh at one another's hair, bristling and stuck full with leaves and hay, pack up our sleeping bags and hike down the hill. We knew what awaited us in the house: thin Swedish pancakes with raspberries, maple syrup, fresh orange juice, sausage. I loved Nanna's cooking, and after she died I loved Mary Ann's almost as much. All I had to do was pick berries, and many of my Vashon hours were spent in the raspberry patch, searching up and down, high and low, for the biggest ones. All five of us kids competed to see who could collect the most. If I ever won nobody knew it because I ate as many as I picked, returning to the house with red stains all about my head, hair, hands, and neck, as well as my clothes. When I was feeling mean I stole berries from my brother's pail. Sometimes our mother joined us, always picking more than we could, moving deftly up and down the rows, as if she knew exactly where the best berries were hidden, an advantage well earned from a childhood spent picking.

THE FARM, NOW, IS GONE, subdivided into lots for another of Seattle's bedroom communities. I don't like to think about the golden field paved and peppered with manicured, expensive houses. I wonder if the crickets still sing out there, and if the stars still whisper back.

Mary Ann and George lived in the old house for many years after Nanna died, but eventually they built a new home just down the road. The last time I was there the old house had been sold, remodeled, a future bed-and-breakfast. I visited Mary Ann and George, who gave me directions to my mother's gravestone in the cemetery. I bought flowers and strapped them to my bike, then rode out the narrow, pot-holed cemetery road, stopping once to buy honey from an old woman who raised bees. She had known my mother when she was a girl, she said. She'd once had a crush on Carl.

At the cemetery I couldn't find my mother's grave. I searched for two hours, intermittently believing that she wasn't really dead, or that my not finding her was symbolic of our relationship. After an hour of frustrated searching, I abandoned the neat linear pathways and clomped across the graves. My mother's flowers wilted in my hand. Fatigued and beaten, I lurched like a drunk to a grave and unzipped my pants to relieve myself, realizing just in time that it was my mother's. I turned, embarrassed. I couldn't cry anymore. I sat on my mother's grave and ate a peanut butter and honey sandwich. I laughed. Out loud and for a long time. When I finished I had the hiccups. It was late in the day and I was cold. On the way home I looked for the bee woman, but she was gone. I would have liked to talk to her again.

VASHON,
1933-1934

JUSTINA, CHRISTINE, AND MISS PETRIL had worked together to sew clothes appropriate for the children's arrival on Vashon. They'd made Doris two dresses, and on the day the ship docked in Seattle Doris was dressed in a plain, knee-length yellow dress, with a lace collar and short sleeves puffed around her shoulders. She wore her only pair of shoes, the leather faded and worn, but her socks were clean and white. Her hair was cut just below her ears and washed clean the morning they arrived. Carl wore a pair of gray overalls with wooden buttons, and underneath a nice blue shirt that Miss Petril had stitched together using material salvaged from Doris's second dress. He wore shoes identical to Doris's except that they were bigger, and he had new black socks. His hair was cut short and parted neatly to the left. Miss Petril had taken great care to clean them thoroughly, from their ears all the way down to the dirt between their toes. She had taught them how to brush their teeth and warned them to do it once every day. Compared to how they dressed in Kotlik, Doris and Carl felt very dressed up, but despite the handsome new clothes and Miss Petril's efforts to help Doris and Carl blend in, they looked like what they were: two Native children fresh from the bush. Doris squirmed and scratched, out of place and uncomfortable in her dress; Carl appeared sheepish and distant. Their eyes were dark with worry.

In Seattle Miss Petril and the children rode a bus to the ferry landing. Neither of the children had ridden in a motor vehicle before, and Doris was terrified because she felt as if she'd been swallowed by a whale. She screamed and flailed her arms until she calmed enough to take notice of the city passing beyond the windows. Exhausted from the journey, she lapsed back into sleep, her head bobbing against Miss Petril's prodigious arm. Carl pressed his face against the window and stared at the towering buildings and crowded streets of Seattle. He kept nudging Doris, wanting to share it with her, baffled that she could sleep during the first bus ride of their life.

Miss Petril was also well dressed for the occasion, in a navy blue, ankle-length wool skirt and a starched white blouse. She looked the prim, controlling, and competent matron that she was, regarding the children with an air of authority. Yet she was compassionate, and while the children slept she watched over them with tenderness, reflecting on their uncertain futures. She questioned whether Charlie Backlund was doing the right thing by sending them away. She thought him heartless for not making the journey himself, but she saw that he would not be persuaded otherwise. She'd known Charlie for many years, and though generally she thought him to be a good man, she knew that his business ruled his life and that he let nothing get in its way. Not even his children.

On the ferry Doris was rejuvenated. They got off the bus and climbed to the upper deck, where Doris and Carl stood next to Miss Petril at the bow, watching with jittery excitement as Vashon came into view. It was a clear day and Doris could see the vast length of the island and the green, wooded hills so foreign to her. She gripped Carl's hand, her tiny fingers around two of his chubbier ones. Neither of them spoke, afraid to violate Miss Petril's warning about speaking Yup'ik in public. They looked at each other frequently, gathering comfort in each other's nervous eyes; they knew, at least, that they were not alone.

When the ferry reached the island Miss Petril made last-minute adjustments to their hair and clothing, giving them each a fast kiss on the forehead when she finished. The bus was one of only three vehicles to disembark on Vashon, and at once Carl and Doris were comforted by the stillness of the place in contrast to Seattle. The bus shifted into low gear and whined its way up the long, steep hill that rose immediately beyond the landing. A boy across the aisle pointed things out to his mother as they passed by: old man Wilkerson's place, the road to a beach, the church, the school he would be attending. The boy stared at Doris when he talked, as if trying to show her that this was his island, and that he knew they were foreigners. Doris ignored him and put her head out the open window. She marveled at the wind blowing through her hair, the rushing in her ears, the whirring green of trees. She stretched her arms in front of her and pretended she was flying. Miss Petril held her tightly around the waist, allowing her this newfound pleasure. Jealous, Carl squeezed his head out the window next to Doris's. He opened his mouth and let the wind tickle his throat. They laughed in delight when a dog attacked the bus, barking ferociously and following for fifty yards. In their excitement they lost themselves, yelling ecstatically in Yup'ik until Miss Petril pulled them inside.

Twenty minutes later the bus stopped at the Agren place, just off the main road. As soon as they stepped down and the bus sputtered away, a door banged and a solid woman and a short man appeared on the front porch. Doris and Carl were stunned by the house, huge and white with glass windows all around, a neatly trimmed grass yard, potted flowers on the front porch. Mr. and Mrs. Agren walked out to greet them, followed by their teenage daughters, Mary Ann and Hildure, by whom Doris was spellbound. Nanna marched directly to Doris and Carl and gave them hugs, then shook Miss Petril's hand. Mary Ann and Hildure began talking to them, speaking very slowly and loudly, as if Doris and Carl were deaf. Carl smiled uncomfortably, looking to Doris for help. In barely more than a whisper Doris told them that, yes, the trip was fine, they had seen many fine things, but that Carl didn't understand very well. As she spoke she watched the ground, embarrassed, though she couldn't have said why. Tears welled up in her eyes. Mary Ann rescued her by asking if they wanted to see the house and the room where they would be living.

Doris nodded and Mary Ann took her hand. They went inside while the adults drank coffee on the porch. Neither Doris nor Carl had seen a house like this except in magazines, and it was hard for them to believe they would be living here. Sweet smells filled the kitchen and dining room, where the table was crowded with crystal glasses, china and silverware. A sparkling lamp hung from the ceiling, glass candles glowing with light. Soft, colorful rugs covered the floors. Everything sparkled, fresh and clean. Upstairs, where their bedroom was, Doris and Carl were astonished by all the things: model airplanes hanging from the ceilings, posters on the wall, flocks of clothes in the closets, perfume bottles lined up on a dresser. Doris and Carl had a room to themselves, much different from sleeping with one's cousins and friends in one room, or tucked in beside Justina in Kotlik. But most surprising was the indoor bathroom, with a hard, white sink and toilet, and a huge bathtub with legs like a lion's paws. Carl and Doris had never seen such a bathroom, had never even heard of one. The first time Carl used the toilet, he pulled the handle with trepidation, closing his eyes in fear. He stared in wonder at his little stool spinning down the drain; he could scarcely believe it. In Kotlik his waste had sat, rank, in a bucket until someone emptied it into the river. In the future he would flush many items down the toilet, watching them twirl and spin out of sight, to places he couldn't fathom. He stopped this finally when a cardboard boat he'd made clogged the toilet, spilling water over the floor and into the living room.

After touring the house the children went downstairs for dinner. They ate beef casserole and fresh green salad with leaves bigger than any they'd seen on the tundra. The food tasted strange to them, so accustomed to fish, seal oil, and moose. But the bread was something special, soft and warm and spread with real butter, which they'd never tasted before. Doris would remember, for the rest of her life, how that first bite felt, the way the bread melted in her mouth. She loved, also, the raspberry pie, which made her tingle inside. It was served with vanilla ice cream that Pop Agren had made just before dinner. It was very different from Eskimo ice cream—*akutaq*, a mixture of king salmon, seal fat, berries, and sugar—which Carl and Doris, like most Eskimo children, loved.

Nanna's pies reminded Doris of Justina, who made pies from the berries she gathered on the tundra. As Doris ate she was saddened, wondering when she would see Justina again. Her eyes drooped and Nanna noticed it was time to put her to bed. She was asleep by the time Nanna placed her gently under the clean white sheets that smelled of wind. Carl came to bed soon after, but he slept fitfully, the sound of crickets foreign to his ears, the smells so different from Alaska.

DORIS DREAMED. Her mother, Dora, walked the frozen tundra. She was a young woman, with tight skin wrapping her wide face, and creases running from her nose to the corners of her lips. Her shiny hair fell like black water halfway down her back. It was cold and snowy, but Dora wore only a summer dress, and she was barefoot. Her village was a long way off, and she was trying to return. The freezing wind burned her skin where it was bare, froze her eyelids solid. Tiny icicles hung from her nose. Every few steps she broke through the snow's hard crust, and her legs and feet bled. Dora sang, her soft voice swallowed by the wind.

"Someday I will come home," she sang. "The ground will thaw, and I will walk along the flowered sea. Someday I will come home."

Dora turned to look behind her. A crimson shape winged through the darkness. She felt its searing breath.

Doris woke, terrified, but she didn't cry out. The smells of her new surroundings, sweet and somehow too clean, offered her no comfort; she shivered in the dark. She pulled Nina close to her and buried her face in the doll's hair, inhaling deeply the smell of bear and fish. For the rest of the night she dreamed of the river, her feet sunk deep and warmed in the mud.

WHEN DORIS ROSE IN THE MORNING, Carl was already down in the kitchen gobbling up Nanna's strawberry pancakes, trying to keep pace with Pop Agren, who chuckled as he watched Carl. Hildure and Mary Ann came into Doris's room to see if she needed anything. They wanted so much to be sisterly, to help her feel at home. But they didn't know how different Doris's life had been, and when Hildure breathed the salmon smell of Doris's doll, she cringed and drew back.

"What is that smell?" she asked, repulsed. "We've got to wash that doll!"

Embarrassed, Doris nearly burst into tears. She didn't want Nina's smell to go away. She clutched her tightly to her breast. Hildure, not wanting to upset her, left Nina alone and helped Mary Ann dress her, brush her hair and tie it with a red ribbon, which reminded Doris of the poodle she had seen at the dock the day before.

Primped, they joined Carl at the kitchen table. Nanna stood erect over the stove, filling their plates with food. Everyone was dressed up, the girls in their finest skirts and blouses, Carl in a necktie that Pop Agren had tied on him. Nanna Agren cooked pancakes in her blue silk dress, two pearls hanging from a gold chain around her neck. They were in their church clothes, but it wasn't Sunday. They were going to have their picture taken.

After breakfast the family gathered on the porch where Nanna's brother, Uncle Elmer, waited with a camera set on a tripod. Elmer arranged them—Miss Petril, Nanna, Doris, and Pop in back; Mary Ann, Hildure, and Carl in front—and snapped six photographs. He said "Smile," and they did, except Doris. She glared, as if that porch on Vashon was the last place she wanted to be, despite Nanna's arm on her waist and a tummy full of pancakes. Carl smiled, but it was the faintest of smiles, a shadow.

As soon as Uncle Elmer finished, Miss Petril hustled Doris and Carl inside to speak with them. She had told them all of it before, but she felt the need to say everything one last time, as if to weld her words into the center of their nervous systems. She was going, she said, back to Kotlik, where she knew Charlie would want to hear all about their journey. Charlie had business to complete, but when he was finished he would come back to live with them on Vashon. They mustn't worry, she said. He'd be down soon. In the meantime Charlie would write letters, and they must try to write back, in English. She told them to study hard, to do well in school, and to be a help to the Agrens. She admonished them, one last time, about speaking Yup'ik, because some people might scorn them for it. She reassured them that everything would be all right.

Doris and Carl stared bleary-eyed at the ground. Carl had noticed that Miss Petril's suitcase was packed. He held back his tears, wanting to be strong for Doris, who began to weep openly. It wasn't Miss Petril that they would miss, for they hardly knew her, but she was their last connection to Kotlik. Miss Petril, her own eyes watery, picked up

Doris and hugged her farewell. She held her for a long, speechless moment as Doris sobbed quietly on her shoulder. Then Miss Petril lifted Carl and held both of them against her full-bosomed body, and she wondered how the children would fare.

She put them down, squeezed both of their hands. Nanna came in and picked up Doris, still weeping, and held Carl's hand as Miss Petril said good-bye to Mary Ann and Hildure, then shook Nanna's hand firmly.

"Thank you for your kindness," she said. "I'll be in touch."

She set her suitcase in the bed of Pop Agren's pickup truck, then heaved herself into the cab next to Pop. She waved as the truck rumbled out the driveway. The children kept listening long after the sound of the engine faded over the hill.

THIS, WITH A BOX of chocolates:

February 3, 1934

My dearest Doris and Carl,
You can't have forgotten how cold and dark it is this time of year in Alaska. It's been a bitter winter and I can't help but be happy that you are in a warmer place, though I miss you both very much. I'm visiting Kotlik for the potlatch— not much to do in Liberty Landing this time of year. I'm sitting here with Justina, who wants me to say how very much she misses and loves you. She tells me to tell you that she has been searching for a fox with wings but hasn't seen one since you left. She says for you to keep looking for the fox down there.
Happy Birthday, little Inaqaq! You're five years old, and I'm sorry that I can't be there to celebrate with you. I hope

you like the little present I've sent along with this letter—
perhaps you can share it with Carl. You've both probably
grown more than I can imagine, and I wonder if I'd recognize
you after all these months. I promise it won't be long before
I'm there. Justina can't come down with me because she is
marrying Gus Mike, who you might remember because he
used to give you candy and tell funny jokes.

Soon, when the ice breaks up, I'll be back in Liberty
Landing for the start of fishing season. After that I'll be down
to see you. I hope you're being helpful with the Agrens, and
speaking English well. It may be hard at first, but you'll both
do very well. You are smart children.

Time to work. Justina says good-bye, and we'll write
again soon. Behave yourselves, my little bears.
Love,
Papa

P.S. Dear Mr. and Mrs. Agren—Thank you for reading this
letter to the children. Enclosed is a money order for the next
three months' expenses. After that the account at the bank
will be activated, and funds will be allocated monthly. Once
again I thank you so much for taking care of the children.
I plan on visiting this summer, perhaps in July if I find
someone to mind the store. Please note the address where
I can be reached after May 1.
My best to you, C.B.

CHARLIE DID INDEED VISIT THAT SUMMER, though only for
a couple of weeks because he couldn't leave the store for long. As his
children had before him, he rode the ferry and then the bus to the
Agrens' house. It was raining when he arrived, had been raining for a
week straight. It had poured for most of Charlie's two-thousand-mile

journey, and he was tired of it. He sat on the bus and watched the dense green of Vashon fly by, and for a few minutes he felt depressed by it all, the rain in this wet place so far from home, where for some godforsaken reason he'd sent his children. Then he thought of Doris and Carl and it cheered him. He had missed them more than he'd expected to.

When the bus groaned to a halt in front of the house, Carl and Doris sprinted from the porch, where they had waited all morning, their ears tuned to the hill over which the bus would come. They wondered what Charlie would be like, if things would be the same, if their dreams of him would match the man he was. A year is a long time for young children, and already their life in Kotlik seemed like a dream. They hadn't slept a wink the night before, and when Carl heard the grumble of the bus his stomach did somersaults.

Charlie held them in his arms, and they smelled the familiar odor of fish and pipe smoke. Doris thought she could smell Justina, and she was so happy that after a few minutes her face ached from smiling. It seemed as if they had never been apart, and never would be again. Carl and Doris escorted Charlie to the house, pointing things out to him as they walked—the raspberries, the swag-bellied cow, the school up the hill. Charlie smiled at their energy, relieved that they seemed happy and healthy. Carl, Charlie noticed, talked a little bit more, and his English was coming along. Doris was bubbly and spirited, and Charlie was surprised by how much she'd grown. Their good spirits softened the guilt Charlie felt, but he knew it was a temporary relief.

Nanna Agren emerged from the house to greet him. As she offered her hand Charlie smelled the sweet, sleepy essence of baking, and he was struck by both her gentle demeanor and the strength of her hands. She invited him in, sat him at the kitchen table with his children and served them thin blueberry pancakes covered in applesauce and powdered sugar. Charlie drank coffee, and the two of them talked as Nanna hustled around the kitchen. Carl and Doris moved from their chairs to Charlie's lap, and he bounced them on his knees.

"Lately it's just been me and Carl and Doris around here," Nanna said. "Mr. Agren has a job down in Tacoma, working on the Navy shipyard—he comes home weekends when he can. Harold's off at school, living in Seattle, and my two daughters, Hildure and Mary Ann, come and go so much these days I can't keep track of them. But they all do their share around here. Including Doris and Carl. They've become quite the berry pickers."

"How many acres do you have here?" Charlie asked.

"Oh, about five, I guess, but not much is farmable. It's pretty hilly. We grow hay on the hill down there, and get plenty of vegetables from the garden. Plus the fruit trees and the berries. Vashon does well with berries."

Charlie nodded, his eyes drowsy and his back slouched. "I gathered that on the drive. Plenty of water, too, I noticed." He smiled, hoping she wouldn't take offense.

Nanna chuckled. "Yes. Rain we have. Especially this year. Seems like summer will never arrive. Do you get much rain in Alaska?" Nanna was rolling out dough as she talked, her eye contact infrequent, flitting. She reminded Charlie of a bird, swooping about the morning as it searched for worms and bugs.

"We do, yes, quite a bit. But not this hard for this long. It rained for most of my journey down here."

Their conversation was interrupted by Mary Ann, who came in the side door carrying a pail brimming with milk. She said hello, then with Nanna's help emptied the pail into glass bottles, which they placed in the icebox.

"Fresh milk?" Nanna asked Charlie.

"Maybe just a bit for my coffee," he said. "What a treat milk is. Do Carl and Doris help milk the cow?"

Mary Ann laughed. "Carl's learning, but Doris is scared to death of cows."

"This true?" he asked Doris, squeezing her leg.

"The cows want to get me, I can tell when they look at me. They're bigger than bears," Doris responded. She spread her arms to demonstrate.

"Ah, so that's it," said Carl, shooting Mary Ann a wink.

Doris and Carl jumped down from Charlie's lap to help Mary Ann, but mostly just got in her way. Charlie saw their mutual fondness. Doris and Mary Ann giggled, at nothing in particular. Mary Ann was fourteen, and spent much of her time helping around the farm, which often meant caring for Carl and Doris. She'd become a big sister to them.

For her part, Mary Ann was surprised to see how old Mr. Backlund was. She had known his age from Nanna, but until she saw him it hadn't really registered in her mind that he was an old man, easily old enough to be her grandfather. She tried to hide her surprise on first seeing him. She liked him right away and she could tell that Nanna did, too. He was a large but unassuming man, who carried himself slowly and with ease. He had a certain grace about him that immediately won her trust.

"Come on, Papa," Doris said during a pause in his and Nanna's conversation. "The rain's let up. I'll show you the raspberry patch!"

"She's there so much that her fingers are stained red," Mary Ann added.

Doris proudly held her hands out for Charlie to examine and he saw that it was true, that her fingers were red from the last knuckles to the tips. She led Charlie by the hand down the short grade behind the house to the raspberry patch. The air felt heavy with water. Carl and Mary Ann followed, and Nanna stayed behind in the kitchen to clean up and work on her canning.

"This is how you do it," Doris told Charlie, matter-of-factly. "Watch out for the thorns, come in underneath, then you can find the ones that are hiding. If they don't come off easily then they're not ready."

She showed him, reaching into the tangled vines, her sleeve drenched from leaves spilling rainwater. She pulled off a fat, wet, dark crimson raspberry that she gave to Charlie. He bent over and let her put it directly into his mouth.

"Here, now take this," Doris commanded, handing Charlie a small cardboard crate. "We'll see who can fill their basket first."

The four of them moved quickly, Doris and Carl giggling at how funny their father looked stooped over the bushes. In less than two minutes Carl blurted out, "Finished!" and raised his box in the air to signal his victory.

"That's not fair, you always win," Doris whined.

"That's because you eat half your berries," Carl scolded back. But then he softened and looked guilty. He came over to her and poured some of his berries into her box. Charlie watched them both, put his hand on Carl's head.

"You're a fine brother," Charlie said, "and a gentleman. I hope you two are always so good to each other."

At noon they ate turkey sandwiches for lunch, with Nanna's raspberry-peach pie for dessert. Afterwards they played croquet in the front yard, until Charlie retired to his room for a nap while Doris helped Nanna in the kitchen and Carl carried wood for the stove. That evening they walked through the back field, Carl and Doris showing Charlie their secret hiding places, their magic world among the mice and crickets. Charlie followed just behind them, his expression often far away and troubled. Carl noticed and it made him nervous. He wondered what was wrong. Doris seemed oblivious, skipping through the tall grass as if she had just learned that she was lighter than air.

It rained on and off all evening, and they opened their umbrellas and wore rain slickers. When they returned at twilight their shoes were soaked, and Nanna made a fuss. She boiled water for tea, which she insisted they drink with lemon and honey before dinner. The children were exhausted, their legs tired from the walking and their heads spinning with the joy of having their father back. Doris could hardly keep her eyes open at the dinner table, but she wanted so badly for the day to go on and on and for her father to stay forever. Finally she flopped her face into the mashed potatoes, and Mary Ann cleaned her and carried her upstairs to bed.

Charlie stayed for two weeks. Each day was a repetition of the last, though for the children there was nothing monotonous about it and for Charlie it was a welcome reprieve from the stresses of work. One day he went to Seattle to buy goods for the store, and when he returned in the evening he brought with him a tricycle for Doris and a bicycle with training wheels for Carl. The children were thrilled, but there was no smooth place for them to ride. The road was too dangerous, the gravel driveway too rough, the grass too soft. The next day Charlie set out to build a sidewalk, and for the next week the children tried to help their father as he dug the earth, set the frame, and mixed and poured the concrete. It was backbreaking work and Nanna worried about Charlie's strength, but he seemed healthy and strong for an elderly man, and it was obvious that he was used to hard labor.

When it was finished they all thought it splendid, a long walkway that extended from the house, along the driveway to the road. Uncle Elmer came to see it, and Doris and Carl beamed with pleasure. They rode the tricycle and bicycle up and down the sidewalk all day, back and forth, back and forth, until Charlie thought he'd go dizzy from watching. Nanna thanked him and he shook his head, saying only, "Mrs. Agren, it's the very least I can do," looking almost somber when he said it.

Charlie spent the next few days searching for a house to buy. He had decided, finally, that he had no choice but to leave Alaska the following summer. *After all, I'm not a young man anymore,* he thought to himself. *And this will be a good place to grow old.* He found a house just up the street from the Agrens', a run-down shack that he immediately began remodeling. He bought new windows and doors, all the necessary supplies, then hired out the work, which he expected to be finished by the time he returned the following year.

Finally everything appeared to be in place. His children were settled and cared for, the future was paid, the map drawn and his place on it marked with an x. He'd loved his life in Alaska, and he would miss it; he'd been there fifty years. But it wasn't an easy life, and he felt ready to give it up. He had his children to think of now. His children and Dora's. He missed her, saw her in the children's eyes, and imagined what she would have wanted him to do. *If she had lived,* he thought, *if she had lived we would have come here together. But she wouldn't have wanted to. It would have been hard for her.*

Pop Agren returned for the last week Charlie was on Vashon. The two of them got along well together and spent the evenings smoking their pipes out on the porch, watching the children play croquet or ride the sidewalk. Never sitting for a moment, Nanna hustled around in the kitchen, bringing Pop and Charlie fresh vanilla ice cream as they sat talking in the cooling dusk. They spoke about Alaska, about Sweden and Finland, about the threat of war in Europe. Charlie liked the sound of Pop's voice, the slight trace of Swedish intonation, the easy way he linked his words. He seemed a natural storyteller, and it was relaxing to hear him talk of his boyhood in Sweden, the crickets filling up the space between his words. Pop Agren was a jovial man, serious at times but usually a jester's glint in his eyes. He played easily with the children and liked to tell them stories of adventure.

Pop liked having Charlie around. He could tell Charlie was an educated man, though in what context he couldn't say and he didn't ask. Charlie had a certain authority and a way of measuring his words before he released them, so that when he spoke you could be sure he meant what he said. And in many ways Charlie had lived the life Pop had dreamed of, the travel and adventure and wild ways of Alaska. Charlie was perplexing to Pop, though not inaccessible. He was an intelligent, wealthy gentleman, yet he had lived among the gold miners and fur trappers and Natives of the bush, had hunted and fished and lived off the land. Charlie defied definition, and because of this Pop liked him all the more. He looked forward to having him around permanently.

As the evenings wore on the family would migrate inside to the sitting room, where they read or played checkers or cards. Doris had recently learned checkers from Carl, who usually let her win, so she was excited to show Charlie what she knew. On his last night he agreed to play with her, and she insisted on setting up the board by herself. She played eagerly, with Mary Ann whispering in her ear, coaching her, the both of them unable to contain their giggles. Charlie sat back in his chair, Carl on his lap, and enjoyed watching his daughter and son. Once in a while Carl whispered advice in Charlie's ear, and Doris would scowl and say, "No, you can't help him, that's not fair!"

When Doris jumped Charlie's last piece she laughed ecstatically and Charlie put his finger to his lips to quiet her. Pop was sleeping, the newspaper scattered across his lap. Charlie yawned and said it was time for bed, that they had an early morning coming. Doris stiffened. For the first time in days she realized that her father would soon be gone. She felt like crying but she didn't want to ruin the evening.

Charlie saw her eyes darken and her jaw tighten. *Such a willful child*, he thought, *so earnest and fierce.* He was comforted by this knowledge, knowing she'd make her way in the world, with or without him. While Mary Ann went to clear the dishes, Charlie carried the children to their room. Doris clung to him, trembling.

He got them into their pajamas, put them into their beds, and turned out the light. He sat on the edge of Doris's bed and waited for his eyes to adjust to the darkness.

"Papa, how long till you'll come back?" Carl asked, his face invisible.

"Next summer will come before you know it," Charlie answered, trying to sound convincing but feeling his words as hollow as driftwood.

"And we'll live just up the street and we can come visit Nanna whenever we want?" Carl was slurring his words as he drifted off. Charlie couldn't see if Doris was awake; he heard her breathing but she was very still.

"Of course, and by that time the training wheels will be off your bike and you can ride back and forth between here and there. There's a cherry tree in back and you can help me pick cherries. I'll teach you how to fish."

Carl didn't answer and Charlie knew he was asleep.

"Papa, I don't want you to go!" Doris's voice speared through the blackness. Charlie was taken aback by its coldness, the conviction of his little girl. She was commanding him.

"I know you don't, Doris. I know. But I have no choice. When I come back everything will be like it is now, okay? Will you try to be good while I'm gone and help Nanna and Pop around the farm? Will you do that for me?"

Doris's voice cracked, softened, seemed to melt into the night like cream into black coffee. "I will, Papa. But I miss you. And Justina. I want her to come too."

"I know you do. She loves you very much and misses you. But she can't. When I come back, when you are older perhaps, we'll go back to visit her. You'll see her again before too long."

"People look at me funny sometimes," Doris said, her voice barely a whisper.

Charlie paused, thinking deeply about how he should respond. She was at an age when she would begin to understand such things.

"That's because you and Carl are very special," Charlie said. "No matter how they look at you or what they say, remember that you're very special. Very beautiful and very rare. Like an Eskimo curlew that everyone wants to catch."

"Okay," Doris said, slurring. "The curlew . . . " And then she was asleep. Charlie sat in the darkness for a long time and listened to his children sleep. He heard the crickets outside, a cough from the next room, the hum of silence as the night calmed. He thought he heard Doris whisper his name in her sleep, but he couldn't be sure.

She dreamed of birds.

9

Charlie Backlund never returned to Vashon. After news of his death reached the island, the Agrens tried as best they could to make their home permanent for Doris and Carl. My mother never easily gave herself to tears, a legacy that survives in most of my family. Even as a child she rarely cried, except in private, and I imagine that when the news of Charlie's death came, she mourned privately, locked away in her room with Nina. She may have talked to Carl about it, but I doubt this because they were still very young and probably incapable of articulating their emotions. How and to what extent they suffered can only be imagined.

Life on Vashon continued as before, though there was an almost imperceptible shift in the matrix of the family. Legally, no adoption took place, not because the Agrens weren't committed but simply because life was busy and adoption an unnecessary formality. With Charlie's death Doris and Carl suddenly realized that they were on Vashon to stay, and that the Agrens were their new family. This meant that both of them, at impressionable ages, shut Alaska, Kotlik, and Justina out of their lives, as if closing a curtain on the stage of a life no longer theirs to live and too painful to recall. Far from Kotlik and their origins, it was easier to forget. Thus began a pattern of half-truths and denial that would haunt Doris and Carl for the rest of their lives.

In their eighties now, Mary Ann and Hildure still gleam with Nanna's energy. Mary Ann is motherly and talkative, corralling me with food and words when I visit her on Vashon. Hildure is sincere and dignified, with an aura of grace. She doesn't think of herself as wise, but I do. Both of them are children of the Depression, frugal and practical. It isn't easy for them, especially Hildure, to speak of my mother or those early days, not because they don't remember but because their frugality extends to words. Fearing that they will tarnish my mother's memory and perhaps the Agren name, their words hesitate. What information I gather is but the shell, the husk, the skin my mother sloughed, like the translucent veil of a caterpillar, shed and shadowed by the first slow beat of a butterfly's wings.

When my mother and Carl came to Vashon, my Uncle Harold had already left home. Later he joined the Army and died as a Japanese POW late in World War II. My mother never knew him well, but she felt the family's sorrow and assumed it as her own. When I was a child my mother often talked of him fondly, recounting stories Nanna may have told her. I was proud of my war-hero uncle, and I bragged about him to my friends. I stared at photographs of him, a skinny, spectacled, serious man, and I tried to imagine his death. Thus my Uncle Harold came alive to me through stories.

Hildure was sixteen when Carl and Doris arrived, a junior in high school, and Mary Ann two years younger. Hildure remembers them disembarking from the bus, looking "so sad and frightened. I just wanted to protect them." For the first year Hildure and Mary Ann were Carl and Doris's caretakers, dressing, cleaning, and schooling them. They were patient teachers and the children quickly grew fond of them. When Hildure began regularly leaving the island after graduating from high school, Mary Ann stayed on, playing a primary role in raising Carl and Doris. She tutored them, made them clothes, taught them the latest dance steps, was their ally in every way.

Doris emulated her older sisters, wanting to look and be just like them. Her fundamental perceptions about the world began to change. Whereas in Kotlik she might have seen a fox and thought of a story Justina had told her about an ancestor, a story in which the fox was the ancestor, on Vashon she learned that a fox was just a fox, and that separations between the human and nonhuman worlds were clear and mandatory. Whereas in Kotlik they had been told about Raven carving out the rivers and had believed it, on Vashon they learned to distinguish fable and reality.

Doris and Carl became model students. In grade-school class photographs, Doris sits near the front, the other girls leaning adoringly into her. She was popular with her classmates, vivacious and fun. The photographs illustrate what neither Mary Ann nor Hildure would have noticed: that each year Doris and Carl appeared less Eskimo, as if their former essence was being siphoned away. In second grade Doris is frowning, angry or afraid, her hair black and straight, cut just below her ears. However, it's not so much her physical features that belie her blending, but the contrast between her and the others, who smile innocently and untroubled, at ease in their bodies. My mother looks as if she has known—is knowing—pain. By third grade this has changed. She smiles semi-confidently, wearing a flowered dress with a white collar and buttoned neck. Canted into her on either side are two smiling blonde boys who appear acutely aware of the girl sitting next to them. She almost blends in, though she is one of four ethnic children in a class of twenty-five.

Carl doesn't mix as well as Doris, perhaps because in his second- and third-grade photos the students are segregated. The tall, blonde kids stand in the top two rows, while the Japanese, Indian, and Eskimo children sit clumped at the bottom. Whether this was the teacher's decision or a coincidence, a clear line divides white from nonwhite. Carl smiles affably and hunches insecurely. As he grew older this changed. Gradually he gained self-confidence, grew tall and handsome, played sports in high school. Sometimes Carl and Doris danced together, learned new steps as they twirled across the barn floor or the lawn. Nanna didn't like them dancing in the house, so they danced wherever they could. As they became preoccupied by their own friends and activities, dancing was one of the few interests they continued to share, all through high school and into college.

As for friends, Carl had many but none of them close. He studied hard and kept to himself much of the time. Doris, on the other hand, enjoyed the comfort of close circles. She had many girlfriends, most of them white: Rita, Roberta, Dot, Mary, Elsie, and Marlene. Middle-school photographs show my mother with Dot and Roberta at the beach, bows and pigtails, posing in their bathing suits as they might for the cover of a magazine: hips turned, chests out, breasts just beginning to bud. My mother is at the center, her arms around Dot and Roberta, who incline toward her. Even then she was a kind of nucleus.

As often happens with children, those early friendships faded, and my mother's high-school years were dominated by a girl named Betty, whom my mother would later refer to as her best friend. Betty was a small, roundish blonde, with a high voice and energy to match Doris's. They were like two bees, constantly buzzing around projects or ideas. They spoke fast and incomprehensibly, often whispering in each other's ears. As younger girls they played with dolls, Doris's Yup'ik doll Nina replaced by a white doll named Betina that Charlie had given her on that first and final visit to Vashon. Before long the dolls were replaced by talk of boys and crushes. They were inseparable, and when Doris began writing a diary in the ninth grade she always began it, "Dear Betty," as if all of her deepest thoughts should be shared with her. When miniskirts hit Seattle in 1942, my mother and Betty wore them together, boldly showing off their legs as they posed for a photo on the hood of Pop Agren's truck. When she was twelve or thirteen, my mother began curling her hair. One might never have guessed she was Yup'ik if, for example, one had seen her walking to school in 1943, wearing a plaid miniskirt and ankle-high white socks, her curled hair in bows, books in one arm and lunch in the other. She would have looked like any other schoolgirl in America, striding up the road.

By Hildure's and Mary Ann's accounts, Carl and Doris had a fair amount of freedom, and Nanna let them explore the island and occasionally take trips to Seattle. But home life was consistent and comforting, the steady rhythm of Nanna working away, the endless chores and hustle of her life. She never complained. Work was necessary and therefore worthwhile. During the school year Doris and Carl had chores before and after school: milking the cow, chopping wood, or cleaning out the hen house. The grass had to be cut, the hedges clipped, and always there was work in the kitchen. In the summer the garden needed tending, the fruit harvesting, the berries picking. Many of their schoolmates were doing the same, including Betty, and Doris and she spent more than a few summers side by side in raspberry patches all over the island.

As the Depression passed, life eased for the Agrens. During the war years Pop had steady work in the Navy shipyard, and this combined with the boarding money and Nanna's cooking brought in a comfortable income. There was rarely money to spare, but they were better off than many. After Harold's death Nanna withdrew inside herself, silently mourning her only son while on the surface continuing exactly as she had before. After the war, during my mother's high-school years, Pop Agren was home more, and during this time they formed a lasting bond. They were both spirited and adventurous, and liked each other's company. Carl and Doris were the last of the children at home, after Hildure and Mary Ann married and moved off the island. Carl studied while my mother socialized. She became a cheerleader and went on dates. She could never settle on one boyfriend; she didn't want to limit herself. When Carl left for college she missed him, but by that time she was so engulfed in her social life that she hardly had time to notice.

On the surface it seemed an uneventful adolescence. My mother grew up in a middle-American family in a period defined by the Depression, conservatism, growth of the middle class, technological revolution, and the fresh green buds of consumerism. Vashon was a safe, easy place, a good place for transformation. My mother looked ahead.

Her high-school portrait is bright, her eyes flashing toward the future. Touched up as photos were in those days, it shows her skin pasty white, a slight rouge masking her high cheeks, her lips cherry red. But they can't hide her teeth, perfectly white and large, her smile beckoning. A string of pearls arcs from her neck. She gazes to the left, as if looking beyond the photographer's yellow ducky to a future as veiled and unfathomable as the past.

Half-breed,

1945

Doris's birthday was yesterday. Sixteen years old, she sits with Betty in the hard wooden chairs of the Motor Vehicle Department, waiting for her temporary driver's license.

"Gosh," Betty says, "it's so exciting that you can drive us now. I can't wait to get my license. Was the test very hard?"

"It was fluff. You'll pass it with flying colors." Doris smiles reassuringly. "You're a better driver than I am."

Betty leans close to Doris and whispers in her ear: "I don't think I could drive in a straight line at all if I got the same instructor you did. He's so handsome!"

They giggle, and the corpulent woman with glasses behind the counter glares at them. "Young ladies," she says, "people are taking tests in here. Will you please hush?"

They bow their heads in compliance, both about to burst with laughter.

"Gee whiz, how long is it going to take them?" Betty whispers after a few minutes. "You'd think you'd applied to medical school or something!"

Just as she says this the stout woman bleats, "Your temporary license is ready, young lady, the permanent one will be in the mail in four to eight weeks. Be sure to carry this with you at all times or your license may be suspended." She shoves the white piece of paper in Doris's face.

"Thank you," Doris says. The woman sighs and returns to her desk.

Outside, Betty mocks the woman's sigh. "What a testy old buzzard," she says. "You'd think we'd asked her to scour the outhouse or something." They laugh as they get in Pop's pickup.

"This is for real," Betty says. "Now you're official. Let's drive down to Ernie's and get a soda. All the kids will be there now."

Doris doesn't respond, and Betty looks at her. "What are you waiting for?" she asks. "What's wrong?"

Doris's face is pale. She stares at the paper and shakes. "It says here, it says, I . . . "

Betty takes the license and reads it. "I can't believe it," she says. "I can't believe they'd write that. 'Half-breed!' How dare they!" She reaches to open the door.

"No!" Doris snaps. Then quietly, "Not now, please, I just want to go."

Doris drives down the hill toward town, thinking *Half-breed, half-breed, Doris is a half-breed,* remembering fourth grade and towheaded Tommy taunting her until Carl punched him in the nose. Betty is talking to her, but she can't hear anything except Tommy's voice in her ears and a distant sound like a great rushing of water.

She drops Betty at Ernie's, sees the gang inside at their favorite table by the window. They wave at her. In the booth next to them is a Navy man, in uniform, with his girlfriend.

"Bye, Betty," she says, and she waves at the gang and turns the truck around and drives. Halfway home she pulls off the road, takes the piece of paper and tears it into tiny strips. She drives on and still the sounds are in her ears.

That night she goes to bed without supper and Nanna Agren worries. Doris dreams of soldiers marching and her brother, Harold, is one of them. Behind him a short Japanese soldier pushes him and beats him around the head with a gun until Harold collapses and the man shoots a bullet in the back of his head. Doris is crying in her sleep, sad for Harold and mad at the Japanese soldier, but then the man turns into Mary, her friend from primary school, who was Japanese and picked berries with Doris all summer and whose toes showed through her shoes because her father was a fisherman without a boat. Mary and Doris were good friends until America joined the war against the Japs and Mary and her family were taken away to an internment camp in Montana.

The dream shifts. Mary is barefoot and carrying her baby brother when they get off a train filled with Japanese people. American soldiers point guns at them, yelling, "Half-breed!" and marching them into a big smokestack and Doris knows the smokestack because she has seen it in news clips about what Hitler did to the Jews. Mary walks toward the gas chambers and Harold is alive again and points a gun at her head. Doris screams when Mary's face becomes Carl's face, walking to the smokestack, and in Carl's arms the baby is her, Doris. The baby screams and when Doris wakes from the dream she is crying but there aren't any tears.

10

A CHILD'S ANGER

An eight-year-old boy sits on the stairs in front of his house, watching butterflies flit from flower to flower. His hair is blonde, almost white, and his eyes are blue and sharp like a cat's. His chin rests in the palms of his too-large hands, and his elbows balance on his skinny, scabbed knees.

In the mountains where he lives the day is clear. He hears blue jays, which he hates because their screeching wakes him in the morning. A creek trickles nearby, and in the distance a dog barks. His mother is inside the house, cleaning. He hears the vacuum moving from room to room, stressing him because it was his job to vacuum. Now his mother will ignore him, angry at him for arguing. Anybody walking by would see a boy watching butterflies.

The boy's eyes lock on a monarch, bigger and brighter than any he has seen yet today. He has been waiting for this one. At least that's what he thinks as the monarch alights on a "donkey's ear" flower less than three feet away. The boy's eyes narrow and his body tightens. He imagines himself as a cat, quick. Today maybe he is quicker than ever because he is mad.

The butterfly's wings move up and down slowly, the orange and black patterns reflecting in the boy's eyes. It cleans its black legs, which bend like thread at tiny knees. Its antennae quiver. The boy watches for a long minute, then in one motion springs forward and with both hands swiftly cups the butterfly.

The boy feels the silky wings on the palms of his hands. He feels the wing dust his mother has told him about; it coats his fingers. She has forbidden him to do this, telling him that butterflies cannot fly without their wing dust. He doesn't believe in magic or he might think the dust has special powers. He likes the way it feels on his skin.

The butterfly beats its wings frantically inside the cage of fingers. The boy stares between his fingers, unsmiling. He feels sorry for the butterfly but he watches anyway. He cannot not watch.

The vacuum whines. To be safe the boy slinks around the side of the house where no one can see him. He sits on a flat granite rock and holds the globe of his hands out in front of his face where he can watch the butterfly tire itself. Soon the wings cease flapping and the boy thinks he can see the butterfly's tiny chest heaving. *That is strange, the boy thinks, that a butterfly breathes like me, that it has lungs and a heart as big as a speck of dirt that is pounding and pounding right now.* The boy tries to feel the butterfly's breath on his fingers. He peers in and sees the butterfly's eyes, but he can't tell where they're looking because they're black and solid and don't seem to be looking anywhere. He imagines himself as the butterfly, staring out of the giant fingers into the blue cat eyes. It scares him, so he decides to proceed.

Very carefully the boy reaches two of his fingers inside the cage and pinches one of the butterfly's wings. He unlocks the rest of his fingers and holds the butterfly dangling and flapping a few inches from his nose. He stares into the butterfly's dark face, thinks he recognizes fear. He still isn't smiling. He doesn't like this anymore but he's gone too far. He can't stop himself.

He places the butterfly on the rock and bends over it, still holding a wing between his fingers. With the forefinger and thumb of his other hand he pinches the butterfly's other wing. Gently he pulls apart with both hands. He senses the fragility of the wings between his fingers, feels the wing dust slippery against his skin. He watches the butterfly's face. The left wing shears away in the boy's hand. He can't tell from the butterfly's face, but he imagines it must have hurt a lot. A yellowish pus oozes from where the wing ripped loose, not blood but something like it. The boy lets go and the butterfly flaps its remaining wing, trying to fly. With every beat it tips to the wingless side, off balance.

The boy is close to crying. He watches for a while longer until he hears the vacuum cleaner stop. He stands, hesitates for a second before smashing the butterfly with his shoe and grinding it into pulp against the granite. He walks to the woodpile under the stairs, where he lifts a single log. Underneath is a hidden crevasse, in which there are four more butterfly wings, along with a menagerie of body parts from ants, ladybugs, grasshoppers, bees, flies, mosquitoes, various and sundry beetles and, most important, his prized possession, the charred carcass of a giant spider that he had found in the bathtub and burned alive leg by leg with the careful use of his father's lighter.

He places the wide monarch wing on top of the other things and replaces the log just in time. His mother emerges from the house and sees her son climbing the stairs. He frowns.

"What have you been doing?" she asks him, suspiciously.

"Nothing," he answers, "just playing."

And she knows he is lying and he knows she knows he is lying, but it doesn't matter because the deed is done and will be done again and again, times without number, repeating itself endlessly in ways neither the boy nor the mother can possibly imagine.

~

LOOKING BACK I see that, as privileged as I was, much of my childhood was filled with anger, and that often my anger involved my mother. My feelings for her occupied a place between affection and distress. I had a sense that I didn't know her, that she wouldn't let me know her. I wanted to be in her life but wasn't sure there was room for me. I fought her reticence without knowing what I was fighting, lashing out blindly and without discretion.

Once, when I was nine or ten, I refused for the umpteenth time that day to do what my mother had asked. Saturdays in our house were Family Work days, when all of us kids were expected to help around the house. Other kids called them "chores," except for chores they were paid an allowance. Family Work was, in my opinion, unpaid labor. I thought it unfair that we weren't allowed to debate the ethics of this—I always wanted to discuss why things were the way they were. I demanded answers. The problem was that I was part of a family that didn't face issues head-on. My mother, from a young age, had learned to deny crucial elements of her life; or, at the very least, she resisted discussing things that were painful for her. My father, the absentminded professor, was her compatriot, having himself grown up in a tight-lipped, disciplined family. Talking to my parents was intensely frustrating for a child as questioning as I was. I sensed that they were hiding things, but I was too young to understand what or why. When I asked, for example, why I had to do their bidding, their response was, "Because we're the parents and you're the child, and we know better than you do. No ifs, ands, or buts about it." I felt like strangling them.

On that particular Saturday I rebelled. I refused to work, and I watched television when I knew it was against the rules. I probably did other things as well, perhaps picking on Brad or Heather, or making what my parents called "disrespectful comments." In any case, when all the work was done late in the afternoon, my mother sat down to have a glass of wine. My father was out of town. When I came in and asked her what was for dinner, she told me I could make my own dinner if I wasn't willing to help with Family Work. I said I didn't want any of her pukey dinner anyway, and that's when she cracked.

Despite my mother's petite build, she was strong and quick. She put down her wine and was after me, chasing me around the maze of our house, up and down the stairs. I had reached the age when I could outrun her, and though I was terrified of getting caught I was fairly certain she wouldn't catch me. From time to time I turned and jeered at her, until tears streaked her face as she gave chase. I knew it had gone too far and I wanted it to end; I was even willing to apologize. But I was afraid of what would happen if she actually caught me. Which she did.

In the upstairs of our house, two rooms were connected by a bathroom and a hallway, forming a large circle around which we could travel. At some point during her pursuit my mother picked up one of my long wooden building blocks and waved it behind me like a weapon as we raced around the circle. Finally she doubled back on me, caught me off guard, and before I could retreat she creamed me over the head with the block, sending me, stunned, to the floor.

This act caught her by surprise even more than it did me. She awoke, as if from a trance, to her child nearly unconscious on the floor. She examined my head to make sure it wasn't serious, felt the large bump swelling, then gave me ice to hold on it. She even turned on the television for me. I wasn't hurt badly, but I was scared. We had crossed into some forbidden place. Over the din of the television, I heard my mother's muffled sobs slipping from her room. I lay there, my head throbbing, wondering what had happened.

There were other times, too, when we butted heads in the cruelest of ways. I remember my roles with embarrassment. Things that hurt to tell. After one particularly vicious argument, I screamed at her, "I hope you die." I'm not sure what she'd done, but I was livid. She had always encouraged me to express my anger artistically, so I stormed to my room and went right to work drawing my revenge. I had a new set of felt-tipped pens that she'd given me for Christmas, forty different colors lined up in an aluminum box with swans engraved on the lid. I used all six shades of red for the blood spurting from my mother's gaping wounds. A boy's knife dripped red into a pool on the ground. Giant butterflies in the sky overhead. Underneath, the caption in blue: "I want to stab you with a knife."

When I was finished I tacked it to my mother's bedroom door. I knew she'd found it when I heard her weeping. She didn't leave her room all day. I felt horrible and confused. I didn't understand my violence, and I was scared that it was an inescapable part of me. I wondered if my biological parents had been murderers, and if it were my destiny.

BRAD BORE THE BRUNT OF MY ANGER. He was much smaller than I, light and bony, and without a hint of meanness. Soft-spoken and compliant, he rarely fought with my mother, which made me jealous. I felt that she loved him more, and as a result I wanted to hurt him. Often, when my parents weren't home, I'd chase him around the house until either I caught him and beat him, or he locked himself in the basement, where he'd stay until my parents returned. Once, when I heard him laughing at me from behind the locked basement door, I kicked a hole through it and grabbed him by the throat. He bit me and I let go. By the time I opened the door he'd escaped and was halfway down the street running as fast as he could. He lived in perpetual fear of me, and with good reason. There were few boundaries to my rage.

One hot summer day, my friend Peter and I were playing guns behind a vacant house when we discovered a hornets' nest underneath the front doormat. We usually didn't let my brother play with us, so when I asked him if he wanted to play, he came running. We told him that "home base" was the doormat, and that to win the game he had to make it all the way around the house without getting shot. The first person to make home base would win. We began the game, and then Peter and I hid just around the corner from the mat, not even playing. Brad came sprinting around the opposite corner and slid, baseball-style, into the mat, elated with his victory. Peter and I ducked back when we heard his shrieks and the powerful hum of hornets, like the sound of snowflakes falling on a power line. When I looked again Brad was sprinting down the street, screaming, a cloud of hornets over his head. He was stung fourteen times all over his body, which swelled like a balloon. If he had any inkling that I had planned the attack, he never ratted.

Somehow Brad has forgiven me for all that; twenty years later we are the closest of friends. He has my mother's capacity for love, the same gentle way about him. But another part of her is missing: the struggle, the unpredictability.

My high-school years were not happy. I was a good student, well liked, but crippled by angst. I look back at that person and wonder who he was, where all of his ire went. Over the years my mother helped me redirect my anger through competitive sports, at which I excelled. Perhaps she believed—and it may be true—that I was hardwired that way, just as Brad was programmed for kindness. I believed that I was to blame, and the fact that we clashed so often caused me tremendous guilt. I felt bitter, ugly, full of hate. My mother's drinking increased, but nobody seemed to notice. I denied that it was a problem by comparing it to worse scenarios. Once I called her a bitch and she slapped me across the face. I raised my fist, so close to striking her back. But the look in her eyes stopped me cold: they were eyes I did not know, dark and seething and confused. How had we come to this?

One day that same year, I put a gun to my head and nearly pulled the trigger. My mother hated guns, but she had allowed my brother and me to keep an old pair of .22 caliber rifles that our brother-in-law,

Ed, had bought at a garage sale and refinished for us. We used them for target practice at a firing range, shot a few squirrels and the side of a neighbor's house, but for the most part we rarely touched them. On that day I was determined to use my rifle on myself. I remember crying in my basement room, the curtains drawn and my door locked, and a pain in my chest so fierce that I thought I'd die. I was tired of masks, every day rising and going about my life as if all was well, while underneath the mask I suffocated. We all wore them—my mother, my father—whether we recognized them or not. I couldn't remove my mask because I feared what lay beneath. And I blamed my mother for putting it on me.

It was a crisp, clear spring day in the Sierras. I looked out my window and saw the aspen trees that my father had planted near the creek. Tall and blooming, their leaves fluttered like the wings of hummingbirds. I remembered my father planting them when I was small, saplings stuck hopefully in the dark, rocky soil. He had tied them upright with rope anchored to the ground, helping them to grow straight. Dozens of trees over the years, and my dad out there watering and wandering his land to check their growth. I saw the creek cascading by our house, Brad and I trying to dam it with rocks and sticks, our bodies soaking wet and muddy. I saw these things as if in a dream, a life passed by and longed for. Now the aspens were grown and my mother hung bird feeders on their branches, watching for hummingbirds as she drank her morning coffee. How beautiful she was standing by the windows looking out, how perfect.

I closed the curtains and loaded my rifle with a single bullet. I had no more tears to cry. My eyes felt stretched and slanted. I felt the smooth wood of the rifle, worked by Ed's rough hands. Slowly I turned the rifle and held it by the stock away from me, looking down the barrel. I brought the cold steel into my mouth, dropped the stock so the bullet would go up through my brain. I didn't want to do it wrong. I edged my right thumb up the stock and placed it lightly on the trigger. The rifle shook in my hands, my fingers quivered.

I was so close.

I don't know what kept me from pulling the trigger. Perhaps it was simply fear, the spineless cry of biology. I unloaded the gun, put it under the bed, and slept, waking only once when my mother came to check on me. She placed her hand on my forehead, sweating with fever. She went away, returned with a cool, wet washcloth that she draped over my head. She took my temperature, gently parting my lips to slide the cold glass underneath my tongue. I fell asleep to the sight of her holding the thermometer to the light, squinting to get a reading. She must have kissed me as she left me for the night. She must have kissed me.

LIBERTY LANDING,
1934

ONE COOL OCTOBER NIGHT Charlie Backlund lay on his bed in the rear of his store and ground his teeth to dust. The pain moved slowly, millimeter by millimeter, through his small intestines, tiny shards and slivers of glass tearing through the soft pink walls. If he focused he thought he could see individual slivers, like dendrite flakes of snow, twisting and turning, blown by the lightest of winds. Each feathery crystal was like a tiny razor blade slicing him as it edged its way through his digestive system. As he breathed, small bubbles of blood-stained saliva launched from the tip of his swollen, protruding tongue, hanging in the air for a split second before they popped and spattered his sheets with blood.

Charlie was dying. As he drifted in and out of consciousness, people came to him, swooping out of the darkness like bright birds, descending on what he knew were the last moments of his life. His mother came to him, a tall, stout woman with a gruff voice, calling his name as he sailed away on a ship. She spoke a language he couldn't understand, though it was vaguely familiar. His father was there, in the background, wisping in and out of the fog like a ghost. Charlie thought he saw him smiling, but then he remembered that the man had never smiled. His brother passed by, his face still shiny and slick from the fire that had burned him as a boy. He was Charlie's only sibling, and when he died their father's anger grew like a malignancy. When Charlie was fifteen his father beat his face black with an ax handle. The next day Charlie left; he packed his mother's portrait in his suitcase, and as best he could left his father's rage impotent on the dock.

Charlie was dying alone. Liberty Landing was a small place, and he hadn't been there long. He got along well with the Natives, but there was nobody in Liberty Landing whom Charlie wanted by his deathbed. There was nobody who could save him, either. As soon as Vincent O'Leary had walked out of the store, Charlie had known he was going to die.

Vincent had come up from Mountain Village claiming that he wanted to settle the argument about the new store. He had tried again to persuade Charlie to close down before Bering got angry. It was a civil meeting, although Charlie hadn't budged on his position. Midway through the evening Vincent had offered a bottle of whiskey, which he'd carried with him from Mountain Village. They drank together, letting go of business matters to talk about happenings downstates: the World Series, the economy, the threat of war in Europe. They even laughed from time to time, and it was late at night when Vincent poured the finely ground glass into a whiskey-filled cup while Charlie was outside relieving himself. Charlie returned, sat down heavily in his chair, finished his whiskey in one quick shot, and immediately began choking. In that instant his throat was scraped raw and his life began to end.

When Charlie looked up from his fit of bloody coughing, Vincent was staring at him from the doorway. It wasn't a malicious stare, but resigned, as if killing Charlie had been a duty rather than an act of violence. But later, as Charlie lay frothing bloody bubbles, he wondered about the look, and why Vincent hadn't just put a bullet in his head. As the night crawled on and the whiskey wore off, Charlie's pain intensified. Vincent's features winged from the darkness as grotesque, sinister phantoms holding glinting swords of glass. He woke with a start when he saw his cousin, Igvaq, sitting on a stool, his body swaying as he rolled a rock around and around in a bowl filled with glass. Igvaq's face was red and swollen, and he stared longingly toward the door of a room where Vincent stood holding a bottle of whiskey. Igvaq cried over the bowl, his tears steaming as they blended with the glass.

Charlie drank more whiskey, which burned like acid going down. As he swallowed he could feel shreds of skin flapping in his throat, like waterborne plants undulating in the current of a whiskey-filled river. It was early in the morning when he faded off again. This time, out of the darkness came the red fox he had seen above the store on his first day in Liberty Landing. It trotted forward, stopping momentarily to look around, ears pointed and tail in the air. It was coming to him. As it drew closer he saw that it was changing, becoming something other than a fox. It was a raven, a bear, a fish swimming upstream. Charlie watched, fought off the agony that veiled his eyes in a viscous haze. When the creature was less than a harpoon's length away, a blinding light singed the air like lightning, and as it dimmed Charlie saw a human figure moving toward him, the body shimmering like a wave of heat in the distance, an apparition, arms outstretched.

Dora. Out of the gloaming she walked, her river of hair restrained by an ivory barrette that Charlie had given her many years before. She came to him, shuffling across ice, and she placed her freezing hand on his forehead.

"I am here for you now," she said.

Dora was as Charlie remembered, her skin smooth and fawn brown, her eyes curving widely across her face. She had a full lower lip that he had loved to hold between his own, and above it large teeth browned on her left side as if only half had gone rotten. Her nose was long and straight, accentuating her elliptical face. She was small-boned, but her hands were short and thick. Charlie had always been surprised by her strength. Now he could feel her hands, cool as ice, soothing his burning forehead.

"Dora," he said, struggling with his breath, "the children are gone. Inaqaq and Ungkak. What have I done?"

A look of knowing crossed her face. Charlie saw that she understood, that she did not judge him harshly. She did not answer; nothing could be said that was not conveyed through her face and eyes. She sat on the edge of Charlie's bed, blew on his face, sang songs in whispers, restrained his arms when his stomach convulsed and wracked his body with pain. Dora told him stories, old stories from before she was born and even long before her great-great-grandmother was born. Where she had heard these stories Charlie didn't know, for he had never heard her tell them. He had never heard anyone tell them.

When Dora spoke, the words became nearly visible in the air, at first as frozen breath that danced in the dim morning light, then later as colorful figures acting out the stories on an invisible stage. Out of Dora's mouth flew Raven, *caw-caw-caw*ing as he dove to scratch the rivers and lakes into the world on Charlie's wooden floor. Soon the floor resembled a giant map, and when this was done Raven lifted off and winged fast toward a mountain, disappearing soundlessly through the wall. One black feather rocked like a cradle in the middle of the room.

When Charlie woke late in the afternoon, Dora was gone and a handful of visitors stood glumly around his bed. He could feel nothing in his legs, swollen and as purple as wine. Some of the people spoke to him but he couldn't understand. One of them picked up the black feather and brought it to Charlie, who held it in the palm of his hand until he died late that evening. His last moments were void of pain; his body had gone numb, as if the glass shards had severed his nerves.

A priest from Mountain Village came upriver the next day, accompanied by Igvaq and a handful of Dora's relatives. Igvaq's mother prepared the body, washed him with soap and warm water, sprinkled tundra leaves over him to make him smell good, dressed him in his one nice suit. Unable to open Charlie's hand, the old woman called in two men to help her. After them came two more, until everyone, including the priest, had tried and failed. Finally they gave up and Charlie was buried with Raven's feather clenched in his fist, as if he held redemption in his hand.

Perhaps Charlie'd had some premonition that he was going to die, for he was well prepared. His finances were in order, he'd had a will written during his last visit to Seattle a few months earlier, and he'd even left money for a wooden casket and a fence to be constructed around his grave. When they opened his safe they found explicit instructions about where he wanted to be buried were he to die in Alaska: on the hill above Liberty Landing, in a flat place where he used to go when he was tired. In the summer, after work, he'd labored up the hill, removed his clothes and slept naked under the evening sun, waking only when it got too cold or when fishermen's voices came wafting up the river. All the world became funneled into those moments, so that he heard Raven and the fishermen and his children calling; and he saw the outline of a fox bounding through the willows and the long grass touching his wrinkled skin and bone-white thighs; and he felt, if only for a second, what it was to be that sun squinting down at him, what it was to be the light.

"How silly I am," he said out loud to himself, looking down at his white, sagging body. "How very incredibly silly I am." But he felt good, and he was glad that he was too old to feel embarrassed.

A SMALL GROUP ATTENDED CHARLIE'S FUNERAL on the hill. Igvaq was there; he'd gotten drunk in Charlie's honor, feeling certain that Charlie would have done the same for him. Most people wouldn't even learn of Charlie's death until months later. Justina would hear about it from the priest as he traveled downriver to St. Michael. She would mourn silently for months because Charlie's death meant that Inaqaq and Ungkak might as well be dead too. She would probably never see them again. Still, she harbored a deep faith in God, and she prayed the children would be delivered back to their homeland.

Charlie's funeral was brief. The day was clear and in the distance early-season snow shimmered on the summit of Mount Kusilvak, where Charlie had once stood as a young man new to Alaska. The priest's voice rose feebly from his throat, drifting like a crippled kite into the sky, tethered to the earth by only a thread of the people's faith.

"Ashes to ashes, dust to dust . . . " and Igvaq wobbled back and forth on his feet, fighting the urge to lie in the grass. His vision blurred and the priest's words came to him as mere background to the sound of rushing blood and the strained beating of his heart. He could not mourn Charlie's death, for he felt as if he was closer to Charlie than he'd ever been. The clamor of his heart told him he wouldn't be long in following. He was thinking this as his eyes closed and he crumpled, out cold, onto the tundra.

When the service finished a few men lifted Igvaq onto their backs and carried him down the hill behind the women. The priest followed.

Two men remained to bury the coffin, and a skinny man named Gus returned every day for the next week to build the fence and the long house that covered the grave. A fine woodworker, Gus had helped Charlie put the finishing touches on the new store. Sometimes Charlie had invited Gus for dinner, and the two of them played cards late into the night.

Gus carved the fence posts, each rounded and sanded smooth at the top, then carried them up the hill where he constructed the fence using tiny finishing nails. The long house he built from wood that Charlie had left in his shed. It was seven feet long, three feet wide, and covered with canvas to protect the wood. Gus spent hours laboring over Charlie's cross, carved out of driftwood he'd salvaged from the banks of the Andreafsky River at its confluence with the Yukon. The cross itself was small and simple, its points rounded and sanded as smooth as skin, but it sat atop a five-foot piece of driftwood, squared off so that an inscription could be etched. Gus was pleased with his work. He marveled at the size of the grave, its elegance, and he thought that if someday a stranger stumbled upon the place, he would think a king had been buried there. Gus returned twice a year to maintain the grave, and soon other people were buried on the hill and he had other graves to tend. When everyone left Liberty Landing, Gus was the only one who stayed. People thought him crazy. He'd carve on his doorstep and watch the fox hunting mice on the hill. He tended those graves until he died, an old man alone with piles of wood chips, like little mountains, just outside his door.

THINGS ACROSS THE CREEK

I never imagined that a dog would someday haunt me, bring me back to my beginnings, lead me through her muddy creek beds and meadows chasing butterflies. I never thought a dog would remind me of my mother, of her ashes never thrown. I didn't think a dog could take up so much space.

Inaqaq. The wild one. My brother and I found her in a shopping cart, for sale, in front of the convenience store from which we used to steal licorice and bubble gum. We'd just come from fishing Squaw Creek, and were covered in mud and slime. Burrs—or "prickly balls" as we called them—peppered our socks and shoelaces. We'd never seen a puppy like her. She had a depth to her eyes that I couldn't explain until I came across the words of Aldo Leopold, describing a dying wolf's eyes as "a fierce green fire." I was afraid to touch her at first, feeling instinctively that she was more than a dog.

Her eyes stared out from a mask of black fur. She was a ball of black and white fur with one extraneous item: a long bushy tail curved around like a question mark. My brother and I learned from the woman selling her that she was an Alaskan malamute, and with that ammunition we ran up the hill to our house to find our mother, who had resisted getting a dog.

The puppy stirred something in my mother. With a few hollow promises to care for her, my brother and I whooped and hollered all the way up the hill toward home with our new friend in tow. For the first month, we slept on the porch under the stars with her nestled between us. The raccoons scurried around nervously beneath the porch, sensing a new and dangerous presence. I don't remember hearing the name Inaqaq before the puppy came into our lives, but I remember my mom suggesting it, and how we knew immediately there could be no other name. We called her Inaq for short; only my mother invariably called her Inaqaq. And invariably Inaq loved my mother best.

One morning during her first month with us, I poked my head from my sleeping bag and saw what I thought was a wolf or a big coyote trotting up the hill. As it came closer, just beyond the creek that trickled by the house, I saw that it wore a collar and looked a lot like Inaq. It stood away, tense and waiting, ice-colored eyes staring through black rings of fur. After a few minutes it sat, drank from the creek, then lay as still as the morning, its eyes never moving from us. It was only a dog, but I felt I was in the presence of something inexplicable and wild. I froze, afraid that I would spook this creature before it unveiled its mystery.

Suddenly it sprang to its feet, twisted a couple of dancing circles, and pranced in place. Inaqaq emerged from my brother's sleeping bag and peed through the cracks in the deck, doing a strained squat that produced a smirk on her long black lips. When she sighted the dancing creature across the creek, her stream stopped instantly and she let out a howl I'll never forget, as if she carried at that moment all the world's sorrow and joy. Her eyes flamed large and otherworldly, and I knew this puppy didn't belong to us. There was something in her that I could never touch. At most, I could admire from a distance, as I did her mother that morning, just across the creek yet distances immeasurable away.

For days Inaq's mother came to visit, staring from a distance, until finally, in one easy jump over the fence, she came to play. She lay there while Inaq stalked her from all angles, chewing at her lips, her feet, her nipples, her tail. More joyful than she ever was with us, Inaq howled every day when her mother left, staring down the hill to where her mother disappeared into the trees.

After a month her mother stopped coming, though Inaq would still stand at the edge of the porch, her head wedged between the posts of the railing, staring across the creek in expectation. She did this until the day she died, looked off into distances with those old-wisdom eyes, as if waiting for the return of something lost. I saw her mother again only in glimpses, scurrying through the meadow's early morning fog.

Inaq grew into a large dog, and the older she got the more she resembled a bear. Her raccoon face became a bear face, her snout long and pointed; her gait became a kind of bear's waddle. When she lost her tail one foggy morning to a speeding Chevy truck, her transformation was complete.

Inaq outlived my mother by a few years. She died below the big granite rock below our house, where she spent her latter days after she was too old to climb the stairs. She was twelve years old and gray around the eyes. After we children had moved from home, she lived alone with my father. Brad called to tell me of Inaq's death, and I gathered from his voice that he was hurting. What bothered him most was that Inaqaq had been dead a week before my father could gather his strength to tell us.

Years later Inaq's mysteriousness makes sense to me, and so does my mother's affection for her. In Inaq my mother found a connection to a home she had barely known. She could look out the window of her house and see her children playing with her Alaskan dog, and some-how this connected the past to the present. I want to believe that Inaq made the void easier for her, brought her closer to her roots.

Six years after Inaq's death, Brad and I walked the streets of Mountain Village with a puppy given to us by relatives. She was a little raccoon-faced thing, like Inaq, starving when we first saw her staked outside our cousin's house.

"She's not going to make it," Brad had said to me, shaking his hooded head. "No way is she going to survive this winter. Look at her ribs poking through."

I knew what he was thinking. Later we asked our relatives for permission to take her and they had agreed, glad, I think, to give us something.

Many village dogs appeared ragged and starving, staked outside in subzero temperatures for days on end. Brad and I shook our heads at each other as we passed bony dogs begging, their ears frostbitten down to tiny flaps; or a man kicking a dog as it cowered at the end of its chain. But in my time there, I learned to resist judging from my out-sider's perspective. Dogs were tools, nothing more. I had never had to haul a dead moose twenty miles through a blizzard; I had never had to live off the land.

As Brad and I walked our puppy, Nunapik, down the streets of Mountain Village, people regarded us strangely. In the villages, people don't "walk" their dogs; they use them to pull sleds. If they can't work, they're as good as gone. On that particular day, Brad and I were just beginning to realize how differently we saw a dog's life. People grinned at us and we grinned back.

Halfway through the walk, as we chuckled at Nuna sniffing and stumbling around the road, a tall white dog joined us and began play-ing with Nuna, tossing her around like a toy and then scurrying away in mock retreat. It had greenish eyes and a lanky wolf frame. The two roughhoused for a few minutes, until suddenly the dog started, sniffed the air, then disappeared down an alley. Moments later two village policeman drove by in a Suburban, windows down and a rifle barrel jutting from the passenger side. The man holding the rifle wore silver aviator shades, like any L.A. cop. His mustache was straight and stiff, and underneath it his lips frowned as we nodded at him deferentially. Brad and I exchanged perplexed glances.

A split second later a shot exploded. My ears rang; Nuna thrashed against the leash. The policemen stepped from the truck and strolled casually to the alley, returning moments later dragging the white dog by its tail, a bloody track staining the snow. They heaved it like a sack of garbage into the back of the Suburban and drove away. Brad and I couldn't believe our eyes. We hurried back to our cousin Matt's house, sure that the police had committed a crime.

"It's Tuesday," Matt said, shrugging. "Every Tuesday the police kill loose dogs. Gotta keep your dog staked, or he's gonna get killed."

Brad and I stared at him, our mouths hanging open.

"They gotta do it," he continued, seeing our confusion, "otherwise those dogs maybe become wild dogs and form packs. Then it's real dangerous for the village. Hasn't happened in a long time, but people still remember wild dogs, so if we kill them it won't happen. Those police, they're just doin' their jobs."

During our last few days there I kept Nuna tied with two separate ropes behind Matt's place, out of sight of the road. I had spent so much time in Alaska trying to imagine how my mother might have been if she had made it back there. I imagined her joy at meeting Justina, her understanding when faced with alcoholic cousins, her ability to rede-fine herself in this culture. But this dog killing, it may have been too much. Watching them drag that dead dog over the snow, I was glad my mother wasn't beside me.

Dogs,
1898

AIVRUN LOVED A GOOD STORY. He would listen attentively for hours to a good storyteller, and he never forgot a word of a well-told tale about hunting or fishing. He was thankful that his father-in-law told stories with the presence of a shaman. In the winters people came from long distances to sit around old Yugisaq's fire, smoke rising from the roof late into the night. Yugisaq's voice turned preternatural, serious and humble, rippling with laughter and trimmed with sounds of animals, the wind and the sea. Inhuman sounds. Voices of ancestors, spirits, elements of nature. The eyes watched him around the fire, full of fear, sorrow, joy, mirth. Listening to Yugisaq was like traveling in time. It was difficult to resist the journey.

Until his dying days, Aivrun dreamed about the first story Yugisaq told him, about losing his dogs on a hunting trip many years before. The images came to Aivrun as if they had been his dogs that had fallen through the ice. He saw them screaming, furiously paddling, the knowing in their eyes and the silence before they sank below the surface. In his sleep he jerked and squirmed as he trudged over the frozen tundra, back to the village many miles away. His sleep calmed as he placed the shining beads beneath the moose calf's eyelids, in its gutted belly. Aivrun never decided if it was a good dream or a bad one, only that when he woke he was impelled to check his dogs.

Aivrun was a dog man. He saw them as essential tools for the hunt, pulling him far into caribou country much faster than he could have traveled on snowshoes. He knew of hunters—elders, most of them— who still hunted without dogs, and he was awestruck by the stories of them walking hundreds of snowshoe-miles in just a few days. But he had no desire to give up his dogs for the old ways.

Aivrun kept many teams over the years, constantly rotating new dogs in and old ones out, keeping them well trained and healthy. He had favorites, such as Kasha and Niqla, who were with him for many years. But when a dog began to slow, no matter which one, he dealt coldly and quickly with the problem.

Kasha led his team for six years. A female given to him by Yugisaq as a wedding present, she was of medium build with a thick coat the color of summer tundra, dirty gold going to brown, black around the eyes. She'd given Aivrun four litters of pups in six years, most of them good, strong dogs. More than once she'd saved his life, when in blinding snowstorms she led the way home as he sat snow-blind on the sled. She had a knack for direction, and she was a good, if not totalitarian, leader, who resorted to violence to keep other dogs in line. Once, when challenged by an aggressive male, she'd ripped the dog's eye out of its socket. He could still run well, and did for years, peering submissively at Kasha from his one eye. Old One Eye, Aivrun called him.

As much as Aivrun cared for Kasha, the time came when she began to weaken his team. He procrastinated for weeks before deciding. Finally, one early February morning, when Nicuuk and the children were still asleep, he took her alone out onto the ice. She didn't flinch as he raised the barrel of his rifle to her face. She stared him straight in the eyes, her head cocked slightly to the side, and Aivrun returned her stare until he saw his own reflection. He pulled the trigger and she dropped soundlessly onto the snow-packed ice, where he left her to be swallowed by the river when the ice broke up in the spring. Aivrun may have felt sadness as he walked up the hill toward his house, but nobody would have noticed; his face was calm, focused on the coming day's work. He went to the dogs and began the morning feed. They howled in anticipation. Fish arced through the air.

My parents met in 1954. My father was working in Buffalo as an engineer for Bell Aircraft. On business trips out west he'd sometimes stop at ski areas along the way. My mother was working as a nurse at the Pitkin County Hospital in Aspen when my father was brought in on a stretcher, blood gushing from a gash in his leg. While the doctor stitched him up, my mother distracted him with conversation, asking him about the four large indentations in his right thigh.

"I was bitten by a large animal," he answered.

My father had, in fact, been attacked and bitten by a large female lion while hunting in Northern Rhodesia in 1953. But my mother, a farm girl, would later admit that the only large animal she'd ever known was a cow, and she thought him quite a fool for letting a cow take a chunk out of him.

Nevertheless she was charmed, and when he asked her on a date she agreed. They dated a few times during his stay there, and somehow during the course of conversation the subject of her Eskimo heritage was raised.

My father, chronically indelicate, looked her in the eyes and asked, "Well, can we rub noses?"

My mother couldn't help but smile, and years later she would tease my father about trying to steal a kiss on the first date. My father visited her in Aspen a few more times, and my mother knew it was serious when he arrived one weekend with a broken leg; he hadn't come to ski but to see her.

After a year in Aspen she moved to New York City, where she was a nurse in Spanish Harlem. She saw my father frequently, either skiing in upstate New York or touring the East Coast, which she'd never seen. She stayed a year in the city, at the end of which she announced to my father that she was taking a nursing position in Sweden. My father translated this as an ultimatum and asked her to marry him.

"I'll think about it," she answered. "I'll call you tomorrow."

And she did. She called him and said that yes, she'd marry him, but that she was going to Sweden for a year anyway, so the wedding would have to wait. Ever since college my mother had been on a whirlwind tour of the world, wanting to see and do it all before she settled down. Nursing allowed her the flexibility to go where and when she wanted, and in five years she nursed in four different places. She wasn't going to let engagement get in the way of her life. She returned from Sweden excited about nursing, espousing the benefits of socialized medicine, ready to take on the American medical establishment. Finally she was ready to be with my father. She lived in Manhattan for another year before they decided to make it official.

Foreshadowing the next thirty years, my parents married on one of my father's business trips. My mother wanted a West Coast wedding so that her family could attend, so my father arranged business meetings in California. In June 1957, they married at a mission in Carmel. Their honeymoon consisted of driving through California, from one of my father's meetings to the next.

~

SIERRA NEVADA CORPORATION, 1984. I'm a junior in high school. In Reno for tonight's ice hockey practice, I stop off at my parents' company to say hello and get some money. My father is usually more generous, so I walk down the hall toward his office and see him before he sees me; he's talking on the phone and smoking a cigarette, which surprises me. I've known from the smell of his clothes that he sometimes smokes, but usually only on business trips when he's stressed. His feet are propped on his desk as he reclines in his chair. He wears a white shirt stained yellow around its collar, his skinny plaid tie loose around his neck and the same tan polyester pants he wore yesterday. Papers litter the floor and a half-eaten pastrami sandwich festers on his desk.

He jerks when he sees me, but I look away to give him a chance to extinguish the cigarette. I walk into his office and raise my hand in greeting. His cigarette is gone, but smoke pours from his desk drawer. He ignores it as he talks on the phone.

"Where's Mom?" I mouth silently, and he points down the hall to her office.

"Fire!" I mouth. "Fire!" and I point to his drawer. He waves me away and turns to the wall, arguing with the phone about lengths of radio waves or satellites or some such thing.

My mother's office is the opposite of my father's, as is her appearance. She's surrounded by plants and African batiks, and she's dressed in a pressed brown blouse and black slacks (she's always preferred "earth tones"). She wears mild red lipstick and some eyeliner, but otherwise her face is makeup-free. She, too, is on the phone. She waves me into a chair, gives me a quick smile.

"We need this contract, Bill. We're prepared to take it on, we can handle it, and you know John is the only person who really understands this landing system." She speaks calmly, but her tone is strained.

"I know we don't have the fastest turnover, nor the best equipment, but we . . . " She's interrupted and her eyes frown.

"Bill, listen. We've been working on this project for a long time now, we've invested too much time and energy to let it go. How can we make this work?"

I watch my mother, the businesswoman. She looks entirely capable, confident in her clean clothes and her light, uncluttered office. No diplomas, certificates of merit, or family portraits muddle the walls. I rarely see her at work, and when I do I'm surprised: she is not the woman who is my mother. This woman could be on the cover of *Ms.* or *Fortune* or *Business Week;* she could stroll suavely down the streets of Manhattan or San Francisco. This is not the woman who makes me breakfast every morning. Watching her talk so confidently on the phone, I feel acutely proud.

"Thanks, Bill, I'll talk to John and we'll try to work this out—I really hope we can make things work. Okay. Yes, yes, okay, bye." Click. The phone is down but she's still not looking at me. She's staring out the window.

"Goddamn it," she whispers, so quietly I wonder if I'm hearing things.

"Mom?" I say, "Mom, what's wrong?"

She snaps from her reverie. "Oh, hi, Colin, oh nothing, just another contract we're about to lose. How are you? Hockey practice?"

I nod. "Are things pretty bad? I mean, are things going to . . . "

"Things are fine," she interrupts. "Don't worry. Now, do you need money?"

"But Mom . . . " I want to know.

"Colin, no!" Her voice is cross. "I don't want to discuss it—I've had enough today. Here, take what you need." She hands me her wallet. "I've got to talk to your father. See you later tonight. Drive safely." She's out the door, down the hall. I've forgotten to warn her that my father is smoking.

I listen for arguing but hear nothing. I take a twenty from

my mother's wallet, return it to her desk, and walk into Reno's tinseled night.

A TIME CAME IN MY MOTHER'S LIFE when her focus shifted. I can't say with certainty when it began, but in my freshman year of high school I remember feeling as if I were losing her. It wasn't as if she ran out on us, but her presence diminished. For the previous five years she had been working full-time with my father, helping him manage their small engineering company while simultaneously cooking us breakfast in the morning, driving us to and from our various sporting events, and often returning after long days to cook us dinner in the evening. Looking back, I am awestruck by her energy, yet ashamed that I didn't recognize how fast it was running out.

My mother's expectations of herself were superhuman. From her early diaries to her final notes, she strove for self-improvement, continually seeking a better, deeper layer of herself. Her challenge was to balance all the elements of her life, but during her final years at the company she felt herself unraveling, losing control of what was most important in her life. In a journal entry, dated May 2, 1985, she wrote:

> I am at the crossroads—feeling trapped—unable to move
> forward with joy but only just getting through each day
> doing what needs to be done, must be done for the survival
> John and I have chosen. The business has become an
> emotional drain. I feel disharmony perhaps because of the
> continual vigilance that must be in order to survive the
> pitfalls of business—it has become wearing to everyone, the
> need to continually push forward—something is wrong and
> I'm not sure I have the capacity to make changes there. The
> strain has spilled over into the other areas of life. John and
> I coexist except at work. There is no play, little laughter,

virtually no exercise together—go to work, come home late.
I often dread the making of dinner or a confrontation with
the boys.

At the top of the page is a muddy smear, an arrow pointing to it and a note that reads, "Inaq's wet foot, in the meadow on a beautiful spring day."

During the ten years preceding this point, my mother explored a plethora of alternative pathways to what she called "developing consciousness." She studied macrobiotic cooking, yoga, meditation, iridology—to name only a few. Her personal library was filled with books about self-improvement and mind/body awareness. She read prolifically when time allowed. Between the ages of forty-five and fifty-five, my mother became a sort of pilgrim, reaching far into the corners of spiritual healing communities, trying to soothe what ached in her; she stretched out her arms to the world and embraced whatever methods promised to heal her. When she came up empty-handed she was not so much angry as disillusioned. She was tired and didn't know which way to turn.

Late in the evenings, Brad, Heather, and I could bribe her into letting us stay up late by giving her foot massages while she read. She'd hand us a bottle of lotion and two of us would each take one of her feet in our hands and rub it until we were exhausted. It was a kind of competition, seeing who could give her the best foot massage, but also we simply loved being in her presence while she was reading, as if she was letting us into her secret world.

Sometimes she read aloud to us as she lay in her upstairs bedroom, one of us on each side of her. She'd prop her head on pillows and stare down through glasses perched on the end of her nose. We'd snuggle in as close as we could get, and I remember staring at her sometimes as she read, not really listening to the words but to the sounds, watching the way her lips moved, or the way her tongue backed up against her long front teeth. She enunciated every syllable, rolled each sound off her tongue like a gift, as if she expected us to keep those words, within us, forever. She always asked if we understood the difficult words, and if we didn't she had a dictionary by the bed in which she said we'd find the answers. It wasn't until her funeral, when a neighbor of ours spoke to me, that it dawned on me that she had a gift with language.

"Your mother was one of the most articulate people I've ever known," the woman said. "She had such a beautiful way of putting her words together."

She loved stories, and when she read them to us she brought her characters to life by changing her voice to match the various personalities or swings in the plot. The book I remember best is *The Secret Garden*, from which she'd taken my name. No matter how many times she read that story she never failed to make me feel as if I were the Colin in the story. She read all the characters exactly as I thought they should be.

She wrote with a remarkably flamboyant hand, especially as a young woman just off to college. She was prolific then, filling journal after journal with bold, swooping letters. Her style varied over the years, became much more simple and even blocked, but always she crossed her T's with a long, sweeping curl of ink. The slant of her words changed dramatically, forward-leaning in her younger years, like a cheetah straining for its prey; then in her later years the letters pushed back on their heels, as if afraid of what lies ahead. In one journal entry, the handwriting is so left-tilting that I have to adjust the angle of my head to read it. The T's are like trees falling, the I's waves going back out to sea, the F's upside down fish hooks:

The continual pressure has kept me from thinking about
what is real and what is important—when Carl was dying

*I shared with him that his dying has given me a new
perspective and a new life in a way. But now I am forgetting
and I don't want to. I would like to focus more diligently on
what I want for the rest of my life.... Just think forward.*

MAY 1985. My last month of high school. I was, even more than
my mother, thinking forward. My Uncle Carl had recently died but I
hadn't been close to him. Though I knew my mother had been deeply
affected by his death, I couldn't comprehend what she was going
through. Girls obsessed me, and I couldn't wait for college. I fought
often with my parents, especially my mother because she made the
rules. Though I couldn't have articulated it at the time, I was furious
at her for her distance, for her subtle alcoholism, for the way her hidden problems manifested themselves as my own guilt. What I really
wanted, more than anything, was to be again the boy with whom she
had shared her stories late at night. I wanted her to read to me, and in
trade I would have massaged her feet until my fingers were nothing
but bone.

What I see now is that my mother had nothing left to give. She had
raised five children, given wholly of herself as she met our needs. And
we had not been easy. She gave and we took, and no matter how much
she gave we always took more, like a nest of chicks whose hunger cannot be satiated. And there were others, neglected children from up the
street, our friends, the vagabonds my father dragged home. She took
care of anyone in need, except herself. In addition, she had the business to run, which increasingly wore her down. She took care of her
employees, opening our doors to them as if they were family. She
excelled in business because she treated everyone as if she cared about
not only what they said, but who they were. My father's strength was
his engineering genius, but as a manager he was incorrigible. My
mother cleaned up his messes and smoothed the ruffled feathers,
essentially saving the company from a likely demise.

My father loved my mother the best he knew how, but his obsession with work rendered him emotionally incognito. He rarely remembered her birthday or their anniversary, and their conversations revolved almost exclusively around work. Nevertheless she loved him. Even late in their marriage, after twenty-five years, she wrote of her "loving relationship with John. Being a wife to John is my number one satisfaction." But she went on to say that "it is demoralizing at times because he is insensitive and does not allot time to reciprocate—so I pull back to avoid hurt—I'm crying all of a sudden as I write this." The areas of her life that she deemed the most important—her children, her marriage, her work—often took more from her than they gave back. Eventually she began reaching farther for fulfillment.

She began talking more about her Eskimo roots, and about contacting her relatives. She conducted business with a Native corporation in Anchorage, and during a visit there met Yup'ik people who knew her relatives.

She was close to making contact with Justina when, in 1984, Carl was diagnosed with cancer. My mother went to Washington, D.C., where he was living, to oversee his treatments. She didn't approve of his medical care, believing that the medical establishment treated symptoms rather than causes. She discouraged Carl from accepting treatments that she believed would strip him of his dignity in exchange for a few miserable months. He chose otherwise, submitting to chemotherapy, radiation, all the standard fare. She came home disheartened and exhausted.

After Carl died a few months later, she returned from his funeral a different person, so distant I barely knew her. I couldn't see it then, but she was scared. She rarely mentioned Alaska anymore, and she pulled away from us like a riptide to the sea.

Her moods varied. She drove me to college in the fall and we fought most of the way. But she wrote to me regularly, sent me care packages at school. She was in high spirits when I came home for Christmas that first year, and we were truly kind to each other. She seemed present again, and I had matured enough to appreciate her. I have a photo of the two of us on Christmas morning, in front of the granite fireplace in our dining room. Muscular from lifting weights, I hold my mother like a baby in my arms. We are sleepy, but grinning. I remember how good it felt to hold her, how good it felt that she wanted me to hold her. *Finally*, I thought, *we are here.* I remember, too, how light she felt, her bones like papier-mâché.

It seems strange now that I couldn't see it, that none of us could. Looking at the photo now it is obvious: she was dying. She felt light because she was. Her cheekbones were too defined; already we could see the shape and contours of her skull. The tendons on her hands like a bird's wings plucked of feathers.

But she loved me. That is what I want to remember about that moment. I want to believe that the hostility had passed; that in later years, had she lived, we would have been the best of friends.

There were storms to come. The following summer I returned home and found her distant again. We were short and cold with each other. I had a girlfriend and spent little time at home. I grew increasingly frustrated with my mother's reticence.

One evening after she returned from work, she refused to discuss with me some silly little thing, my curfew or maybe borrowing her car. Avoiding confrontation, she ignored me.

I exploded. "If you won't even talk to me, why are you here? Why don't you just leave? I'm sick of this!"

Her lips trembled, her jaw flexed, her eyes turned in on themselves. She looked me straight in the eyes, held me there, spellbound, for an endless moment. "Maybe I will leave," she said, coldly. "Maybe I just will."

Then she turned and walked out the door, down the stairs to the street, up and over the hill and out of sight. I was chilled. I didn't know what she meant, but I felt it. She had threatened me with her death. Earlier that afternoon the doctor had given her one year to live. She didn't know how else to tell me.

Dreams,
1935

DORIS DREAMED. On her sixth birthday she ate the chocolate cake that Nanna Agren had baked for her, then cried herself to sleep because she missed her father and Justina. She dreamed she was soaring at a great height on Raven's back, clutching black feathers that she feared would pull loose and send her falling to the winter earth below. She wasn't cold. The feathers felt good against her body.

Raven flew north. Doris wasn't sure where she had climbed on, but she thought it must have been on Vashon. Now she was being carried back to Kotlik, to her father and Justina. She slept sometimes, in her dream, and when she slept she had dreams within her dream, layer upon layer of her life's moments coming back to her, arranged in patterns she hadn't seen before. When she woke again on Raven's back, she knew that home was near. Raven glided downward, and as he approached the earth she began to see things she hadn't seen in a long time. "The rivers, oh yes the rivers!" she exclaimed; she had not known how much she had missed them. She saw the greenish lakes, icebergs floating and bumping like miniature continents. Raven dropped lower and Doris saw animals: white rabbits just beginning to turn a shade of brown around their necks, moose lumbering awkwardly through the snow, and a bony wolf—*kegluneq*—without the strength to make a kill. Doris felt sorry for the wolf, willed it to be fast and strong, and in her dream's mind's eye the wolf sprang to life and gave chase. She turned away, not wanting to see the end, but knowing anyway.

When the Yukon came into view, Doris nearly fell from Raven's back. She saw Kotlik downriver, the tiny slough that broke from the river like the branch of a tree, and in the village, smoke rising in wispy, sinuous lines. The ice had broken up and she saw boats venturing out into the ice floes. She pulled at Raven's feathers, urging him to drop lower and lower, steering him. Over Kotlik, Raven's feathers began to tear away. Cold air bit at Doris's skin. She looked down to where her father's store had been, but it was gone and so was his house and his dog team and his sled and his boat. In the place of the store was a freshly dug grave, and around it people crying.

Raven spiraled from the sky. Doris saw a woman who resembled Justina, but her face was withered and old. In her arms was a girl, pale and stiff. Raven exploded in a puff of black feathers, and the last thing Doris remembered was falling into Justina's arms, into the body of the little girl.

Doris awoke crying, calling out in her sleep. Often Carl would be sitting next to her, whispering in Yup'ik and stroking her head. "It's all right," he would say, "I'm here with you." Doris would look into Carl's magnanimous eyes and see his fear, and she would feel sorry for frightening him. In their first year on Vashon, sometimes they cried together, hunched quietly in a corner. Or they would sneak away to tell each other Yup'ik stories about Raven and Bear Woman and the old Bearded Seals. It felt good to laugh together and talk without feeling stupid and shy. But after Charlie's death, they ceased talking about Kotlik or anything connected to their past. Justina, Nicuuk, the immeasurable, flowing Yukon and animals in the sky: all of it became a vast dream, a geography determined by the rising and falling of the sun, the ever-receding impossible past.

UNCLE CARL

Carl was a phantom uncle, more alive to me in stories than in real life. Though his story and my mother's are interwoven, their lives diverged as soon as they left Vashon. My mother bragged about Carl; he was the type of brother I should aspire to be: kind, generous, compassionate, and, most important, gentle. He was big but unimposing, with soft brown eyes and a large head. He smiled easily, and when his mouth wasn't smiling, his eyes were, so that it was rare to see him look unfriendly. One could tell, just by looking at him, that he was a gracious and kindhearted man.

In their early years my mother and Carl's relationship was intimate, probably because of their dependence on one another. They were each other's lifeline to their past. When they arrived in Vashon, Doris taught Carl to speak English over the course of two painstaking years, and later, when Carl became the stronger student, he tutored her. More important, they were playmates. In my mother's senior year of high school, she wrote of him coming home from the army for Christmas vacation: "Carl came home tonight and I had so much fun with him. Lately we have gotten much closer together and I was happy because he suggested we get some clothes alike. Things like that mean so much to a girl."

They also enjoyed dancing together. My mother's early journals are peppered with exclamations about new dances she had learned, and her attraction to a man seemed largely determined by how well he stepped across the dance floor. Home for Christmas from her freshman year at the University of Washington, she wrote:

> *I never realized how wonderful brothers can be, especially when they are as handsome and such super dancers as Carl. We acted like a couple of kids in love by dancing every dance possible together and dreamy and cuddly. We dance just perfectly together. It is so easy to follow his new, graceful sweeping steps. People would watch us and comment on the way Carl dances. But darn all the girls who would come up and ask if I could please arrange to have a trade with Carl. They just adore the way he dances. I wasn't really mad. Mostly proud. When the Rumba and Samba were played Carl and I were one of the few couples who participated.*

That same Christmas my mother wrote about Carl's generosity when on Christmas Eve he gave her a new pair of skis: "I could do nothing but hug him and cry (for the first time in my life) in sheer happiness. Just to think that Carl spent the majority of his monthly army wages to get something that pleases ME!"

Uncle Carl never lived near us, and his visits were rare. He came with his wife, Ann, and his only son, Kip, who was Brad's age and also adopted. Carl was immaculate. He wore pressed slacks, clean white shirts, and his black hair was trimmed and combed. He was handsome, tasteful, soft-spoken and polite. But he wasn't stuffy, and he and my mother remained playful with each other throughout their lives. I can imagine my mother and Carl dancing around the dining room of our house. In the early years it was common for my parents to rise from the dinner table and waltz around the room. My father was an adequate dancer, and I can see him dancing with Ann while Carl danced with my mother, all of them having a ball while the children looked on with embarrassment.

Later, when Carl moved back east to work for the State Department, we rarely saw him. He and my mother kept in touch, but infrequently. Toward the end of Carl's life, just before his cancer diagnosis, I heard my mother speaking with him on the telephone. She mentioned Kotlik and the possibility of returning together. She told him how afraid she was of going alone. I doubt Carl said no, at least not definitively. He may have said he would think about it. When my mother got off the phone her eyes were glassy. I think she sensed that Carl would never make it back to Kotlik.

Carl, even more than my mother, was reticent. Though I was comfortable with him, I sensed his unavailability. His shadowed eyes defined him in ways I couldn't comprehend. Part of this was a dark side: Carl drank, too, harder than my mother. He drank enough in his early twenties to destroy his first marriage, to a woman about whom I was never told. The first marriage was volatile and brief, and Carl had numerous extramarital affairs.

My mother, to the best of my knowledge, never cheated on my father. Her lifelong best friend, Norma, with whom she shared many of her deepest secrets, attests to her fidelity, though she admits my mother had many opportunities.

"Your mother just said, 'You know, Norma, that kind of thing just doesn't interest me.' And she meant it. She didn't judge an affair as wrong, but the thought of it simply didn't excite her."

Nevertheless, the parallels between my mother's life and Carl's are unusual. Two years apart in age, they were bound together as children by the intense pressure of cultural adaptation. Both became good students, went to college, had successful careers. They both adopted children. They drank. And each died at 57, of the same cancer, the secret of their past wrapped like a nut inside the shells of their improvised lives.

Sending the Seals to Sea, 1930

NICUUK WAS VERY OLD FOR THOSE DAYS. Nearly sixty years she had been alive. Still she was constantly working with her hands, though she slept more than she used to. Lately she had been weaving grass baskets, and today she was decorating them with dyed seal guts, as her three-year-old great-grandson, Ungkak, looked on. *He is a very patient boy,* Nicuuk thought, *just sitting there watching me.* Ungkak loved to watch how quickly his great-grandmother's fingers, old and wrinkled as they were, moved with the grass, and how perfectly she placed the colored seal guts, the forms emerging as if by magic. He sat with Nicuuk whenever he could, especially when the men were away hunting as they were today. Sometimes she told him stories about the olden days, how life used to be before the big ships and the Russians came.

Ungkak was a quiet boy, always the one to sit back in the corner and listen, but often when Nicuuk talked he would politely interrupt to ask her questions.

"But Grandma," he would say, his tenor voice slow as he tried to find the right words, "If there was no store, what did Papa do then?

And where did the peppermint sticks go? And what about the mail that comes by the ships?"

Nicuuk would nod to Ungkak but keep her eyes on her work. "You are right to ask," she would say, "and you ask wise questions. This was so far back that even your papa wasn't here, and neither was I. Raven had just carved out the rivers, and bears wandered among the people like friends. There was no store until the Russians came, and we lived off the land and never even dreamed of peppermint sticks. But there's much sweetness in the land."

This day as Nicuuk worked she was silent, and Ungkak didn't push her. He knew better than to speak too forwardly with an elder, even if she was his great-grandmother. He knew she liked to tell stories, and if he waited long enough she would speak. She sat with three baskets in front of her. The two large ones she planned on giving to her grand-daughters—one to Justina, one to Dora—to use in their kitchens. The small one she'd made especially for her great-granddaughter, Inaqaq, who was just a year old. It was family tradition to pass down a basket from the oldest to the youngest female, symbolic of passing on the skill of weaving, of craftsmanship, of motherhood. But before all that, before she became a woman at all, Inaqaq would use the little basket to store seashells collected from the beach.

Nicuuk worked many hours on Inaqaq's basket, decorating it with seal gut she had dyed in strips of blue and red and yellow. She could have bought the dye in the store—many people were doing that now because it allowed for a wider variety of colors—but she liked doing it the old way, the simplicity of the colors she knew how to make. Anyway, she had never even been in the store. She heard all about the new things one could buy—canned berries, Swedish cookies, Swiss chocolate, white porcelain dishes and silver knives—but she preferred to do things as she had always done them. Nicuuk made the dyes from berries, alder bark, and other plants she gathered on the tundra. She took pleasure in her long walks through the knee-high grass, soggy meadows, and endless hummocky plains. Usually she returned with her baskets brimming with the tools of her trade. She soaked the seal guts for many nights, making the color rich and deep.

Inaqaq's basket was four inches high and round. The lid had a shell interwoven on top to serve as a knob. Ungkak was fond of animals and often brought home wounded birds or baby mice to care for, asking Nicuuk for advice on how to feed them. So all around the basket Nicuuk had woven Ungkak's favorite animals: a small blue bird perched on the tail of a red fox running after a yellow caribou. Nicuuk was nearly finished with the basket, and her mind wandered as she crafted a girl riding on the back of a raven.

The seal guts reminded Nicuuk of the Bladder Festival, and the year Aivrun was chosen to carry the *kangaciqaq*, the wooden staff to which wild celery was bound with long grass. She remembered how Aivrun had been nervous about his role because it had never been filled by a white man, but that he was honored and proud. To her it seemed that Aivrun wasn't a white man anymore. He spoke Yup'ik, lived as they did, and to her he even began looking Yup'ik as he aged, the skin on his face dark except for the white, wormy scar. Aivrun worried that he might make a mistake in the ceremony, but Nicuuk knew he would do as well as anyone.

Nicuuk loved the Bladder Festival, even though it was a men's ceremony in which she wasn't allowed to participate. As a girl she had resented not being allowed to dance with the boys in the *qasgiq*. But she watched whenever she could, shouting with pleasure when the man carrying the flaming stick crawled from the sky hole in the *qasgiq* and ran toward the sea with the bladder carriers in pursuit. Dressed in a woman's squirrel parka, the hood of which could easily catch on fire, the running man appeared to be borne along by flames. Nicuuk was mesmerized by the sight of it, unafraid because she trusted he would never be burned.

Year after year Nicuuk helped with preparations for the ceremony. When she was only a few years old, Nicuuk learned to help her mother, Ciklak, with the seal bladders. In the springtime, her father, Yugisaq, took his spear and hunted seals with the other men. Sometimes he killed a large bearded seal, sometimes spotted or ringed seals, but inevitably he came back with something. When he returned, it was Ciklak's job to gut the seal, including the bladder. Nicuuk would help Ciklak with this, her tiny arms buried deep in the seal's gut as she searched for the bladder. She loved the feel of the seal's insides, especially if it wasn't long dead. Years later, in hard times, she would dream of crawling inside a seal to escape from the world, the wet warmth all around her.

When the bladder was removed, Yugisaq filled it with air by blowing into it. Then the bladder was tied and hung with seal guts from a tall pole outside, where it would dry over the course of the summer. Every time Yugisaq brought a seal home they did this with the bladder, until, if the season was good, they would have nearly a dozen seal bladders hanging from the pole. When it came time to move from fish camp back to the village, they took the seal bladders and carefully stacked them in large bags. By then the bladders had dried and deflated. When the people arrived back at the village they had been keeping the bladders for months. All in preparation for when the water froze over, which was difficult to predict. Usually it was late October, maybe early November. Nicuuk was always excited to get back to the village, even though it meant winter loomed. She liked helping her mother prepare the dry, crinkled bladders, soaking them in water and oil to make them soft and slippery, like flat jellyfish.

Nicuuk paused from her work when she heard Ungkak shift in his chair. Then, very suddenly, surprising even herself, Nicuuk began telling Ungkak about the time Aivrun had carried the burning pole at the Seal Bladder Festival.

"You have heard," she began, "about the Bladder Festival. But maybe you have never heard about when your great-grandfather, Aivrun, carried the burning stick to the sea."

Ungkak sat up and leaned toward Nicuuk, hanging on her words. His eyes were bright and wide, waiting. He had heard stories about Aivrun, and he knew about the Bladder Festival, though he had never witnessed one. The Bladder Festival began to disappear with the coming of the white man, whose church disapproved of such ceremonies. As the Yup'ik took on Christianity many of the old traditions disappeared. Some villages still had a Bladder Festival, and Ungkak had heard many stories about them.

"Aivrun was a great hunter, and for many years he brought back twice as many seals as anybody else. We gave much away because we had more than we needed, even in the lean years when people were starving. It was said that a hole in the sea had swallowed all the seals. Whenever Aivrun came home with a seal, people would say that he had gone down into that hole to pull one out.

"But that wasn't it, I don't think. I think he knew how to think like a seal, and that when he went out in his kayak he knew where the seals would be. Don't ask me how he knew, but I think he did. His kayaks were beautiful, he spent long hours making them stable and fast. Using beads that Yugisaq had given us on our wedding, I sewed the beads into the shape of a seal, and this rainbow-colored seal he tied onto the bow of his kayak, for good luck.

"Aivrun liked to hunt alone, and though he sometimes joined the men on their hunts, he had his best luck when he was out on the sea by himself. People said it was dangerous for him to go alone, but he did and almost never did anything go wrong. You have heard, I am sure, about the many days and nights when he didn't come home, when for more than a week he was missing, and all that time it was blowing and there was rain and snow and swells on the sea ten times as big as you, little Ungkak.

"When he did come home he came on foot, dragging a seal behind him, chunks of it cut away from when he'd had to eat. He'd been caught in a storm far out at sea, as he circled an island twenty miles north of here, looking for seal. He'd killed one just before the storm hit and decided to land on the island when the water got too rough. It's a cold, rocky place, that island—I've been there—with very few places to hide from the sea. He turned his kayak upside down, wedged it between some rocks, and there he spent the next four days, cutting into the seal once a day to satisfy his hunger.

"On the fifth day the storm let up, and he decided to try for the mainland. But halfway there a violent squall swamped him, breaking his kayak in half. He saved two things: from the bow he cut his beaded seal; and the seal he had killed floated beside him like a buoy, saving his life. He and the seal were washed to shore, and he spent the next three days dragging it home. When he got back he acted as if nothing unusual had happened. But he was embarrassed that he'd wrecked his kayak. That same night he started building a new one. 'And this one,' he said, 'will never break.' This, you know, is the one your uncle still uses when he hunts seals. Maybe someday you will use it, too."

Ungkak nodded when she said this. He imagined himself in his great-grandfather's kayak, paddling through violent waves as if they were nothing.

"But, oh, I was talking about the Bladder Festival, and here now I am talking about many other things. So I will tell you about the Bladder Festival, which was not so long ago that I cannot remember, the year after a famine when it was very important that the seal hunt be good. That is when they asked Aivrun to carry the burning pole, for they knew he was a blessed hunter and they wanted his luck to be everyone's.

"There weren't many seal bladders that year, but Aivrun took what we had and hung them, inflated, with the other bladders, from the ceiling of the *qasgiq*. There, all of the men gathered, and the boys like you, and they danced for many days and nights. They sang songs, danced, beat the drums under those bladders. I could hear them all the time, and I wished I could go dance also, but I didn't because it was the time and place for men. Sometimes I would go in, with another woman, bringing food, and when we came in someone would call out, 'Qua—qua—qua,' and we would freeze in place until someone said it again and we were released. That was the custom, and I liked going in there, the smell of smoke and sweat thick. I wanted to stay, but it is a man's place, so I would go."

Nicuuk turned from a basket to look at Ungkak, who was holding Inaqaq's basket, turning it around and around as he listened. His eyes drooped.

"Little man," she said to Ungkak, "you are sleepy. Perhaps I will tell you the rest of the story later. Will you sleep now?"

Ungkak shook his head. "I want to hear," he said. "Please tell me about great-grandpa. I'm not sleepy."

Even as he said it his eyes fluttered, but Nicuuk was enjoying the telling, seeing in her mind's eye the details of those days, when she had been young and Aivrun was alive and not filled up with whiskey.

"I will tell, but you must listen," she said. "Otherwise the words will float around, unheard, their sounds falling away one by one, until the story is lost. Did I tell you, yet, about the wild celery?"

Ungkak shook his head.

"After dancing under the bladders, the men took them down from the ceiling. Whoever had bladders took his spear and fastened his bladders to the spear's tip. The bladders, you see, were the seals. And just as seals are startled by sudden noises like the falling of sea ice, so it was said that the bladders would be startled by sudden noises. If anyone made a sound during a quiet time in the ceremony, people would say that it was the sea ice collapsing, and that it would scare the seals, which was not good for hunting. There was a time for dancing during the festival, but also much silence and discipline. You couldn't just run around and do as you please, as children do nowadays at potlatch.

"That year, Aivrun's kayak was left hanging from the ceiling at the back of the *qasgiq*, for good luck. Boys, like you, were sent out to pick wild celery from the tundra. They brought their celery back to the *qasgiq*, where it was set out to dry, and if you fell asleep inside the *qasgiq*, someone would light some wild celery on fire and put it under your nose. Maybe I should do that to you now to keep you awake."

Again Ungkak shook his head. "I am awake," he said. "I am!" He wanted so much to hear the story, but it was late in the day and he was warm from Nicuuk's fire.

"There was a pole," Nicuuk continued, "a wooden staff, and it was dyed with red ochre and covered with strips of caribou skin tied downward. The wild celery, when it was very dry, was tied to the top of the pole, and then the pole was stuck into the ground in the center of the *qasgiq*. Aivrun carried that pole as he ran to the sea.

"I remember that morning well, because I was up early and heard the drums stop, and then a long silence. I thought I heard the ice groaning out on the river, as it does when it begins to thicken and tighten against its banks. I bundled up your grandmother, who was still just a baby, and we went out together, down below the *qasgiq* where a trail led to the sea. Already there were other women and children there, waiting to see *nalugyaraq*, when the hunters returned the bladders to the sea. It was very quiet, even the youngest baby wouldn't cry, and we all stood out there on that cold early morning, the sun never rising but its light an orange glow that capped the horizon like a crown of fire.

"Then a low hushed song came from the *qasgiq*, and as all heads turned to see, a lamp was lit just above the sky window of the *qasgiq* and in the light was the shaman, who was old and had very strong medicine. Next to him, staring into the flame, was your great-grandfather—I could not have mistaken him for he was wearing my clothes!"

Ungkak's nearly closed eyes popped open. His lips quivered at their edges, breaking into a small, tentative smile. His head cocked to the side in question and his eyebrows lowered. He said nothing, but he was aching to know.

"It was the tradition," Nicuuk continued, "that the man carrying the pole dress in the clothes of a woman. The parka was easily burned, so the man had to be very careful. If Aivrun burned my parka it was bad luck; it meant maybe I would not have long to live. But if the parka was not burned then it was a blessing. I had faith that Aivrun would not burn my parka.

"After the shaman performed the ritual, he lit the top of the pole, the wild celery. I could smell the smoke as it drifted by us, the ones who were watching. The smell was so strong that it burned my nostrils. When the pole glowed orange with heat, Aivrun took it from the shaman, shouldered it, and circled the sky window. He looked so calm but I knew that he was nervous.

"Then, with a signal from the shaman, Aivrun ran down from the *qasgiq*, though he wasn't actually running but only looked as if he was running, as if he was performing a running dance. When he began to move the flame grew, and behind him the men with the seal bladders on their spears chased him, and when they were close they whipped the flame with a bladder and the flame roared and sparks flew into the air and it seemed as if Aivrun was a comet flying low over the earth, or a raven on fire.

"Aivrun ran toward the pond. I said earlier the bladders must be returned to the sea, but the village was inland of the ocean and it was too far to go there, so the pond was used in place of the sea. Aivrun circled the pond, which was the sea, but all I could see was a fire in the low morning light, and behind it the men running with their seal bladders.

"After a while Aivrun moved to the center of the pond, where the men had made a hole in the ice. Aivrun took the pole from his shoulder and stuck it straight up in the ice, and the flame began to die. I could see his face in the light and I could see that he was glad to be finished, that he was happy that he had done it well, that the other men were satisfied as they gathered around the hole and began deflating the seal bladders. They pricked the bladders with a bone needle to deflate them and stacked them one on top of the other until they all were in a tall stack. The shaman then put a seal spear through all of them, and he said a few words and then with the spear he pushed the bladders away under the ice.

"They said good-bye this way, to the souls of the seals, and thank you. And if it was done right then the people knew the souls would return in other seals, and the people would always have enough to eat. That's why it was so important for your great-grandfather to do this right, for if he had failed it could have gone badly for the village. Are you listening, little sleepy-eyed seal?"

Ungkak was tired, but he knew now that he would hear the end of the story. He loved hearing about Aivrun, whom he had never known, and it was rare for his great-grandmother to speak so openly about him.

"What about your parka?" Ungkak asked. "Was it burned? Or is that the end?"

"After releasing the bladders, later in the afternoon, everyone came together for a celebration and a dance, if the fur parka wasn't burned. When Aivrun and I came there, he was made to stand in the center of the room while the elders inspected the parka. When they saw that it wasn't burned one of them let out a great shout, and the drums began to beat and we danced the old-time slow dance that lasted a long time. Since the parka was not burned it was a great honor for Aivrun, and it was said he was blessed by the shaman, what we call *qaniqumayaraq*. We danced much of the night, and though Aivrun didn't usually like to dance, he danced because he had to. I think he even liked it."

Nicuuk stopped talking, and Ungkak could tell she was finished. She sat very still, her eyes closed and her breathing soft. Ungkak dared not move. He heard a dog barking by the river, and nearby the creaking of a boat's wooden planks. He smelled salmon smoking, and he pictured the red strips of flesh hanging from the lines at fish camp, imagined Aivrun stoking the fire with a long pole, his eyes jumping around as he herded popping coals back into the pit. *They are strong eyes,* Ungkak thought, *but sad.*

Ungkak pulled back, startled, when Nicuuk's eyes blinked open. She smiled. "Have you any questions, little Raven-without-a-voice?" she said.

"Why is it we have no Seal Bladder Festival?" he asked. "When can we have one again?"

Nicuuk thought to herself, *He is too wise, maybe, for one so young. Too many questions to burden his heart.* But she answered, "There will be no more Bladder Festival, for the Russian shamans have told us it is no good, that we insult their god. Many things are not as they used to be—you will see this as you get older—but we go on as best we can, and if we have no Bladder Festival we can at least remember it, and someday perhaps it will come again."

Now it was Nicuuk who was sleepy and Ungkak who was not. She leaned back, eyes closed, and Ungkak spun Inaqaq's basket around and around, blurring the colors of the animals. He heard the thick breathing of his great-grandmother, and he watched her for a while, awed by the deep creases in her face. When her breathing became a snore, Ungkak smiled, touched her forehead, and went out into the day.

FLIGHT OF THE OUZEL

No moon. Brad and I sneak from the house at midnight, armed with flashlights but not using them. We cut through old Big John's front yard and duck under the log fence that surrounds the meadow. Horses graze there, and through the pitch darkness slip the snorts of the herd. As we draw nearer we see the dark outlines of horses standing and lying down, all bunched close together. In the cold air, breath streams thickly from their nostrils. I pull carrots from my pocket, hand one to Brad, and slowly, quietly, walk flat-footed toward the horses.

After a flurry of movement, they adjust, smell the carrots, maybe our familiarity, and come to us through the dark. Brad searches for the Appaloosa, and I feed my carrot to the palomino I've been horsejacking for months. I pull a halter over her head, wrap the lead rope over her neck and tie it on the other side, creating makeshift reins. With a grunting lunge I'm aboard and kicking to catch Brad, who is galloping into the night.

Riding at night is like swimming in the dark, only better. I hear the horse's legs pounding earth. I clutch the mane, my legs gripped tight

around the heaving mass. Once before, the palomino had sent me flying into the night, and I'd belly flopped onto the meadow and thought
I was dead until my air returned in gasps.

I catch Brad just before the beaver ponds at the meadow's north
end, where we stop to let the horses drink. I hear Brad breathing but
we don't speak. After a minute we turn upstream, toward our favorite
fishing hole. The horse's breathing spreads my legs in and out, and I
am tiny on her back.

Willows line the banks of Squaw Creek. We tie the horses downstream from our fishing hole and walk along the bank. When we reach
the water we take out our knives, cut two thick willow branches, and
begin carving the sharp tips and the notches an inch up so the fish
won't slide off when we pull them from the water. Satisfied, we remove
our shoes and socks, roll up our pants, and wade into the frigid, knee-
deep water. In the middle of the creek I whisper okay to Brad and we
turn the flashlights on. I point my light at the creek bottom and walk
slowly upstream. The first fish to enter my beam is too fast and my
spear digs into mud. "Shoot," I mumble.

"Ssshhh," Brad hisses back. I hear his spear slice water and then
the slapping of a fish against rock. "Huge," he whispers loudly.

"Ssshhh," I hiss. "Shut up!"

I continue upstream a few feet before a big trout moves into the
flashlight beam. It stops and hovers in the light, trapped like a deer
in a car's headlights. I hold off, my spear raised above me, my body
tense. It's a rainbow, maybe fourteen inches, undulating pink and
silver in the light. I see it closely, a tear in its fin, gills pumping,
bulging eyes. For a long moment I think that I won't kill it. I stand,
spellbound. Then I plunge the spear through the water and into the
fish. I watch it skewered like that, the spear stuck in the river bottom,
the fish thrashing to escape.

When I reach Brad downstream he has speared two and is almost
finished cleaning them. I sit with him and hold his light while he

admires my fish, then slices and guts it. We string them on a piece of kite cord and head back to the horses.

When we get there his horse has pulled loose, so we ride the palomino double across the meadow, I in front and Brad in back holding the fish in one hand, my shoulder in the other. We ride slowly, and I smell the fish and hear our breathing. I give the horse one more carrot before I slap her rear and send her back into the meadow's night.

MY FATHER FIRST SAW THE MEADOW IN 1952, when he went skiing at Squaw Valley. At the time, the ski area was tiny, with one lift and a jig back, a one-person chair on which the skier sat sideways. Lift tickets cost a few dollars; mostly just the locals skied there. The one road in was dirt, and the town consisted of a post office, a general store, and the Bear Pen, a two-story bar with antlers nailed above the door. From the moment he rounded the fourth curve in the valley road and saw the snow-covered meadow surrounded by mountains, my father knew that Squaw Valley would become his home.

Five years later, he and my mother packed their bags and drove west for good. They bought a small cabin just above the meadow, which ran the length of the valley and was split by a creek winding its way to the Truckee River. Behind our house, up Shirley Canyon, were hundreds of square miles of wilderness, including what is now the Granite Chief Wilderness Area. Shirley Canyon consisted of leviathan granite slabs, towering trees, and mossy forests cloven by the rock troughs of upper Squaw Creek, which fed the aquifer beneath the valley floor. Because of the prodigious Sierra snowfalls, Squaw Creek raged in the springtime. The meadow waited below, swallowing as it covered itself in waist-high grass and wildflowers. From their cabin, my parents could see the entire length of the valley, all the way to the looming cliffs of Granite Chief Mountain.

My father, John Peter Chisholm, still tells of watching the meadow in early mornings, coyotes trotting through the chilly fog that hovered, ethereal, just above the grass. Squaw Creek was a meeting place for animals, and my parents watched deer, beavers, raccoons, coyotes, and bears navigate around one another on their way to morning drinks. Mountain lions, too, they knew from the tracks, but they never saw one, even so long ago. I can imagine my father, there on the deck of his A-frame cabin, his hands down the back of his underwear scratching his bottom, his then-red hair ruffled and his cerulean eyes surveying his place. He did that every morning, gazed across the valley like a king regarding his domain; though as the years went on the changes in the landscape registered on his forehead as deep, curving grooves that came and went and then finally, one day, became the permanent contours of his face.

For my mother, I think, moving to Squaw Valley was like taking a step back toward the wilder landscape of her Alaskan youth. As the years went on she spent more and more time exploring the wilderness that surrounded her home. However, I believe that she never forgot the wide open vistas and waterways of Kotlik, and despite her love of Squaw Valley and Shirley Canyon, she was always a person displaced. Though she learned to love the mountains, her heart was with the ocean, with water.

By the time Heather, Brad, and I were adopted in the late 1960s, Squaw Valley was long gone as a paradise. The winter Olympics had come in 1960, bringing with them all the growth required to house a world community. In those two weeks Squaw Valley was transformed from a little-known ski town into a world-class destination resort. Part of the meadow was covered with sawdust to serve as a parking lot, and the mountain was stripped of its trees to create new ski runs. The Olympic Village was built at the base of Shirley Canyon; Olympic rings hung like gold from the rafters of the concrete and steel ice arena. More chairlifts were constructed to connect the valley floor with the upper mountain. Suddenly the locals were sitting on millions of dollars of real estate and the entire Lake Tahoe basin was transformed into a year-round recreation boomtown.

My parents saw it coming, and from early on my father and other locals fought the Ski Corporation for every stand of trees they clearcut. After the Olympics, the valley became an Olympic ghost town. The monolithic monuments fell into ruin, until virtually all of them were demolished. We still had the meadow and Shirley Canyon, and for many years after I was born, my parents lived under the influence of their early visions of Squaw Valley. I think they thought the worst of it was over. It was twenty years down the road before they realized how wrong they had been.

MY MOTHER LOVED HIKING to the water ouzel falls. When Heather and I were old enough to walk, she'd pack a lunch of peanut butter and honey sandwiches, strap Brad on her back, and off we'd go up the trail into Shirley Canyon. It was a long hike for children, maybe two miles, and it seemed to take forever to get there. Along the way my mother would point things out to us: the Three Gray Ghosts, four-hundred-year-old Jeffrey pine trees; the Big Flat Rock, a piece of granite flat as a pancake and as wide as our house; the Bathtubs, huge granite pools scooped out by a millennia of surging water; squirrels, hummingbirds, pinecones that came up to my knees. We marveled at her observations, and it made the journey go faster. We were excited, too, because we knew the water ouzel falls was our mother's favorite place.

After coming through a thick ferny forest we'd break through the trees, crest a small rise, and go left to the falls, a series of cascades stretched across a sloping slab of white granite, like a long smooth water slide. The main drop was about five feet, and behind the water was a wide horizontal cave, in which water ouzels built their yellow and green, grapefruit-sized nests, made of moss, interwoven with pieces of driftwood and anchored to rock. Sometimes, when the water flow was low, diminutive flowers grew from the moss, coloring the inside of the cave. My mom once told me that the water ouzel's house was alive, and that someday she'd like to live in a house like that, the breathing belly of home.

She'd stare for hours at the waterfall, waiting for the water ouzel to appear, while I romped with Brad and Heather on the sloping ramps of granite that shouldered the creek. She'd sit in her yellow bikini, her knees drawn up to her breasts, her journal resting on her shins. She'd sketch the water ouzel falls, the trees, her children.

The water ouzel (or American dipper) is a bird worth watching; I learned that from my mother. Virtually unaffected by weather, they sing all winter long, seemingly aloof to freezing temperatures or violent storms. As John Muir noted, "The ouzel sings on through all the seasons and every kind of storm. Indeed no storm can be more violent than those of the waterfalls in the midst of which he delights to dwell. However dark and boisterous the weather, snowing, blowing, or cloudy, all the same he sings, and with never a note of sadness."

Once my mother snowshoed up Shirley Canyon in midwinter to see how the birds were faring. She was gone all day. When she returned at dusk she was as happy as I'd ever seen her. "The falls are frozen," she said, "and through the ice you can see the nests. Like looking through glass into someone's home at night." Later, she told me, an ouzel had pecked a hole in the ice and disappeared downstream. When it returned it was carrying a tuft of moss. "Piling on the blankets," she said.

Ouzels are slightly smaller than robins, with slick bluish-gray feathers, sometimes brown on the head and shoulders. Their beaks are long and pointy, their tails erect. They're seen often dancing on mid-river boulders, their legs bending as they bob up and down, like women in an Eskimo dance. Their real beauty for me, though, is in their acrobatics. They fly like bees or hummingbirds, their wings invisible and their movements quick and vertical. In flight they commune with water.

When I was five years old, at the water ouzel falls with my mother, I saw an ouzel dive into the white water downstream where the creek narrowed. I thought it had drowned, but in a split second it reemerged from the water. My mother and I were speechless as we watched it dive in the same spot for an hour, returning to its nest periodically to deposit whatever it had found beneath the water's skin.

Often ouzels are seen wading mid-stream, dunking their heads underwater like blue herons picking at a river bottom. Invariably the water ouzel is seen in, by, or above water. Perhaps that is what my mother so loved about the ouzel: its fidelity to place. The Shirley Canyon water ouzels were born in the falls, made their living along the creek's mossy banks, and died when the water carried them away. I think my mother saw in the water ouzel how she wanted to be and could not.

IF SHIRLEY CANYON WAS MY MOTHER'S PLACE, the meadow was my father's. He took long walks along the banks of the creek, and together we skipped stones across the wider pools down near the beaver ponds. Some days after work he hiked with my mother in the meadow or up Shirley Canyon, which were both under constant threat by developers.

"Sons-a-bitches," my dad would mumble, when yet another condominium complex blocked our view to the meadow. We saw it happening all around us, the whole Tahoe basin becoming a kind of wilderness suburbia. We were part of it, simply earlier versions of the masses moving in, inevitably building our paradise in the backyard of someone else's, but back then we didn't see the irony.

The final blow hit one summer when I was home from college. The Poulsens, Squaw Valley's founding family, sold a large portion of the meadow to a development corporation. What was a ski area without a golf course? the developers reasoned. They planned an eighteen-hole course and a nine-story hotel. A small group of property owners, my father included, took the developers to court, charging that the proposed development might contaminate the aquifer. They won a few concessions, but eventually were overpowered by the developers' economic force. During the time we were losing the meadow, we found out that my mother had cancer.

On darkest nights my brother and I dressed in black and ran through the meadow pulling stakes and throwing rocks into the darkness—mostly stupid, hopeless games. But we felt helpless and angry and didn't know what else to do. We'd stand on the porch, looking down at the black thing growing into the sky, and talking about how great it would be to have a rocket launcher. I can't say I wouldn't have used it.

My dad kept fighting, in public hearings, in court, on his evening walks if he happened across a pro-development neighbor. When he read in the newspaper that vandalism—what some might call environmental terrorism—had occurred in the meadow, he pulled Brad and me aside.

"You horse's asses," he said. "If I ever find out you're doing any of these things . . . " He shook his head, took off his glasses, and pinched the bridge of his nose. Brad and I looked at each other, silent. There was nothing to say.

"You know we can lose everything," he said. "You have no idea how much power these people have. We can lose everything. Goddamn it!" He turned and stormed into his office, slamming the door.

For the first time I saw that my father was scared, and that I didn't understand the complexity of the issue. The developers had enough capital to bury my father in court. In the end, I think what hurt my father most was his powerlessness. He stood with my mother on the porch of our house, his arm around her too-thin shoulders, watching surveyors stake out the meadow, and he knew, finally, that none of it would last.

~

HORSES NO LONGER RUN FREE IN THE MEADOW. The once-tall, flowing meadow grass is covered by nature's equivalent of Astroturf. Golf carts race around. On the far side of the meadow stands the nine-story hotel. Covered with black reflective glass, it resembles Darth Vader's Death Star. My father calls it the Black Elephant. Rooms start at $158 a night. Eighteen holes of golf goes for $100.

Squaw Creek often flows a dirty trickle, out of place beneath the wide, dry banks. The ski area sucks up massive quantities of water for its snowmaking machines. My father argues that the aquifer can't supply enough water for the golf course and the artificial snow. There is constant concern about shortages, and talk of water-use restrictions.

Still the growth continues. Developers lobby for new hotels; the ski area has expanded into the upper end of Shirley Canyon. The base of the chairlift, a slab of concrete and steel, sits about two hundred yards from the water ouzel falls. The ultimate irony, it seems, is that the Ski Corporation owns the falls.

The fight continues. When I call my father on the phone to ask how he is, he answers by telling me the latest developments in the valley's ecosystem. He realizes that Squaw Valley will never again be what it was when he first came there, but he believes that what is left is still worth fighting for. He knows there are very few unspoiled places left, and all of them are threatened. He recognizes cancer when he sees it.

LATE SPRING IN SQUAW VALLEY. BRAD, my dad, and I hike up Shirley Canyon. Dad is getting old and his knees are weak, but once in a while we talk him into going. We hike along the south side of the creek, by the Bathtubs, where Brad and I strip and swim. It feels good to be running around naked on the rocks with Brad, my dad watching like time has reversed itself twenty years. Farther up the canyon we stop for water on the Big Flat Rock, and my father points out the fire ring we used when our family camped up here.

An hour later we come to the water ouzel falls. I'm nervous being here with him, wondering if he is thinking about my mother and the ashes never thrown. Spring water rushes over the falls, but I see at least one nest underneath. I haven't been here in years, but it looks exactly as I remember it. My dad points to a large stand of trees up from the falls, says, "That's where it is, the lift. Through those trees. We're lucky they didn't plant it right here." I can't see it, but the thought of it being so close is unsettling.

We sit on the rocks and watch the falls, hoping for a glimpse of an ouzel. We can hear their singing, so we know they are there. It's strange being here with my dad, because most of my childhood memories of this place are associated with my mother. After a while with no luck, I sit back and close my eyes, listening to the water and the ouzel's song. I hear my dad's breathing, and I wonder what he is thinking.

"Colin, Brad, look," he says softly after a few minutes, "The ouzel."

I rise up and there it is, hovering just above the water twenty yards downstream. It darts to the side and lands on a rock in midstream, where it begins its dance of bobbing head and rising tail, intermittently extending its wings for balance. I think of all the winters this bird has endured, singing through the storms, and how good it is to come here and find the ouzel still in place, still building its mossy nest and flying low over the water.

My father clears his throat. The ouzel looks up, alert, then whirs into the air back upstream and disappears into the waterfall.

"Beautiful," he says, "isn't it?"

"Yeah," I answer. "It is."

"You boys know," my father says, "your mother, she loved this place."

It is the first time since her death that I've heard him speak of her, and I let the words hang in the air for a while around my head, the ouzel's singing blending with the roar of falling water. I think about the ashes, about asking him why he can't throw them, but then I realize it doesn't matter. It is good enough just to be here with him and the water ouzel, and I think that someday after he is gone, I might take a handful of ashes from my mother's grave on Vashon and sprinkle them over these waters. Maybe we will have his ashes, too, and we can throw their ashes together into the creek. Maybe that is why he has waited all these years.

I picture their soft flakes of bone, borne along the current over the water ouzel falls, winding down the canyon and into the depths of the meadow, where someday long grass may grow again.

Aivrun,
1914

He looked around at the land that had sustained him and his family since Raven first carved out the rivers and shallow, lush valleys. He couldn't remember a time when the land hadn't been in his heart, and in the worst of times he went to the land to heal. But this time it was different. He knew this when he knelt by the shore of a small lake far out on the tundra, when the person staring back at him from the water was wholly different from the one who stared in. His once-yellow, sharp eyes were dull and somber. His chestnut skin sagged prematurely, like an old man's. His cheeks were ruddy and swollen. Aivrun felt the weight of his head and it seemed unbearable. He was fifty-one years old.

He carried a shotgun. It lay beside him as he gazed into the water, and when he began vomiting he noticed it between convulsions, dry heaves that continued until he was spitting blood. Gasping for air,

Aivrun regarded the shotgun and thought how easy it would be, how simple. He wasn't afraid. When the retching subsided he picked up the gun and placed the double barrel in his mouth, pointing upward at his brain. *So easy,* he thought. *So damn easy.* His finger trembled on the trigger, pressed lightly but just shy enough. Ducks quacked overhead. What stopped him he couldn't say; perhaps it was Nicuuk and the children, but she was distant to him now and the children were grown. *It might just as easily have been the ducks,* Aivrun thought afterward. As the ducks called, he drew the barrel from his mouth, swung the shotgun around and fired. It took only a second, and when it was finished his life was saved and three ducks lay dead on the tundra.

Aivrun walked all day. He killed another four ducks and could have had more but his bag was full. He walked upriver a few miles to the place where he and Nicuuk had made love for the first time, a tiny beach hidden by thick alders. He'd known the place since his early days in the delta, and he'd killed his first bear from those same bushes. He remembered Nicuuk standing naked before him, her hair loose, river water dripping from her hard, goose-bumped nipples and her flesh glowing in the waning light. For the first time in his life he had dropped to his knees in front of another person. He had kissed the seal brown birthmark just below her navel, and she had shuddered when he moved to the wet black of her sex and the sound of the river filled her.

It was difficult for Aivrun to think of these things; he felt himself wanting Nicuuk again, yet nothing stirred in his groin. He felt dead already. He stayed in the place for only a minute, not wanting to remember more. He couldn't help thinking of what a failed husband he'd become, how heavy the silence was between them. He still loved Nicuuk, but he was unable to show it. He didn't blame her if she didn't love him any longer.

Even as he belittled himself while walking across the tundra, Aivrun was helpless against his illness. He pulled a stained silver flask from his coat and drank. Whiskey had long ago stopped burning as it went down, but still it warmed his chest. He worried about the rawness of his throat and about the blood he spat up every morning, but there was no going back. He could no more quit drinking than he could give up hunting. He knew that when he returned to the village that evening he would go to Joe's house to play poker and drink. More often than not, Aivrun passed out and spent the night on Joe's stinking floor. At times, when he was lonely, Aivrun might stay in for the evening and talk to Nicuuk about the children, but those times became increasingly rare as the years passed.

From his and Nicuuk's place on the Yukon he hiked another five miles to the highest hill around, from where, when he was nineteen years old, he'd seen his first caribou migration, the wide sweeping flux of motion across the tundra, the ground shaking under him and a low rumble filling his ears. As a young man in Russia he'd grown up in the country, dreaming of the great north. But even in his most vivid imagining he'd never seen a world so elusive to description. He could feel it, could feel the rolling, endless horizon in his gut, but never in his rare letters home could he bring the place to life. When he saw that first rush of caribou covering the land like water breaking from a dam, he felt something shift in the person he was, as if the energy of the herd was cutting the cord that tied him to any past, releasing him into a future that relied on nothing but the land, the shifting of seasons, the water, the ice, the open air.

Aivrun had spent most of his adult life in the wilderness. He often left the house early in the morning, hunting seal, whale, and duck in the spring, fishing all summer, then moose or caribou in the fall. In the winter he worked a trapline, taking red fox and wolf and wolverine, which he traded for food and supplies, or gave to Nicuuk for making clothing. He hunted with a reverence for the animals he killed, having learned from Yugisaq a profound sense of the sacred. When he took an animal he thanked it, not with a great show of deference, but inwardly, with a quick bowing of his head and a silent movement of his lips, even as he moved to skin the animal or reload his rifle.

Once, while working his trapline, he'd found one of his steel-jawed traps with a bloody fox leg dangling from the sharp teeth. The fox had chewed off its own leg. Aivrun was shaken. Though it was late in the day, he tracked the wounded fox, following the trail of blood where it wandered into thick brush. Two hours later he found the den, nestled high above the riverbank on a south-facing slope. He perched himself above the den and waited all night in the stiff cold for the fox to show itself. In the dim light of morning a fox poked its head from the hole. Aivrun waited to see that it was the wounded one, silently asked forgiveness, then blew the fox into the next world.

He lifted the small, mutilated body to check its sex, found the swollen nipples and swore to himself. He set about making a fire, breaking dead branches from bushes and placing them in a pile below the den's entrance. The fire blazing, he warmed his freezing hands and feet, ate a strip of dried salmon, then worked to smoke the pups from the den. It didn't take long, as the den was built on a hill and the smoke drifted naturally into the tunnel. Soon the light red pups emerged, their eyes barely open and each no bigger than Aivrun's hand. He waited until all six were out in the open, then as quickly as he could, brought the butt of his rifle down on each of them. It wasn't as easy as he'd hoped. With the first blow the other pups tried to escape. Aivrun was forced to kick the fleeing pups back in front of him where he could crush them. As one tried to flee back into the den, Aivrun crushed it with his mukluk, the sickening crunch of its skull raising bile into his throat. After a few long seconds the pups were dead, the hard snow all around covered in carnage. Aivrun dropped to his knees and vomited. He pulled himself together and headed home, utterly exhausted. Looking back one last time, Aivrun was shocked to see another red fox glaring at him from twenty yards away. It had to be the father. Aivrun thought to kill it, but something in its eyes held him back. The fox would go on, if it didn't end up in another one of Aivrun's traps. Though Aivrun knew he had done what was necessary, he felt awful, and he would never again hunt without remembering. In the future, if anything went awry on a hunt, he would blame it on that day; the ancestors were punishing him for his brutality. He never again let his traps sit for more than a day.

Aivrun walked. Freshly thawed, the tundra was soggy and still brown from the previous year. He walked and he drank and the ducks were heavy in his bag. The spring air felt good and he thought if he could just keep moving then everything would be all right. If he just kept walking he would run out of whiskey but it wouldn't matter because he could hunt and live off the land and keep right on going until he was at peace. He saw Mount Kusilvak, fifty or more miles away, and thought if he walked to the top of the mountain he could look down on the tundra and the animals and the great river and he would be strengthened and go home to Nicuuk and be a good husband and live out his days teaching his grandchildren to hunt. He walked faster, filled with a new, albeit dim, sense of hope. But then came the tug from his gut, the knocking of his need on the door of his pain. He ignored it, willed it away, but soon the knocking became a pounding, then a scream that pierced his spine and drilled to his brain. His hope withered, and he grasped desperately at the nearly empty flask. He finished it in one long gulp, realizing before the whiskey landed in his stomach that it would not be enough. Not even close. He yelled wildly and hurled the silver flask into a clear, glassy lake, where it bubbled and sank.

Aivrun nearly ran back to the village, not noticing until he was there that he'd forgotten his ducks. The thought of wasting the birds filled him with shame, but it was too late, his need too fierce. When he reached the village he walked up the hill toward home, saw smoke rising from the chimney. He passed quietly by the house, not noticing the plaintive eyes watching him.

At Joe's, a game of poker was just beginning. Joe slapped Aivrun heartily on the back and took a pull from the bottle. The smoke was thick. Aivrun drank and played along, and though he was more reserved than usual, nobody noticed. Aivrun stared at his cards and wished he had killed that last poor fox.

LOOKING FOR HOME

15

W hen we were children, my mother used to tell us that Squaw Valley was named for the Indian women, squaws, who stayed behind in the valley when the men went hunting. It was years after her death before I learned the real origin of that word, used by the mountain men to describe a woman's genitalia, in the crudest of terms. "I'm goin' to git me some squaw," they would say. An offensive term to many Native Americans, squaw is only now being recognized as such, with states such as Montana removing the word from official registries and maps. Most likely my mother was unaware of the irony, but perhaps, on some level, it had to do with her disillusionment in Squaw Valley.

Hawaii was my mother's home away from home. She went often, beginning when she was a nurse in her early twenties, the last time about a year before she died. She loved the island of Kauai because it was the least crowded back then, its beaches and forests still pristine. But any island would do, and she visited most of them. In Hawaii she was among people who resembled her: Hawaiians and Asians, dark-skinned, high-cheeked people with whom she had more in common physically than with her own husband.

She talked often about retiring in Hawaii. If she were alive today, she'd probably be living in a small bungalow near a beach on Kauai. For much of her life she went there at least once a year, if only for a week or two. When I was small, our family lived there for months at a time, not far from the Spouting Horn, where the swelling of the tide forced water in great blasts through a hole in a seaside cliff. Every morning my mother woke early to go snorkeling. Sometimes my father joined her, but usually she went alone. She wore flower-print bikinis, and when she returned from the sea her eyes sparkled and her teeth glowed; she looked to me like a bouquet of freshly cut flowers. She held me and I tasted the salt on her skin and smelled the ocean. For the rest of her life my mother talked fondly about those months we lived in Hawaii, the warm, rainy nights, when breathing was like inhaling a flower's heart.

There was a span of years when we took our Christmas vacations in Hawaii. I remember one year in particular, when we stayed for a week on Oahu's Waikiki Beach. My parents had gone into debt to finance the trip. We had eaten beans and rice for six months prior, and there were to be no Christmas presents. All seven of us stayed in a shoddy, one-room hotel a few blocks from the beach. I remember walking by the Royal Hawaiian, the giant pink hotel that crowns Waikiki Beach, and wishing that we had enough money to stay there. I was disgusted by our dingy hotel, with its cockroaches under the bed, scorpions in the bathtub, and brown stains on the sheets.

My mother couldn't have been happier. She had a beach nearby, warm rain to walk in, fresh seafood and friendly faces all around. She seemed always to be smiling, buying us little trinkets, rings made out of fish bones, or raw sugarcane to suck on.

On Christmas Eve we kids complained about not having a Christmas tree. We were used to snowy Squaw Valley holidays, with presents piled underneath a tall tree, Christmas caroling in boots and hats and mittens. To appease us, my mother bought us a two-foot-tall Styrofoam Christmas tree covered with various and sundry hard candies acting as ornaments. Even then I recognized it as tacky, a poor excuse for the real thing. My mother was hurt by us not liking the tree she had spent too much money to buy. While we bawled, she went by herself to walk along the beach.

When I was twelve, I went to Hawaii for what would be my last time. Having failed to convince my father to accompany her, for the last few years my mother had gone by herself. This year, however, she'd decided to bring along one of her children. Heidi and Michelle were living away from home, Heather was busy, so it came down to Brad or me. She made us a deal: one of us got to go to Hawaii, one of us got a new bike. I suckered Brad into taking the bike and two weeks later found myself sitting next to my mother on a jet bound for Hawaii, eating salted macadamia nuts and reveling in the fact that for once I had my mother to myself.

We didn't stay at the Royal Hawaiian, but neither did we stay at Cockroach Central. We were just off the beach in a sheltered, clean hotel that had a bird of paradise, my mother's favorite flower, growing right outside the window. It was a wonderful, peaceful time for the two of us, she so happy being there and I feeling lucky just to be with her. We walked the beach, snorkeled, ate seafood dinners by the sea. She watched as I took surfing lessons. On a remote beach halfway around the island I nearly drowned while bodysurfing, before a lifeguard pulled me to safety. When we returned to the rental car somebody had broken in and stolen most of our belongings.

A few days later I went out to bodysurf while she guarded our things. She asked me to return in an hour to trade places with her, but I got caught up in the excitement of the waves, surfing for two hours while my mother sat stewing on the beach. When I finally returned she could hardly speak. I had drained the magic from our trip. After that, my mother continued to frequent Hawaii, but she usually went alone.

As with her life and her love, my mother's dying wishes were split between places. She wanted her ashes spread in the water ouzel falls up Shirley Canyon, and in the waters off Kauai. Perhaps she imagined my father going there to spread them, her ashes dropping from his wet fingers into the boat's wake, and the fish rising to feed on her, nibbling at flakes, their tiny teeth speckled with the gray stars of her skull and skin and bones.

My mother's heart was with water. *Meq*, the Yup'ik say. Or *imarpik*, the sea. For thousands of years her people had lived by and from the sea, and no distance could remove this from her being. When she married a man who loved mountains, I think she knew he would never change. Knowing she would probably never leave Squaw Valley, she made do with the water she could find. And every year, Hawaii. The need pressed on her, growing with the years. I imagine her in a Sierra winter, home alone with five young children, gazing out the window at the snow covering the circle of mountains. Did she imagine the smell of flowers and fish? Did she feel sand underfoot? Did she feel water, in waves, washing over her?

RIVER AND SEA,
1909-1931

SINCE HER EARLIEST DAYS Dora loved the sea. She was a shy, recondite little girl, willful and independent. Once, in the springtime, when she was three years old, she wandered from the house clad only in her undergarments, searching for the source of the sound she had heard all morning. It was the ice breaking up, the sea tides swelling and smashing the ice as they pushed upriver. She half-crawled, half-walked from the house as her sick mother, Cu'paq, slept through the early morning. Ordinarily Cu'paq would have been up sewing and cooking, but she'd been awake all night with a cough and fever. Her husband was up and gone, hunting the first ducks of the season.

Dora emerged from the house in the day's first light. The air was cold, winter-chilled, the ground frozen. She was barefoot, but she didn't notice the cold, only the crunching and grinding of the ice as it awoke. The house was set back twenty yards from the river, so it didn't take her long to get to the bank, where she stood, perplexed, next to her father's wooden boat, upside down and badly in need of repair. She saw no creatures, no animals or birds. No people made this noise, no machine that she could see. Yet it was louder now, the snapping and cracking, the wheezing of air. Dora saw the fractures in the ice from where the sounds came, and it frightened her because she thought it must be something under the ice, a creature or sea monster trying to escape.

But she didn't run. Curious, she sat still, freezing yet determined to wait for the creature to emerge. She thought of the stories she had been told, of the salmon that were their relatives, of the river and sea from which they came. She thought perhaps it was the river itself trying to break free, and suddenly it occurred to her that she should help. For the first time in her life she realized the river was alive, and that it was very much a part of her.

Dora moved onto the ice. Her tiny feet stepped carefully, leaving tracks in the night's fresh dusting of snow. She didn't know what she was going to do, but she had to do something. She was twenty feet out when she reached the first crack, less than an inch wide and too deep for her to see where it ended. She kneeled on the ice, peered into the crevasse, saw nothing. She sniffed it, touched it, blew into it, and finally put her ear over it to listen.

After a few minutes she heard a cracking and felt, under her cheek, the ice shake. A cold blast of wind gushed from the slot into her ear, surprising her. She saw that the crack was bigger now, and she wondered if blowing had helped. She blew into it again and waited. Nothing. She whispered into the crack.

"Hello, down there, whoever you are, river or fish or uncle. You must tell me how to help you. Should I blow some more, try to melt the ice? What is it you want? I will sing you a song."

She sang a song that Nicuuk had taught her: "The fish and the loon went to the moon, and the river wept in sorrow. And the river it cried, and said to the tide, 'Where have they gone, in this world's last dawn, and how will they know that I've died.'" She sang it many times over, and after a while the river spoke back to her, moving and shaking and the crack growing wider. And though she grew cold until she couldn't feel her feet, she sang and thought of nothing else but the singing and the voice and breath seeping from the dark seam.

Dora was startled from her singing by her mother's shrill voice. She turned and saw Cu'paq running to her from the house, and she said quietly to the river, "What is wrong? What have I done?" Cu'paq stopped at the shore, wailing. Her way was blocked by a gaping crevasse that had opened behind Dora, marooning her on a floe of ice cut off on all sides. Dora waved at her mother.

"It's talking to me, the river is talking," she said.

Cu'paq's pale face drew tight against her bones. "Don't move," she yelled. "Don't move an inch! I'll be right back!"

Cu'paq ran to the Ivanoffs' house, but all the men were out hunting and only old woman Ivanoff remained. Cu'paq realized that she would have to rescue Dora by herself, and a strange sense of power filtered through her fear. She borrowed the Ivanoffs' wooden ladder, dragged it to the shore, and easily made a bridge over the crevasse. Dora watched with curiosity, thinking it some kind of game. Cu'paq grabbed her in her arms and retreated carefully back across the ladder. Safely on the other side, Cu'paq scolded and embraced Dora, holding her tightly, rocking her.

"You are so bad, Dora. You must never go out on the ice alone. Never! Do you hear me? You could get yourself killed."

"Mama, did you hear the river speak? I thought it was a monster coming, but it was the river trying to get free." Dora's voice was sleepy, her words slurred. Cu'paq felt Dora's feet, as cold and hard as ice cubes. She ran fast then with Dora, knowing the danger.

"You may not have drowned, little rabbit," Cu'paq said as they rushed into the house. "But you're almost frozen."

"The river blew on me," Dora murmured, her eyelids drooping. "I could see its heart, the river, a salmon."

Dora slept long and hard. Cu'paq cared for her, spooning warm tundra tea into her mouth, rubbing her feet and hands slowly in luke-warm water, then immersing her in a hot tub. Later she wrapped her in furs and laid her next to the fire. Once, in her sleep, Dora cried out in the night. "I'm coming, river. Coming!"

IN LATER YEARS Dora loved hearing her mother tell the story of her rescue from the ice. Of course the story changed over the years, the crevasse wider and the temperature colder, the ladder more dilapidated and the river hungrier. But Dora would forever harbor a crystal-clear memory of those minutes when the river spoke to her. After that day she learned the river and the sea better than most of the village people, even the hunters and fishermen. She didn't know the ways of all the animals and fish, but she knew the more subtle elements, the hidden characteristics that showed themselves to only the most patient observers.

She knew how the colors changed after rain, and how the river smelled, thick and organic, like mushrooms freshly pulled. She knew how the river danced with the sky, how it rippled in the rain and froze in a thin veil of skin when the first cold came. She saw the shorebirds in the river's reflection, knew not their names but their colors and sizes and sounds. She knew what the birds plucked from the river's depths, the eddies, the grassy banks. She knew the differing textures of mud. She even knew how the Yukon tasted, like fish in summer, dirt in spring, and bears and sweet tea in the fall. She couldn't have said how a bear tasted, but she had seen bears swiping at fish, seen them wading and playing in the water, and she had tasted the water then. Ever after, she knew the taste of bear in water.

Dora loved fish camp in summers, though she wished she could go out on the boats to set nets instead of staying at camp where she cleaned and prepared the salmon after they were brought in by her father and brothers. She worked with Nicuuk and Cu'paq, and her sister, Justina, cutting strips of king salmon and hanging them on drying racks. She loved when the first fish were brought in, shining silver and the scales reflecting tiny rainbows of light. She was awed by their size; when she was little many of the fish were bigger than she. And she was mesmerized by Nicuuk and Cu'paq preparing the strips, cutting so quickly with the *ulu* that Dora could hardly see their hands. She loved the bright red of the meat and the patterns the fish ribs made along the slabs, like ripples in a red sea.

But fish camp was more than just fish. It was travel, when they packed the boat and traveled downriver a few miles, near where the Yukon flowed into the Bering Sea. It was the smell and taste of saltwater; the squawking of gulls; scouring the beaches for shells and seaweed; searching for wild goose eggs in the alder bushes and grass. And, for Dora, it was swimming. When she was ten she began swimming in the river, though it was not a common practice among her people. She did it in privacy, for if people had known, she would have been scolded. She'd find a private cove thick with bushes, strip naked and slide into the water like a snake, so quietly that she couldn't even hear herself. She loved to lie naked in the mud, rolling around, rubbing her skin with it, then slipping into the water to clean herself. She longed to swim in the sea, to know what it felt like to be thrashed by the waves. Once she had snuck to the beach at night, had been naked and up to her knees in the sea when fear turned her away. She wasn't afraid of the sea, but of night, of being swept into the darkness.

As the years went on, Dora became more and more reclusive, spending much of her time alone by the water. In the summers, after returning from fish camp, she hiked for hours across the wet, hummocky plain of tundra, hypnotized by the innumerable small marshy lakes and meandering creeks. In the winter she ice fished, sometimes by herself when the hole was already cut, but usually with her father, Anthony, who would cut a hole in the ice, start a fire, then sit watching as Dora fished. She'd peer down the hole and remember the river's voice, and it made her feel good to know the river was still there, always there, no matter how hard the winter or how sad the village life. She caught mostly burbot in the winter time, ugly fish but good to eat. Cu'paq didn't like it when Dora went alone, but Dora was willful; if Cu'paq said that Dora couldn't go, Dora wouldn't argue but would sneak out anyway. Finally Cu'paq realized it was better just to let Dora go, keeping an eye on her when possible.

Because Dora was a loner, most of her peers had married and borne children long before she had any interest in men. She had decided in her youth that she would never marry, that the river and the sea were all she wanted. She found men unattractive and boring, and she swore to stay a spinster for all of her days. She saw how content Nicuuk was by herself after Aivrun died, and though Nicuuk had mourned, Dora thought she could detect a change in Nicuuk, a deep calming. She wanted to be just like her grandmother when she was old.

Everything changed when her father died. Her family had nothing to live on, and her brothers had started families of their own. Everyone was hungry. That was when Charlie Backlund lent a hand. He had been good friends with Anthony, the two had hunted and fished together every year, and when Charlie saw the family's situation he offered them a place to live. He was old, his head covered in white hair and his rosy cheeks sagging into jowls. The family had known him for a long time, and Dora could not remember a time when he was not there, minding his store. She thought of him as her father's friend, and as such she treated him with respect.

Gradually Dora and Charlie became close friends, despite their difference in years. They didn't speak much or often, but they enjoyed each other's company. They walked together in the summer evenings after Charlie closed up the store, and sometimes he took Dora fishing on his new boat, made of metal instead of wood. It was the village's first boat with an outboard motor, and Dora was thrilled by how fast they moved over water, bouncing over swells like a skipped stone. Sometimes they journeyed upriver to a favorite place of Charlie's, a high hill overlooking the river, thick with salmonberries, birds, and bears.

They were walking along the river when Charlie asked Dora to marry him. Surprised, she felt guilty that she couldn't respond joyfully. She'd grown to love Charlie, but not in a romantic way. She thought of him as her surrogate father. Nevertheless she agreed to ask her mother, and when Cu'paq responded positively, Dora could think of no reason to refuse. She loved no other, and Charlie was a good man. He could take care of the family. She wanted children, though she wondered if Charlie's age would hinder them. She answered him two days later, while they were fishing from his boat, hauling the nets in. He smiled broadly, nodded thank you, and continued pulling the nets.

Ungkak was born a year later, Inaqaq two years after that. They were named after their ancestors, as was the custom. Dora was happy as a mother, though she felt hardly older than a child herself. She longed for the private time she had enjoyed by the river, and she replaced the solitude with picnics and walks with the children. As soon as Ungkak was able to walk, she strapped Inaqaq on her back and strolled every summer day along the river. She pointed things out to him along the way, and he would sit and stare for minutes, even more awed than his mother had been as a child. He especially loved the birds, pointed frantically when he saw one he recognized, trying to include his mother in his joy. He loved their sounds, the chuckling, throaty call of the brant, the wild near-screams of the loons, the wolf whistle of the bristle-thighed curlew, and his favorite, the strange airy sound—like an ocean geyser—of the sandpiper. Ungkak could sit for hours watching the birds over the water, his lips mutating as he tried to imitate calls. Sometimes Dora showed him the things the birds ate, or where they built their nests, but before long Ungkak knew more about the birds than his mother did. He would often point out longspurs or curlews, so well camouflaged in the tundra that she marveled at his eye. It was the beak, he said; the curlew's beak gives it away.

On those walks Dora taught the children the joy of swimming, holding them one at a time between her hands and pulling them through the water. Inaqaq took to it quickly, screaming with delight as Dora lowered her into the water. But Ungkak preferred the muddy banks, where he dug clay and formed imaginary creatures, humans and foxes with wings, or birds with the heads of men. He remembered the stories Nicuuk had told him about the bear woman, and he made a bear with human hands, as well as two bear cubs. He'd make his clay creatures and set them in a hidden place where he thought he could find them when he returned. But usually when he came back the creatures were gone, so that Ungkak came to believe they had come to life, that his great-grandmother's stories were alive.

Much of their time by water was spent in silence. Ungkak liked to watch his mother sitting by the water, and she in turn loved to see her children slithering around in the mud. Ungkak knew it was a secret, shared pleasure, and he told no one. Even Inaqaq, only two years old, seemed to understand the sanctity of their outings. It was as if they were in a vacuum, as if sound had been sucked from the air. They moved through the water as if swimming through space, where planets exploded and galaxies expanded in perfect silence.

During winter the silence grew, and Ungkak learned to hear the hum of falling snow. With no water lapping at the banks, no birds singing, no distant yells from fishermen, Ungkak's ears buzzed. With Inaqaq on her back, bundled in furs, Dora took Ungkak fishing. She taught him to tie fishing knots as they sat by the hole waiting for the day to warm. Ice fishing was an exercise in endurance, sitting cold, sticks held over a hole where the line disappeared into darkness. Ungkak was amazed every time a fish was caught, because he couldn't understand how fish could survive under the ice. Dora caught fish regularly, and Ungkak couldn't figure out how she did it. He held his line as she did, moved it around in the same circular way, yet he rarely even got a bite.

"How come you get all the fish?" Ungkak would whine at his mother. "Show me how to do it."

"It's all in how you think," she would say. "You must focus your thoughts, imagine the fish near your hook, ask for it."

Ungkak was too young to understand, but it made him feel good when his mother shared such grown-up thoughts with him.

The afternoon of Dora's death, Ungkak walked alone to a small eddy hidden by thick alders. He stripped his clothes and slipped into the freezing water. He held his nose and submerged himself, floating motionless just below the surface. The muddy bank touched his legs, the current pulled at him, but he wasn't scared. He heard the silence leaking into him.

16

How can anybody know how she will handle death? And why are we often disappointed by weakness, as though the people we love and respect should bow down to the great reaper and say, "Take me, for I am at peace with the world"? As though it should be quiet, clean, and dignified.

I know little of death, but I suppose in my own way as much as anybody does who hasn't died. I know how I hoped my mother would die, that it would be tranquil and that I would be at her bedside, weeping. Death, and dying, like love, are easily made cliché.

My mother spent her final months cloistered from the world and from the people who loved her most. Our home was a peaceful place in summer, the skiers' din replaced by birdsong and wind and water. Aspens thrived along the creek, shading my mother's favorite room, speckling the brown tiles with shadows of leaves that flitted around the room like golden fish in a murky pond.

In the corner of that many-windowed room was a spa, a luxury my mother allowed herself when she remodeled the house seven years before her death. In the mornings of her final years, my mother would make herself a cup of coffee, then slide into the hot tub for a soak. I'd come downstairs, smelling the eggs or hot cereal or French toast that she'd made, and there she would be in the water, her back against the Spanish tiles, a mug of coffee in her hand, talking with my father or sometimes just sitting with her eyes closed.

During her last summer she still soaked, but less often as she grew weaker and spent most of her time upstairs in her bedroom, reading or sleeping. My mother never told me she had cancer. Instead, she had my oldest sister, Michelle, tell me. She insisted on talking about her illness as if she would overcome it. But to do so, she said, she needed all the healing energy she could muster, which meant that she didn't have much time for other people. I tried to accept this, but the sicker she became the more desperate I was to connect with her. I would gravitate to her room, hoping she would want company, and if I found her awake I'd sit next to her on the bed or sprawl on the floor. Sometimes she'd let me stay for a while, but often she'd look at me, tiredly, and say, "I need to be left alone."

"But Mom, how about if I just sit here for a few minutes?"

"I need peace and quiet, now don't argue with me. It will just make it worse."

"I'm not arguing, I just . . . "

"You are arguing. Now go, I need to rest." She was getting upset.

"But Mom . . . "

"Go!" she half-yelled. "Now!"

It went on that way the whole summer, my guilt growing every time we clashed because I felt so wrong for pushing her, yet I couldn't help myself. As her need for solitude increased, so did my need to be with her. I felt abandoned. I wasn't the only one; my mother, in her dying, distanced herself from virtually everyone in her life, except perhaps my father. I tried to convince myself that her strength would pull her through, that if she was really going to die she wouldn't push us away. I was forced to lie to our friends and neighbors, saying she was fine in order to protect her privacy. When I left for my second year of college, I was relieved to get away.

Two weeks later my mother was hospitalized, but still she insisted that her children didn't need to come home. She denied access to even her closest friends, allowing only my father and my oldest sisters to visit regularly. We spoke on the phone, the hard edge between us gone. She spoke gently, tried to share with me how she felt, how her pain was; we talked as long as she could bear, which was never long enough because the morphine made her drowsy. Still she said I didn't need to return home yet, and I believed her.

In mid-September Michelle called to tell me to come home. I caught a flight to Reno, where my father met me, and as we drove through the flashing neon of the casinos I felt as if I were in a dream, and that all the lights and noises and sad gamblers were a stage to a play in which I had a leading role, but I couldn't remember a single one of my lines.

"How's Mom?" I said, trying to improvise.

"Your mother," he said, his jaw clenched, "is going to die. Probably very soon."

And that was it. He drove, looking straight ahead, and though I thought I saw him brush away a tear, none fell.

The hospital was pink, like a casino. Set up against the sagebrush hills of Sparks, its windows flashed with the violet glow of twilight. It had been raining. As I stepped from the car I smelled sage, one of my mother's favorite smells. I was glad for it, and I hoped the windows of her room were open. Then I smelled the thick stew of hospital food, that too-sweet smell, that empty-calorie stench that you can find only in hospitals and public schools. I knew my mother wouldn't eat that food, but it didn't matter; she wasn't eating anymore.

From her fifth-floor room, my mother could see the Sierras, the mountains she had lived in for thirty years. When I walked into her room an alpenglow blanketed the east shoulder of Mount Rose; pink light streamed through the windows, eddying just below my mother's high, gaunt cheeks. She was sleeping. She had changed much, her hair thinning and wispy like thread. Her lips were drawn back tightly against her teeth, and her already petite frame had withered, her bones probing through skin. Her hands looked delicate, transparent, but still, somehow, strong. I was nineteen years old and new to death; I felt repelled. I was afraid to touch her.

It is only now, more than ten years later, that my mother, in her death, appears beautiful to me, her bones as light and hollow as a bird's, her skin a veil of rice paper, her being so light that she is ready to float from the bed and out the window, her body dissolving into pink sky. Now I would hold her as she went, just to feel that incandescence pass through me, to know death and to embrace it as I would like to be embraced when I pass from this world.

There is no knowing how it was for my mother to look out from her shrunken body and see her children gathered around her. But when she woke and saw me there, next to her bed, her eyes flickered and she smiled apologetically, as if her infirmity begged forgiveness. We didn't talk much, just held hands and watched the alpenglow wane from the Sierra crest. At one point I buried my face in the crook of her shoulder and wept. She cried with me, and I knew she wasn't grieving for herself, but for me, for all of her children and the pain she was causing. All of her life she had avoided hurting others, and the most difficult aspect of her dying was watching others mourn for her.

For three days our immediate family gathered, along with Hildure and my mother's best friend, Norma. The first day we had a conference with the doctor, who informed us that our mother was going to die soon, with or without surgery. Without surgery she had at most a month to live; with surgery she might have six months, maybe a year. My mother asked us what we wanted her to do, and when after a family meeting we presented her with our desire—we chose surgery, desperate to extend her life at any cost—she broke into tears, nearly hysterical that we had not reaffirmed her belief that modern cancer treatment is futile. She overruled our decision, unwilling to relinquish control of her life. She'd seen Carl chopped, stitched, cooked, and, finally, plugged into life via medical artifice; this she could not bear.

On the day before I left again for college, she called another family meeting, at which point she finally acknowledged what we all knew to be true.

"I know this may not come as a shock to any of you, but for me, I suppose I haven't wanted to admit it. I'm going to die soon. There are things we need to discuss."

Too much for Brad, he left the room. I followed and found him pacing the corridor, his face white and tense.

"Brad," I said, choking back tears. "Come back in. It's okay to cry, and it's okay to tell Mom how you feel. I know it's not easy. But we're leaving tomorrow. This is it. We've gotta go in there and tell Mom we love her."

Brad's eyes were moist, but he wasn't crying and he wouldn't look me in the face. "It's just hard . . . ," he said, turning his head upward and looking out a skylight.

I remember wanting to embrace my brother, standing there before me looking so frail and full of hurt. All of our lives I had been a bully to him, and though I loved him I had never showed it. Now, I just wanted to hold him, to say I was sorry for all of those years, to tell him we would be okay after Mom was gone.

But her dying was different for Brad, and even then I knew that he would take it hardest. As the youngest child he was the last to leave home. He'd spent the last year as her only child, and in that time they became closer than ever. Of all her children he was the most like her: compassionate, accepting, generous. And inward. A part of Brad was inaccessible, a private place to where he escaped during tempests. During family arguments, when the talking turned to shouting, he seemed to disappear from the room, backed away in a corner as if every stinging word was aimed at him. His opinion often went unspoken, his feelings squelched by whoever could talk—or yell—the loudest. In photographs from our childhood he appears worried, as if he's pretty sure that any second things will go to hell.

I see him now in that hospital corridor with the same expression, his green eyes gazing through everything he sees. He is eighteen years old, is just leaving home for college, is having his world turned upside down, and he's never learned to cry.

"I know it's hard," I answered him. "But Mom needs us in there. This may be our last chance to talk to her. So anything you want to say, you've got to say now. Okay?"

Brad nodded, still staring at the sky. We walked back into her room, where my mother was talking quietly to Heather, who sat red-eyed on the bed. My mother fixed on Brad, as if gauging the degree of his pain, and in her eyes I saw an inexplicable sorrow, so intense that time seemed to stop for that moment, and everything, all of us and all of anyone, became just those ebbing eyes looking out to her youngest child, to whom she had to say good-bye.

My mother beckoned us to her bed, searching our eyes. "We have lots of hard things to talk about, don't we?" she said. "One thing I want you boys to do this afternoon, with Michelle. She'll take you out to buy some new clothes, pants and a jacket. Both of you have outgrown those jackets I bought you years ago. I want you to look nice. Will you do that for me? Buy a couple if you want to—you'll need them for college."

For my funeral. Those were the unspoken words. Brad, Michelle, and I drove to a mall that afternoon to buy clothes for the funeral. It was one of those ubiquitous places: B. Dalton's Bookstore, See's Candies, Macy's, Sears, McDonald's. We strolled, not talking, through the crowds. We found a tacky men's clothing store and Michelle helped us select the appropriate attire, all the way down to the shoes. I bought a tweed blazer, khakis, two ties. Sick to my stomach, I couldn't wait to leave. My last day with my mother, and I was in a shopping mall in Reno.

When we returned to the hospital my mother asked Brad and me to model the clothes for her. I didn't argue. We stood before her in our funeral clothes, I in brown, Brad in gray, and she nodded in approval.

"Thank you, boys," she said. "You look wonderful."

I could have screamed.

Later, alone in the room with her, I said to my mother what I never had before. "I love you, Mom," I croaked, the words barely liberated before I broke into sobs. In our family, emotions were expressed in action rather than words, or they were repressed. In any case, I'd never said "I love you" to another human being.

I departed for college the next day. I didn't want to go, but she insisted. She told me she would call when things got worse, and that I could return one last time before she died. One last time. The reality was that she knew we would never see each other again. Just as she held people at a distance in her final months, so in her death did she push us away. Perhaps she did so to shield us from that final ugliness: her incontinence, her drugged stupor, her coma. Heather, Brad, and I returned to our colleges. Michelle, Heidi, my father, Hildure, and Norma remained with her in that final week. Hildure was alone in the room with my mother when she slipped away. My father was out walking through the sagebrush hills.

Michelle called with the news. "Colin, she's gone," she said, and that's all I remember of the conversation. I had believed my mother when she said I'd see her again. I asked that the cremation be delayed until I viewed her body. I flew home the next day and drove through the heat of Reno to a funeral home adjacent to a Chevy dealership.

There were fake flowers in the lobby, velvet paintings on the wall. A man with a wandering eye and slick hair directed me to the "chapel," a sort of mini-church like the ones in which people have shotgun weddings in Reno. My mother was lying on the plastic altar, a sheet draped over her. I walked bewildered down the aisle, until I froze halfway. The air smelled stale and antiseptic, like my high-school biology lab. I choked down vomit and willed my legs forward.

When I reached my mother I was trembling. I lifted the sheet from her face and stepped back, holding my breath. She was white, skeletal, cold and hard. I stood with her for a while, saying prayers to a nameless god, then decided to leave when I imagined that she'd moved her arm. I leaned over, closed my eyes, and kissed her cheek good-bye.

The funeral was like any other, except for the snow. Flakes the size of quarters clotted in the autumn sky. My brother and I wore our new jackets. He didn't cry. I think I did, but perhaps what I remember are the tears of others that I wished were my own. When I left the church, each snowflake stung my cheeks and forehead like a barbed kiss. I held my palm out to the storm and gathered them in.

DORA'S DEATH, 1931

CHARLIE BACKLUND marched down the boardwalk toward his house. His big limbs jerked awkwardly at such speed, accustomed as he was to slow, calculated movements. Through the ruff of his hood his face appeared dark and fearful, the corners of his eyes heavily furrowed, his brow drawn down.

A rare, perfectly clear evening in Kotlik, the stars fluttered through a twilight that washed over the snow in waves of amber. In the crisp air Charlie's breath came heavily in puffs. The dogs, for once, were settled, except for the plaintive howling of a pup who'd strayed too far out on the ice. As the light trickled from the sky, a green glow flickered over the low, snow-covered hills. Charlie noticed neither the stillness nor the changing patterns of light; he was focused inwardly, his mind struggling to fathom the impossibility of his wife's survival. When he reached home and stumbled in the door, she would be there, lying on the bed where she'd been for nearly two weeks, her forehead drenched in sweat, her sister and mother and children beside her. They would look at him with hope, as if he might have found a way to save her, to pull her back from the cold grip of tuberculosis.

At first, in December when she became ill, Charlie was hopeful. Dora was strong and the doctor from St. Michael thought she might recover. But when February slammed down its frozen fist, Dora faltered. Charlie panicked and asked her to let him take her to Seattle, or at least Anchorage, where there was superior medical care. But Dora refused, not wanting to leave Inaqaq and Ungkak, and also secretly afraid that she would never return from the white man's hospital. By the end of February her breathing was labored, and by early March she was too weak to move. Charlie, beside himself with grief and helplessness, worked long days at the store, coming home every two hours to check on Dora, who was attended by Cu'paq and Justina. Sometimes Charlie took Ungkak with him to work, giving him little chores such as dusting the canned food or wiping the glass on the counter. Ungkak was too young to know what was happening, but he was old enough to sense that his life was about to change. His eyes hung in dark, worried circles.

Ungkak was out front gathering wood with Justina when Charlie arrived home. "Look, Papa, how much wood I can carry," Ungkak said. "Soon I'll carry more than you or Justina." Justina smiled tentatively.

Charlie chuckled. "There's no doubt about it. Two sticks is a lot for a boy who weighs less than the ax that cuts the wood! Now get yourself inside before your nostrils freeze!"

Ungkak waddled inside, and Charlie turned to Justina. "How is she?" he asked. "Any improvement?"

Justina looked him in the eyes and shook her head. She reached down, grabbed another stick of wood, and turned to enter the house. "She's not eating anymore," she said. "I don't know what else to do."

"I suppose now all we can do is wait," Charlie said, and he turned his eyes away.

She nodded, then walked into the house. Charlie stacked some wood in his arms and followed her, noticing suddenly that the dogs had stopped howling. He shivered at the tongueless gray of nightfall.

Charlie and Dora's house was big by the village standards. A large living area harbored an iron stove, and a separate kitchen contained another smaller stove and oven. The house had two bedrooms under opposite ends of the A-frame roof. Charlie and Dora's room was south-facing with a long window that overlooked the river and scattered rays of sunshine across the walls. After he and Dora married, Charlie built the house himself, traveling to Seattle to select the lumber, windows, and the stoves. For nearly twenty years he'd lived alone in a one-room log cabin and never thought twice about it. But the cabin was too small for a family, he rationalized; at heart he was building the house for Dora, whose marriage to him still seemed too good to be true. He'd already written himself off as an old bachelor, and when Dora had accepted his affections he felt like the luckiest man on earth.

When Charlie entered the room he saw Cu'paq bent over Dora next to the stove, where he had moved her bed for warmth. He dropped the wood next to the stove and walked around the bed. Cu'paq was draping a cold cloth over Dora's forehead to bring down the fever. Charlie had never gotten used to how similar Cu'paq and Dora looked, but he had found it appealing because it foreshadowed Dora's old age, when he would be long dead. Whenever Charlie saw Cu'paq he was reminded of his own age, older than his wife's mother, and it struck him as odd that nobody in the village seemed to care, while in the Lower 48 it was scandalous to marry a woman so much younger.

Cu'paq glanced at Charlie and nodded hello. She'd been up with Dora most of the previous night, and her eyes were bloodshot. Her grief showed itself in the way she held her body, her usually erect posture hunched. She was forty-one years old but looked sixty. She had aged a great deal in the six years since her husband had died. And she had lost her brother and many cousins and friends to tuberculosis. As she sat there watching her oldest daughter expire, she thought to herself, repeatedly, *I am tired of all the dying. Soon I will have no tears left to cry, and when that happens I will be ready to die too.*

Charlie leaned over and kissed Dora on the cheek; he felt heat rising in ripples from her face. She was asleep, lapsing in and out of consciousness, and when Charlie said her name she didn't respond. He bent his head, closed his eyes, and clasped his hands in prayer, whispering words inaudible to Ungkak, who stood beside him. Ungkak followed his father's example, leaned against the bed, and pressed his palms together. He knew no prayers, so he sang a song that Dora had taught him. His voice was high and faint, and when Charlie heard it he stopped his prayer to listen.

Aa-ay'urrii,
Aa-ingay'urrii
Issantu-u issantu-u
Kituryantu-iq.

The song was a chorus for a story that Dora used to tell him, which she called "The Lonely Loon." It was about a loon left behind on a lake that was nearly frozen over. The loon kept trying to dive where the other loons had gone, but each time he came up alone, and cried out, "Oh poor me, oh poor little me! So sad I am, so sad, and so so lonely."

Finally, on the loon's last, desperate dive, he came up to find the other loons all around him, safe from the encroaching ice.

Justina held Inaqaq in her arms and watched from the kitchen doorway. She began singing along with Ungkak, just loud enough to blend with his voice without drowning him out. They sang and Charlie began crying into his hands. Dora woke for just a few seconds and heard the voices and wondered if she was hearing angels. She saw Charlie, his face in his hands, and she wondered what was wrong with him. With great effort she reached out to him, touched his arm. He jerked his head up, startled, but she had drifted off again.

Charlie sat all night next to the bed, his head resting on Dora's lap as he fell in and out of sleep. Dora dreamed of Nicuuk, dead the year before. In the dream Nicuuk was young and danced naked on the beach. All around the sky was red and the sea boiled into heaping piles of foam and the thunder of drums came from every direction, so loud the earth shook and Nicuuk moved in rhythm with the rise and fall of the land. Her muscles were lean and strong, her smooth skin resplendent with sea spray, her breasts speckled with sand. Nicuuk sang as she danced and the song was a high, wailing lament, her voice wavering and dipping with the story. She sang a dirge for her husband, Aivrun, and the gun of whiskey he'd put to his head; she bemoaned the white man's disease, and people dying by the thousands and all the children without parents and grandparents and no chance to know of their ancestors; she sang of her mother and grandmother and the sorrows of all the women in her family who had given birth to children, only to have them die young; she sang of the women's strength and endurance, and she prayed for her great-granddaughters to keep that strength. Nicuuk fell to her knees in the sand and raised her hands to the sky and keened for her grand-daughter, Dora. Her voice softened as she sang of Dora's early years, when she and Dora would wander through the tundra collecting berries, and how at day's end Dora's face would be stained red and blue from the juice. Nicuuk swayed on her knees, her arms waving back and forth like grass in the wind, and her voice grew louder and higher until she was screaming, and the wind raged and the drums pounded and Nicuuk wailed Dora's death song again and again. The tide covered Nicuuk's feet. Her voice swooped down again, subdued for Ungkak and Inaqaq, alone like the lonely loon. The water rose quickly and Nicuuk didn't move. She had to finish the song. Nicuuk sang and her tears dropped into the sea, and she let the tide swallow her before she sang the final words. The drums stopped, the sky cleared, and the sea and tundra were as hushed as winter on the moon.

Charlie woke early the next day just as Dora took her last breaths. She never regained consciousness, but Charlie heard her final, whispered words: *Charlie,* she said. Then *Nicuuk. Inaqaq. Ungkak. Aana. Kinkamkin.*

Meq, she said. Water.

And then she slipped away into the morning.

17

OLGA

On my first visit to St. Marys in 1989, I stayed with Justina's daughter Olga, who was thirty-five and had two children, four-year-old Wayne, and Justina, an infant. Olga was married to John, a *kass'aq* like myself, who worked in the oil fields and was absent much of the year (in my time there I never met him). Olga immediately reminded me of my mother, not only physically but in the easy way she handled herself, warm yet slightly reserved, and with an inner confidence. I felt at home in her tiny house, with its small living room/kitchen, a bathroom and two bedrooms, one of which I slept in, my head against one wall and my feet crammed against the other.

Like my mother, Olga was small-framed. She had fine, thin fingers, small-boned but strong, like the hands of a weaver or a surgeon. She was a pretty woman, the scars from teenage acne that dimpled her cheeks only enhancing her character. She wore her hair short, and her dark eyes were inquisitive and accepting. She moved about in fast, efficient motions, and spoke similarly using quick, truncated sentences, albeit in perfect English. She wasn't high-strung but merely industrious, and after her chores were done she would sit with me for long periods of time, talking as we waited out February storms.

Both Olga and Natalia were well educated and had earned degrees from the University of Alaska. Both had married white men, which somehow eased my transition into Yup'ik culture. Though a strong advocate of Yup'ik tradition, Olga was also very much a Western woman, educated about the outside world. She seemed to have found a peaceful balance between the two worlds. We discussed at length her studies, life in the Lower 48, and popular culture. Her intelligence reminded me of my mother's: wide-ranging, curious, and sharply perceptive. She was usually a step ahead of me in conversation. Our relationship was casual from the start, thanks to Olga, who treated me with the familiarity of a sister.

As a mother she had seemingly limitless energy and patience. Wayne was rambunctious and demanding, and Olga complied with his desires while also caring for Justina and entertaining me. In the evenings she read Wayne books or told him Yup'ik stories. She felt it was important that her children learn Yup'ik, and she lamented the loss of the language among the young. She also shared her feelings about returning to Kotlik after living in the outside world. It wasn't easy coming back, she said, but in the end she wanted to raise her children among their own people.

Weather permitting, Olga and I sometimes walked together in the early evening. She'd bundle up the kids and we'd stroll up the hill to the school, from which we could see far up the Andreafsky River, streaming serpentinely by the village into the Yukon a few miles downstream. The Andreafsky is St. Marys' lifeline, its road to other villages, fish camps, and the sea. Its sinuous course begins nearly a hundred miles upstream in the Caribou Mountains, and because of its designation as a Wild and Scenic River, there is limited development on its banks.

"More grizzlies than mosquitoes," says my cousin, Fred, who hunts caribou near the river's headwaters.

One evening as Olga and I watched the sunset from the school and Wayne rode his plastic sled down a nearby hill, she told me what she knew of my mother. "Ever since I was a little girl," she said, "my mom told us stories about Inaqaq and Ungkak. I grew up knowing I had two cousins in the Lower 48, and I always hoped I'd meet them someday. It was hard for my mom, I think, because she'd taken care of them like they were her own kids, so when they went away she worried about them a lot. I wish we could have known her."

We descended the hill to Olga's house, where we ate macaroni and cheese for dinner. Olga read Wayne a story and put him to bed. We stayed up late that night, and as Olga folded laundry and I washed dishes, I told her about my mother's life. She listened intently, once in a while asking a question, and when I was finished we sat silent. I could tell she was thinking hard, so I asked what was on her mind.

"I guess just about your mom taking such a long time deciding to come back. You say you don't understand it, and that makes sense because you haven't lived here. But I think I can understand a little what she might have gone through. It would've been hard to have her mom die, be sent away from people that loved her, and grow up in a completely different culture. I mean, even for me, it was hard to go away, when I went to college. It's a culture shock. And then you get used to it and when you come back here it takes a lot of getting used to. A lot of people can't do it. They go away, can't handle it, come back all messed up, don't want to be here but don't want to be anywhere else, either. It's a strange thing that happens, caught between worlds."

In bed that night I lay thinking for a long time. I could hear Olga cleaning up in the living room. I fell asleep imagining my mother in my place, sitting at the table with Olga, drinking tea, both of their smiles illuminating the room with a luster that spilled through the windows and dappled the night sky with a blue-green effervescence.

A few days later I left St. Marys en route to Kotlik. Sorry to leave Olga and the coziness of her house, I promised to visit again before too long. I told her I'd write. But something strange happens every time I visit my Yup'ik relatives. It's difficult to explain, but I feel as if my life shifts entirely, as if when the plane lands in St. Marys or Kotlik my regular existence is so distant that I fear I'll never return, as if my old life is nothing but cosmic dust. And when I return to that old life, suddenly my time in Alaska seems dreamlike, and my Yup'ik relatives a figment of my imagination. This makes it difficult to write letters, and talking on the phone is awkward and expensive. Between visits I lose touch, and before I know it years have passed. It seems easier to forget. What I'm afraid of I can't say, but it's related to my mother's anxiety about going back, to Olga's fear of being caught between worlds. Up there I'm exposed and emotionally raw. I look into Justina's eyes and see my mother.

TWO YEARS PASSED LIKE A DREAM and I'd written only once to Olga. She didn't write back, and the next thing I heard she was dead. Thirty-seven years old, of cancer. My father went to the funeral, but I couldn't leave my job. I thought of Olga's son, Wayne, who was close to the age Carl was when Dora died. Olga's cancer was the same that killed Carl and my mother, the same that killed Matt Andrews' son, Glenn. The list goes on and on, a legacy of cancer. Though possibly genetic, its origins are more clearly linked to the hepatitis B virus, a major killer among Eskimos before the introduction of a vaccine in 1983. Heidi and Michelle, my mother's only birth children, worry about cancer even after testing negative for hepatitis B.

Olga's death seemed unreal to me until I returned to St. Marys six years later. Her house was rented to strangers, her children had moved north with their father, and a new weariness registered in Justina's and Natalia's eyes. I missed Olga when I was there, in the Yup'ik world; now, back in my regular life, she seems reborn. I will always think of her alive up there, and because of this it is difficult to return, for each time I will have to accept her death again, and grieve for her, and for my mother. I procrastinate calling or writing, afraid of the news. All of the dead and the dying become the same.

ON RAVEN'S BACK, 1934

JUSTINA PRAYED IN THE CHURCH EVERY DAY that December, hoping to send her daughter's soul to heaven before Christmas. Clara was Justina's firstborn, three years old when she grew sick in the spring and never made it through the summer. Justina knew many people who had lost children, and she had prayed alongside them and thought she knew a mother's pain. But now she knew she hadn't. She hadn't known how it would take her sleep away, and that for many months she would walk as if in a dream, and that Clara would come back to her every day and ask to be held, crying for her mama, and that when Justina reached out to touch her the sick little girl would fade like river mist.

Justina didn't know there would be so many faces, the dead long gone surfacing again, calling to her in the night or in the glaring sun of fish camp. The voices were everywhere: the sea, the walls of her home, the tall grass whispering.

Justina never forgot Inaqaq and Ungkak. But after so many years they were dead to her, and though she hoped they might someday return, she didn't believe they would. When Charlie died, they had died with him. They were marooned, detached from the center like a child plucked too early from the womb, and it was impossible for her to comprehend their survival. She prayed for them, but more as souls in heaven than people on earth. She was familiar with death, and she grew strong.

But then Clara died. Tiny red-cheeked Clara, who, as soon as she could stand, ran for the sea as if she could walk on water. Always running, tripping, falling over and never getting hurt. Laughter followed her like a shadow, her antics retold over meals and workbenches. The time she tied a leash to a dead salmon, then dragged it around the village asking people to pet her rabbit. "But it's not a rabbit," someone had told her, and she had said, "Not a regular rabbit, a water rabbit," and no one could convince her otherwise. Nobody knew what killed her, not even the nurse or doctor who traveled through. She died slowly, and it was hard for people to watch. When she finally expired one early August morning, a veil of silence descended on the village.

Justina had visions. One night she woke from a brief, fitful sleep to Nicuuk, long dead, standing over the bed, her hand on Justina's forehead. "We have lost so much," she said. "I saw Clara, riding with Inaqaq on the back of Raven, heading to the moon. The moon was laughing." Nicuuk pulled a grass basket from behind her, and in it was water reflecting a moon. When Justina looked up, Nicuuk was gone. She shivered in the murky morning light.

She went to church and prayed for Clara and Inaqaq and Ungkak. She had forgotten that Inaqaq was nearly the same age when she left as Clara was when she died. She wondered if Inaqaq and Ungkak were alive, and she prayed that they would return. She pictured Inaqaq lying on her back in the tundra as she spied cloud animals. It felt good to see her this way, and she thought that she would have to teach this to her own children, that she would tell them about

Inaqaq and Ungkak. That way when they returned, people would remember them.

Christmas came and went, Clara went to heaven, but still Justina could not sleep. Raven returned to her in the night, flying circles around the moon, Inaqaq alone and pulling feathers as she clutched desperately to his back.

DRIVING EAST

18

A year before she died, my mother drove me to college, one thousand miles across Highway 50, "The Loneliest Road in America," through Nevada and Utah, and into the Colorado desert. I had her to myself as we sped through basin and range, over small desert passes, the scent of wet sage thick and exhilarating, my new life just beginning on the open road before us.

I liked to drive, and my mother indulged me for most of the twenty hours it took to go from Squaw Valley to Colorado Springs. I let my mind drift into the desert as we drove, the window down and my arm riding on the door, regarding myself in the rear-view mirror, hair blowing in the wind, thinking, "I am really going somewhere now. I am really moving forward." I was addicted to the motion, the long expanses of Highway 50, the passes dropping straight into endless sections of asphalt, disappearing into shimmering waves of heat. My mother and I tried to predict how long those stretches of road were, and always we came up short by a long shot. At the top of a pass we'd both make a guess, then press the odometer and speed down the mountain in search of the answer. My first lesson in desert travel: distances are always farther than you think.

My mother was quiet for much of the trip, but her silence was natural, appropriate to the dry, seemingly barren landscape we were crossing. She turned to me every once in a while to ask me to slow down, and I would let up for a while and then forget myself again, until finally she said, calmly and matter-of-factly, "I'm just going to say it once. You get a ticket, you pay for it. Okay?" I never even saw a police car out there.

In the long silences that passed between us, I'd watch my mother as she gazed out her window to the mountains and desert passing by, breathing deeply, her lips straight and relaxed. She seemed content, as if the drive were taking her back in time, thirty years earlier when she had first driven that road with my father. She told me not much had changed on that road, with its overpriced gasoline and mind-boggling distances between towns. Dying communities were still dying.

My parents had stopped at a hotel in Ely and my mother had gambled for the first time in her life. When we passed through Ely she pointed out the casino. "That's where I lost my first dollar," she said. "And your father kept putting quarters into those machines." I pictured them, him with his red-haired crewcut, tall and slim with a sly grin; and my mother's smile filling her face, her brown hair cut shoulder-length with wavy, crafted curls.

While growing up I scorned Nevada. I had difficulty seeing beyond the overgrazed ranch land and barbwired nuclear dumping grounds. But my mother had an unusual appreciation for the natural world, often mesmerized by unlikely beauty. It rained intermittently across Nevada, and I remember how she gulped the air as if it were water.

"Sage in the rain," she'd say, shaking her head in amazement. "The smell of sage in the rain."

The car growled up through the mining town of Austin, and I tried to imagine growing up in a place like that: one gas station, general store, hotel, post office, bar, run-down school. Through every small town— Fallon, Austin, Eureka, Ely, Delta—I'd say to my mother, "How can people live here? What do they do?"

Finally she answered, "They see it through different eyes than you. Maybe they are even happy to be here." I didn't understand what it meant to see through different eyes, but I know now that while we were driving that last drive, she had many sets of eyes. When she watched the rain falling as we dropped into the Great Basin, she was seeing ten different shades of green light mixed with the sulfurous glow of lightning; meanwhile, I was wondering how far it was to Colorado Springs, imagining the girls I would meet in my free, fast-approaching future. Yet I sensed the importance of those last hours together, and I was beginning to grow new eyes of my own, whether I knew it or not.

At each summit my mother would say, "Do you want to stop, get a breath of fresh air?"

"If you want to I will, but I'm fine," I'd answer, shrugging. And we'd keep on driving. We stopped once, on Pancake Summit above Eureka, because we liked its name. We got out of the car and walked up the hill a few hundred feet. Sage bushes sprinkled raindrops on my ankles. My mother picked a small bunch and held it to her nose. She stared off into the juniper and piñon forests below us and hummed under her breath. She smiled when I said that I didn't know there were mountains in the desert.

BY THE TIME WE PASSED THOUGH GRAND JUNCTION we were irritated with each other. She kept glancing at the speedometer to check my speed, and we were tired because we had driven fourteen hours straight. She wanted to quit and I didn't. We stopped for the night and went to sleep aggravated. The next day, driving through the canyons of Colorado's western slope, we argued about everything from rest stops to music. She would have preferred no music at all, while I wanted loud Jim Morrison. I couldn't wait to be out of that car, and I was sure that she couldn't wait to be rid of me.

In Glenwood Springs we stopped at a rest area and my mother told me about her and my father's early days in Aspen, when after her nursing shifts they used to come to Glenwood Springs for the hot springs. I tried to imagine my mother and father as young lovers, but I was irritated with her and could only see an old woman, irritable and unpleasant. She wanted to take the long, mountainous route through Aspen, but I was in a hurry. She said she would go there on her way home.

Barely speaking, we arrived in Colorado Springs at night and got lost trying to find the hotel. When we finally found it, I was too wound up to sleep, so I left her and went to the college. I walked around the dormitories, the athletic fields, the classroom buildings, imagining myself in this new place. I did a lap around the track. I forgot about my mother, and when I returned late to the hotel she was asleep with her clothes on, lying on the made bed with a book open on her chest. I felt guilty and wanted to tuck her in and kiss her good night. But when I touched her she shrugged me off. I lay in my bed, hardly sleeping at all. When I woke in the morning she was up and gone, eating breakfast alone in the hotel coffee shop.

We spent the next few days busy with college orientation, she touring around with parents, going to lectures, buying me sheets, toothpaste, underwear. I was caught up in meeting people, registering for classes, going to parties. Afterward, I stood on the sidewalk outside the dormitory and hugged my mother good-bye. My anger was gone. The car was packed and sat idling by the sidewalk. She kissed me and held my hand. "You let me know if there's anything you need," she said. "I'll write you letters and you write back. Okay?"

I nodded and felt tears building. But I didn't let myself cry—not in front of her. She squeezed my hand, then turned, got in the car, and drove away, waving out the window. I felt that something inexplicable was gone to me. When her car disappeared around the corner, Pikes Peak loomed before me. I pictured my mother driving back through Nevada by herself, saw her propelled, a tiny speck of dust across the great expanse of gray-green desert.

Looking back now, I see road signs. I create a map of my mother's life, and on this map are places she never mentioned, landscapes where she had walked but left no tracks. There are blank sections on the map, vast swaths of land that are dark and deeply forested. I see where she entered, the unsteady, meandering walk of a child, and though I search and search, I can't find where she came out. I know she did, though, somewhere, because I see, as if from a great distance above the earth, lonely Highway 50 stretched across the desert. She was on that road, drifting like a phantom away from me.

BEARS

LARGE PAW PRINTS ZAG INTO THE DARKNESS. The starry darkness. Snow. The sow weaves tiredly as she sniffs the night. *It cannot be far off*, she thinks, *it cannot be far away*. Even as she thinks it, she has no idea what "it" is. Refuge? A place to lie down without threat? Home? A place by the mountains and the sea, a place with fish and berries, a place for her cubs to romp on the tundra. A place to be a bear, to think like a bear, to shed the soft-skinned, weakly limbed shell of human.

Two small sets of prints follow. Young cubs. They do not think too much, just follow their mother into the darkness. They watch the stars, as bears do. It reminds them where they come from, where they must go.

A bear is a star is a bear.

The stars are silent, placid, even as they explode out of the ever-expanding darkness. The bears know this, want what the stars have, what is hidden behind the light. They trudge forward over snow only because they cannot go skyward. From time to time one of the bears stumbles, unaccustomed to these legs, these long-gaited, fur-covered limbs, and the nose that registers even the moles burrowed deep beneath snow. There are brief moments when they forget who, or what, they are, and suddenly they are crawling along on pink, frozen hands.

They scramble; blood soaks into snow. Time is running out.

The sow stops in her tracks, frozen midstride. She looks at the sky and sniffs the air. The cubs stop behind her. A new, lofty snow cools the sow's belly. All around, the night wavers with white, ghost shadows. The quiet is yawning, sorrowful, bittersweet. The bears hear it and know what is coming: a brilliant darkness, a deafening silence. They are not filled with dread, but gladness. The sow sniffs because she must, though she knows it doesn't matter, that soon the hunters, her once-brothers, will come. Even in her flight she wants to embrace them, to show them how it feels to be more than one, to welcome even the enemy into her heart.

She plows through the snow. The cubs pad in her wake. Soon the hunters crash through the bush, two brothers armed with spears and a need so thick the sow bear smells it. The brothers are tall and strong and filled with fright. They hunt their need. They must kill the nomad that is their sister and the bear she has become. But they fear what they will find beneath the skin.

The bears watch the stars. They see the Great Bear padding over the horizon, and they are calmed. The hunters' spears fly straight to

the heart. As the last bear falls, time stops. The bear is weightless, floating above the snow. The earth stops turning, the stars blink. Silence
hangs like an eclipse over the world.

A raven screeches, time grinds on. The bear slams to the ground,
the earth shudders. The hunters, the brothers, approach the dead bears.
They are bears, all right, the first is relieved to see. They take out their
knives and begin skinning. The older brother's sharp knife is halfway
down the smallest bear's gut when the fur becomes skin and the long
snout mutates into the fine nose of the hunter's nephew. He looks to
his brother, who has sliced open the chest of their beloved sister. His
tears fall like rain onto his sister's still-warm heart. The stars of the
Great Bear implode, their light sucked back into the vortex of sky. The
hunters run, not to the village but away. Footprints in the snow. Paw
prints in the snow.

Two bears swim through the liquid night.

EPILOGUE:

THE BOGOMILS

WHEN I WAS GROWING UP I rarely thought about searching for my birth parents. I imagined what they looked like and wondered if they were anything like me, but only in passing moments. I didn't want to hurt my parents, nor did I wish to disrupt the lives of my birth parents. When people asked me if I wanted to find my "real" parents, I'd snap back, "I see my real parents every day—I live with them." I saw that question as a threat to my identity, as proof that some people couldn't help but see me as some kind of bastard.

Nevertheless I searched, if not physically, then emotionally. While traveling in Bosnia in 1987, I became fascinated by the Bogomil tombs. The Bogomil movement was a twelfth-century heresy that set itself apart from Catholic and Orthodox religion, aligning with the Ottoman Empire and the invading religion of Islam. The heresy was an ascetic, puritanical revolt that challenged Christianity with an alternative view of the universe in which God and Satan have equal, opposing power. The purpose of spiritual life was to liberate soul from body, light from darkness.

I was twenty years old when I learned about the Bogomils, and I was immediately attracted to their mystery, their rebellious origins, and their challenge to Christianity. But more than anything, I was drawn to their hands.

I remember walking across the yellow grass that covered the field where the tombs were plunked haphazardly about. It was dusk, a golden light reflecting off the low, crumbling hills. I strolled among the ancient graves, quiet, the only sounds the nearby peasant farmers putting away their tools and calling good night to each other across the open fields.

The tombs were marked by massive slabs of stone, no apparent design to their shape. Their magnificence was not in their size, but in the figures carved into them: eerie, phantomlike human shapes, their disproportionately large hands reaching outward as if in infinite welcome. I looked down at my own hands, my thick palms and long, big-boned fingers. They were the same. The Bogomil hands were my own hands; my hands were Bogomil hands. I felt absurdly intimate with that place, as if those graves were the graves of my ancestors. I looked around to see if anyone was watching, found myself alone, stepped forward to the stone. Shivering, I placed my hand against a Bogomil hand, which dwarfed my own and felt warm and familiar.

JUST BEFORE I WENT TO YUGOSLAVIA, a year after my mother died, my father gave me a folder that he had salvaged from my mother's files. In it were details of my life that my mother had collected over the years: medical records, newspaper clippings, letters I had written, childhood paintings. And a small piece of notebook paper, on which was scribbled information about my birth parents that my mother must have obtained when she collected me from the hospital. She may have thought that at some point I might be curious, and when she deemed it appropriate perhaps she would have given me the paper.

At first I was shocked. All along she had known my birth parents' names, ages, physical characteristics, professions, religions, even hobbies. My birth mother was born in 1942, of Yugoslavian origin. She had brown hair and blue eyes; she was short and stout, thick-boned like myself. She was one of five children, a registered nurse, enjoyed music and sports. At the time of my birth she worked as a nurse in California. The paper said nothing about her having Bogomil hands, but I didn't care; in my imagination, her hands were magnificent.

My birth father was two years her senior, born in Canada. He was six feet tall with a 180-pound frame. He was blue-eyed, blonde and fair, of Irish and English descent. He had a B.A. in journalism, and at the time of my birth was a graduate student. The note reads that he "enjoyed music, the arts, and sports." He had one brother, an identical twin.

In terms of their relationship, the note says little. Nevertheless, it is revealing: "She did not give any details about her relationship with your birth father except that she did not plan to marry him. He knew about her pregnancy and about the adoption."

Rough sketches. Now I knew just enough about my parents to tickle my curiosity. I imagined their meeting, creating absurdly romantic scenarios full of Slavic accents and stone-hard bodies coming together in the heat of a postrally 1966 night. They met in cafes, in parks, in smoky nightclubs where she told him about the radical Bogomils over the low background jazz. They thought they were in love, but what they were in love with was not love, but the idea of love that the era spawned. They were in love with ideals, with possibility, with the rock-and-roll and jazz that moved with them in the wet, loose-limbed night. She was in love with the poet, the quiet stranger who spent his days locked away in a library. She imagined being a professor's wife at Berkeley, sushi dinners with Allen Ginsberg and Gary Snyder, summers in Lake Tahoe. He was in love with her slight Bosnian accent, the romantic and tragic history of her family's flight from war-torn Yugoslavia and Tito's postwar tyranny. He loved the intensity of her eyes, like a cat's. He found her beautiful in a way that only peasants can be: sturdy, her skin worn tough but fine and dark like leather, a creased smile, a scar near her left ear.

Or maybe it was only a one-night stand. Stoned after a Doors concert, two strangers wander into a nearby alley and in thirty stand-up seconds create me. I can live with that.

Even with the new information and all my imagining, my search began slowly. I held on to that knowledge for eight years before I did anything with it. From time to time when visiting cities around the country, I would look up the names in local phone books on the outside chance of finding a match. Once, in Colorado Springs, I found my birth father's name. I gathered enough courage to call the number but reached a busy signal; later, I couldn't get myself to try again. It took many years for my curiosity to boil over, and it was my mother's story, finally, that heated the water. At some point while researching her Yup'ik past, I had an epiphany: that my life is more like hers than I'd ever imagined; that I am in danger of repeating her mistake.

These things are never black and white. What I thought would be easy has not been. Names change, records are closed, and qualified search professionals are expensive. But those are just logistical problems. The real barriers are my own fears: of rejection, of finding them dead, of tearing apart their lives, of hurting my father, of unearthing a past that harbors more pain than joy. The very same fears that plagued my mother, that held her back for fifty years.

SIX YEARS AGO I registered with a central adoption computer, which matches searching birth parents and adoptees. The initiative must come from both parties. For a year after I registered, I thought about it every time I fetched the mail. I began digging into records and doing computer searches for my birth parents' names. A year later, with the help of a private investigator, I found a man who I thought was my birth father, same name and birthplace, living in Southern California. I wrote him a letter, trying to confirm whether he was, in fact, my birth father. Every day for a month I went to the mailbox expecting a reply. Finally it came, six weeks later, one typed paragraph:

Dear Mr. Chisholm,

I am returning your letter because I am not your father. I'm not six feet tall, nor do I have blonde hair or blue eyes. I haven't graduated from college. I do not know anybody by your mother's name, and I've never been to Daly City, CA [where I was born]. Plus according to your birth date, I'm not old enough. Sorry and good luck.
Sincerely,
Mr. X.

My initial reaction was disbelief—I had been so sure this was the man. Then I was angry at him for lying. Then just tired and disillusioned. Without realizing it I had become attached to a figment of my imagination. The letter was the loss of a man I had never known and might never know. I chose to believe him, unwilling to press a man who even if he was my birth father didn't want to know me.

My birth mother was next. I found all the registered nurses in California with her name—more than twenty—and sent a letter to every one of them. A shot in the dark. The return letters trickled in. Most of them came unopened, stamped RETURN TO SENDER— NO CURRENT ADDRESS. Some of them were kind letters from women who understood my search, women who had children of their own and wished me luck. Each time a letter came, a hollow hope slipped into my gut, and my heart rate rose. I imagine the letters that haven't been returned, like a flock of geese scattered by a storm, each bird alone but trying to get back to the ancestral summer home.

There are still letters out there, perhaps lying unopened on a wooden desk in Wisconsin or filed away in a farmhouse in Wenatchee. These things take time; I can wait. I have my mother's stone bear, its eyes red and the arrow sturdy on its back. I use it as a paperweight, holding down all the letters that come back to me, standing like a sentinel over the small white mountain of my hope.